COVENTRY LANCHESTER PO

3 8001 00033 99

D1760019

LANCHESTER LIBRARY, Coventry University
Gosford Street, Coventry CV1 5DD Telephone 024 7688 7555

− 2 JUN 2007

This book is due to be returned not later than the date and
time stamped above. Fines are charged on overdue books

This bo

Fines a

Production systems design

David Bennett, MSc, PhD, CEng, MBIM
Aston University Management Centre

Butterworths
London Boston Durban Singapore Sydney Toronto Wellington

All rights reserved. No part of this publication may be reproduced
or transmitted in any form or by any means, including
photocopying and recording, without the written permission of
the copyright holder, application for which should be addressed to
the Publishers. Such written permission must also be obtained
before any part of this publication is stored in a retrieval system of
any nature.

This book is sold subject to the Standard Conditions of Sale of
Net Books and may not be resold in the UK below the net price
given by the Publishers in their current price list.

First published 1986

© Butterworth & Co (Publishers) Ltd, 1986

British Library Cataloguing in Publication Data

Bennett, David
    Production systems design.
    1. Production management
    I. Title
    658.5   TS155

ISBN 0-408-01546-2

Library of Congress Cataloging in Publication Data

Bennett, David
    Production systems design.

    Includes bibliographies and index.
    1. Industrial engineering.   2. Production management.
    I. Title
    T56.B396   1986   658.5   86-11786

ISBN 0-408-01546-2

499/93100

Photoset by Butterworths Litho Preparation Department
Printed and bound in Great Britain by
Robert Hartnoll (1985) Limited, Bodmin, Cornwall

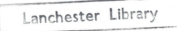
Lanchester Library

Preface

As industrial competition increases it becomes more apparent that improved levels of output, efficiency and quality can only be achieved by designing better production systems rather than by merely exercising greater control over existing ones.

The design of a production system comprises a linked set of widely ranging activities and involves problems common to a variety of situations, regardless of the technology and process being used. In contrast, the concepts, techniques and solution procedures developed in response to specific needs have emerged separately and are rarely presented within a single volume using a common framework.

As a consequence of this, both students and practitioners are usually obliged to refer to a number of very specialized texts. These often contain an unnecessarily high level of detail and sometimes treat the subject matter in an abstract way rather than within the context of production systems design. General texts on production and operations management can provide a broad coverage of some, but not all, of the required material but they tend not to focus on the specific problem of designing production systems. They, therefore, lack the framework and depth of treatment necessary for use in connection with a specialized course being conducted in the latter stages of an engineering or management programme. For the same reasons they also fail to meet the more immediate requirements of the industrial reader.

Production systems design has been written to answer the need for a text which provides a focus on the *design* aspects of production as opposed to planning and control or more general issues. It draws heavily on material developed at Aston University Management Centre where for some years a specialized option has been offered to final year undergraduates and as part of the MBA programme. Students on both courses have already taken an earlier, introductory, course in operations management using a more general text. Readers are, therefore, assumed to have a basic knowledge of production and operations management or, alternatively, they may refer to the necessary introductory material when appropriate.

Acknowledgments are due to SERC (the Science and Engineering Research Council) and ESRC (the Economic and Social Research Council) who supported some of the work which gave rise to the contents of several chapters. Thanks are also owed to the many people who assisted in the book's preparation by providing ideas, helping to arrange visits, and offering constructive advice. Specific reference here should be made to colleagues at Chalmers University in Sweden whose help was especially valuable.

Finally, staff in all the firms which were visited to gather case material deserve particular mention since they contributed much of their scarce free time and exercised great patience in answering a multitude of questions. Their co-operation must be recognized as being a major factor in providing the knowledge shared by all readers of this book.

David Bennett
Ashby de la Zouch

Contents

Chapter 1

Background to production systems design

1.1 The role of production in a modern business environment

Today many organisations are realizing that production is an important factor which must be taken into account when formulating a corporate strategy. This realization represents a reversal of the more traditional view that production just plays a supporting role to marketing.

Although it is true that marketing must establish what is produced, such a view is partly based on a further attitude that profit is more dependent on an item's selling price than on its manufacturing cost. Within a less competitive environment this attitude might go unquestioned. However, the modern consumer is now extremely sophisticated, expecting from the product a range of performance and quality attributes as well as the best value for money.

These attributes can only be satisfactorily derived by adopting a strategic view of production. Incorporating production issues into the strategy of the organization greatly improves the chances of providing customers with products which have the features they want. It also means that production cost considerations are built in to the wider decision-making process. In this way the most cost-effective solution can be designed from the start, so avoiding the need for a separate and subsequent cost reduction exercise.

A further consideration which must be taken into account when formulating a strategy for production is the fact that delivery and availability have become increasingly important features of a product. Nowadays customers insist on immediate ownership of standard products, partly as a result of 'instant' credit facilities, and short delivery periods are even being demanded for products made to order. To meet the demand for better delivery and high availability, a completely new approach must be taken towards the design of production systems. Not only is there a need to raise

1

process output, but inventories must be lowered, delays minimized and material movement reduced. The system must also be responsive to changes in product design and demand pattern.

Such capabilities are not only achieved by devoting attention to the technical system. Organization is also an important factor and, perhaps most important of all, maximization of the contribution made by each person working within the system.

In order to meet such a complex and demanding set of objectives, managers have first to define the parameters for production and must design the system in terms of its technical and physical characteristics, its human resource requirements and the organization of work. They then have to control the flow of materials, and in many cases some of the other resources, through the system. The overall task of production management can thereby be divided into two broad aspects – design of the production system itself and then its subsequent control. This distinction between system design and control is important, the former relating to the selection and arrangement of physical and human resources and the latter to the routine problem of managing the ongoing material processing activities.

1.1.1 Design and control

A common criticism of organizations today is that they frequently place too much emphasis on the problems of control, the assumption being that the underlying production system cannot be readily changed. However, while effective control is doubtless necessary, the way in which a production system is designed will enable or preclude the possibility of achieving the best results.

This emphasis on control may be evidenced by the amount of specialized production and operations management literature covering such topics as capacity planning, production planning, forecasting, scheduling, inventory control, material requirements planning (MRP) etc. In almost all these cases an 'operational research' approach, based on optimization, is taken where solutions are found, but only within a prescribed set of constraints.

A classic example of this approach within inventory control is the well-known *economic order quantity (eoq)* for which a formula has been derived which seeks to minimize the total cost associated with producing and stocking batches of material or products. Costs are assigned to ordering (setting-up) and stockholding which it is assumed cannot be changed; an attitude which totally ignores the possibility of modifying the production system. In practice, the use of the 'eoq' formula at best results in only minimal improvements in terms of total cost. On the other hand, however, it can even have detrimental effects, tying down production facilities on 'economic runs' while ignoring factors such as customer priority[1].

Use of the economic order quantity formula is only one example of where an emphasis placed on control has yielded little real improvement in terms of overall efficiency. Many of the other topics mentioned earlier, such as MRP and scheduling, have received considerable attention and many techniques and formulae have been derived and adopted in various industries.

On the other hand, contrary to the claims usually made, they often prove not to be the panacea for the many problems they are intended to solve. This was shown, for instance, in an international study which discovered a lack of significant reduction in the inventory ratio during 1966–80 among most industry groups and companies, despite widespread adoption of sophisticated production and inventory control systems[2].

Proof that system design is important has often come from some unlikely sources rather than from the traditionally dominant industrial nations. The Soviet Union, for example, has demonstrated that greater efficiency can be derived in component manufacture through designing systems which are product rather than process orientated (group technology). The Scandinavian countries have shown that rigid and highly paced flowlines can be replaced by parallel, flexible systems with long cycle times (autonomous work groups).

The most significant examples of radical thinking probably originate in Japan where, in such areas as quality, material control and production technology, the Japanese capacity for innovative thinking has been amply demonstrated (e.g. quality circles, the Kanban production control system, quick-change tooling etc).

It is, in fact, an analogy originating from Japan which clearly illustrates the alternative philosophies which might be adopted by management[3]. The analogy which is drawn is that of a pond, as shown in *Figure 1.1*. The water level in the pond represents stocks, while the projections in the bottom are the underlying constraints (e.g. set-up times, lead-times, etc.) which would require a covering of water in order to hide them.

Raising the water level to obscure the projections is, so the argument goes, the same as finding 'optimum' solutions to the problems of production and inventory control. Although it may appear that a satisfactory result has been achieved, the underlying constraints still exist, having only been covered over.

The 'Japanese' solution (originating at Toyota) is to deliberately and systematically reduce the stocks.

'By lowering the water level (stocks) in the pond, the highest points at the bottom would appear above the water surface, thus by scraping off the projecting parts, the effective depth of water would become greater. Continuously lowering the water level would make new projections appear, and by scraping them off we could finally make an entirely levelled bottom of the pond'.

This approach can be described as one of *improvement* rather than *optimization* and requires close attention to be paid to the production system design elements.

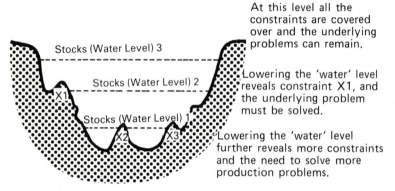

Stocks (Water Level) 3

Stocks (Water Level) 2

X1

Stocks (Water Level) 1

X2   X3

At this level all the constraints are covered over and the underlying problems can remain.

Lowering the 'water' level reveals constraint X1, and the underlying problem must be solved.

Lowering the 'water' level further reveals more constraints and the need to solve more production problems.

Figure 1.1 The 'Pond' analogy to using stocks as a means of covering the constraints in the production system (after Shingo[3])

1.1.2 Production system elements

The point has now been reached where the components of a production system can be examined in detail, taking as a starting point the definition of the system being 'a facility which manufactures physical goods from raw materials using machinery and labour'. This idea may be further refined by taking into account the whole range of inputs, both tangible and intangible, apart from just raw materials, which are required by the transformation process. Thus financial capital, consumable materials and supplies, skill and knowledge (of products and processes), services from outside contractors, etc. can all be regarded as resource inputs.

This refinement may be taken even further by considering the possibility of intangible as well as tangible *outputs*. In the case of manufacturing companies, they may also supply advice and service as well as producing physical goods. Indeed, in certain such cases (for instance, some oil companies and computer manufacturers) these particular outputs may assume greater importance than the primary physical product.

This situation is taken to its logical conclusion in the case of pure service producers, such as consultancies, brokerages etc, where there is no tangible output whatsoever (save perhaps for documents and reports). Strictly speaking such organizations can still be regarded as using production systems (or, more accurately, *operations systems*), but they are generally outside the scope of this book. Nevertheless, many of the ideas discussed are relevant in some way to pure service organizations so their usefulness in such instances may still be evident.

There is similarly some relevance to the case of service activities of manufacturing companies or where service organizations have a significant 'facilitating product'. Furthermore, the growing importance of the internal support services of any organization to its efficient running should be recognized since they can greatly influence the effectiveness of the more productive elements of the system.

Most analyses of production situations suggest that there are three key tangible resources employed, namely labour, physical facilities and materials (in days past, often referred to as the three M's – men, machines and materials). It is more appropriate, however, to consider the last item – i.e. materials – separately since their dynamic nature makes their subsequent control, rather than system design, the most significant activity.

If this argument is accepted, then the essential components of the system which converts inputs to outputs are labour and physical facilities (machines, buildings, equipment). It is the choice of these, together with their organization (including motivation and remuneration) that determines the system's ability to process materials and produce the desired output efficiently.

We need, then, to discuss the segmentation and organization of work and the way it is allocated to the labour resources. Worker remuneration and other aspects which may influence the efficiency and effectiveness of the labour resource must also be examined.

The physical arrangement of the facilities requires consideration since it is a key factor which determines material flow (and consequently throughput times, inventories, etc). In connection with this last point, the application of new technology must be an important consideration, since it is rapidly influencing the way in which the physical system can deal with the changing demands of the market.

Lastly, the design of the internal support services certainly merits examination. In particular, the quality and maintenance sub-systems are important components which determine the performance of the overall production system. The various elements of a production system and the ideas just described are illustrated in *Figure 1.2.*

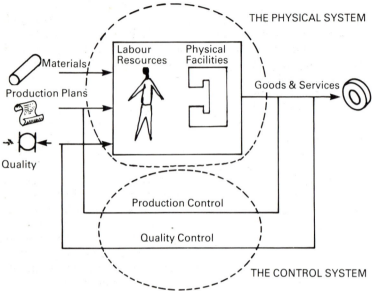

Figure 1.2 The elements of a production system

1.2 The historical perspective of production

In order to understand the rationale behind the different approaches to production system design, it is useful to examine their historical perspective.

It is possible to trace back to the Industrial Revolution some of the thinking which even today is influencing designers of production systems. As well as the 'technological' developments, which at the time contributed significantly to industrial progress (and which will be described later), some notable 'organizational' principles were also established by writers such as Charles Babbage[5] and Adam Smith[6].

1.2.1 Scientific management and behavioural science

After the early principles were established, it is widely accepted that some of the most influential work on organization was carried out during the late 1800s and early 1900s under the general heading of *scientific management.*

Most notable among the 'scientific management school' at this time was Frederick Taylor. While working with a number of American companies, Taylor sought to prove his belief that a scientific approach to planning and the management of work could produce significant benefits in terms of output and efficiency. The main thesis on which his 'principles of scientific management'[7] is based is that individual workers can be selected and allocated to jobs they perform best. A financial incentive can then be applied in order that the workers' best results are achieved to the financial benefit of both the individual and the firm.

Taylor's approach, therefore, accepts and builds on the ideas of Smith and Babbage, which advocated division of a job of work down into a number of functional tasks and the promotion of a high degree of specialization on the part of each worker.

A 'Tayloristic' approach to designing production systems can, therefore, be identified. At the micro level (e.g. productive work), this implies breaking a job into a number of short tasks which can be allocated to the most appropriate operators and performed in a repetitive fashion, normally with a direct financial incentive. At the macro level, the Tayloristic approach requires that jobs in all parts of the organization are performed by functional specialists. So, in most manufacturing companies, are found process planners, quality controllers, stock controllers, machine setters, and even separate specialists for the various functions of maintenance (i.e. mechanical, electrical, etc).

Taylor's argument for taking the division of labour logic this far is justified by his example comparing the 'frontiersman' with the 'surgeon'. The former was a generalist – being an architect, housebuilder, lumberman, soldier and doctor – while the latter has been taught and trained under close supervision in an almost identical way to the factory operative working under scientific management principles. It is in making this comparison that Taylor claimed that functional specialization could still have tasks associated with it which could be developing and broadening, thereby reducing the risk of producing a workforce of 'automatons'.

Despite Taylor's share of critics, and despite the passing of almost a hundred years, his influence on the design of production systems is still profoundly significant. For instance, his 'principles of scientific management' was one of the most likely sources of inspiration for Henry Ford when he conceived the manufacture of the Model T using flowline techniques and even today this form of production system still has widespread acceptance when large production quantities are required.

Even when demand is lower, Taylor's principles can still be applied by routing discrete batches of parts between functionally arranged departments where specific operations can be carried out. Despite the dissimilarity of parts, the similarity of process can provide for division of labour, specialization of skills and the application of direct financial incentives.

It would be wrong to assume that the scientific management school formed the complete picture as far as the historical perspective of production organization is concerned. As early as the 1920s, a second and in many ways equally well-founded school began to emerge, which is now often referred to as the 'behavioural science school'.

This school probably originated with the study conducted over a five year period at the Hawthorne Works of the Western Electric Company in the USA[8]. Intended originally to be a straightforward investigation into the effect of different lighting levels on output, the study developed into series of experiments which increasingly demonstrated that human behaviour was an important factor affecting output and which had been grossly under-estimated by the advocates of scientific management.

1.2.2 Groups and socio-technical systems

One further consideration relating to the way in which productive work might be organized is the fact that a set of tasks can be carried out by people working either as individuals or in groups. The scientific management school presumes that wherever possible tasks should be performed by individuals since only in this way can the division of labour principles be adopted and individual incentives applied. Moreover, even in the Hawthorne studies, tasks were still by and large carried out by individuals working independently so in this respect the organization of work could still be described as 'Tayloristic'.

The idea of using cohesive groups of workers in high volume industrial production is of relatively recent origin, although group work has long been a feature of systems where products are made for customer order (i.e. job or custom production). However, one application where group working is well developed is in the British coal mining industry[9].

Traditionally the mining of coal took place using 'pillar and stall' working where the seam was extracted at a number of single places only six to eleven yards in length. The groups who worked at one of these places comprised about nine persons, selected by their own members, who were completely responsible for coal production. Group members had a wide range of skills and some rotation of jobs was possible.

When mechanized 'longwall' mining came into widespread use from the 1920s, faces of 160 to 200 yards (146–183 m) were introduced and an alternative form of work organization was adopted using the factory approach of strict division of labour. However, this form of working proved to be a problem due to the unpredictable nature of the job compared with factory work. The associated reduction in skills also gave rise to diminishing safety levels and absenteeism became more common.

To tackle these problems an alternative form of working, called the 'composite work organization and wage system', was introduced which had many similarities to the traditional way of working. Skills were widened and rotation between jobs and shifts was made possible, while bonuses were paid to the groups rather than to individuals. The result was that smoother changeovers from one shift to the next became possible, as was previously the case using traditional methods, and more importantly productivity increased.

So significant were the effects of changes to work organization in mining that they gave rise to a massive research programme conducted by personnel from the Tavistock Institute of Human Relations in London. They referred to their methods as the 'socio-technical systems' approach, since the situation they were dealing with was neither purely a technical system nor a social system and, therefore, required a completely new form of research methodology.

The coal mining studies, while very important, relate to a rather unusual form of work compared with the more familiar manufacturing activities with which Taylor and the Hawthorne Researchers were involved. The systems of group working which were developed were obviously appropriate in the mining environment, but they could not be proved as being appropriate in the context of a factory producing a wide variety of complex products.

With this question in mind, the Philips Company in Eindhoven, Holland, conducted a series of experiments during 1960 in their television receiver factory[10]. Philips, like most other large volume manufacturers, were using assembly line techniques where, in much the fashion conceived by Henry Ford, jobs were divided into short cycle tasks which could be quickly learned and enabled unskilled workers to reach a high level of proficiency. The intention was to create a regular flow of production with high output levels being ensured by a wage system geared to effort.

However, at the time of the experiments, the Company was faced with a number of problems for which the techniques used so far did not provide suitable answers. The problems, which related to output, quality and morale, caused the researchers to question the organization of the unskilled work and the sophisticated wage system. Both these factors were being influenced by changing mental attitudes, full employment and better basic levels of education which conflicted with the rigorous division of labour.

Firstly, the researchers found that waiting times could be reduced and, therefore, output increased, as the number of workstations on the line was reduced. In the experiments this was achieved by breaking down the single line with no bufferstocks into five groups, each of which was separated by a buffer, as shown in *Figure 1.3*. In this way less time was lost waiting for material and due to balancing and system loss (these terms will be fully explained in Chapter 5).

Secondly, it was found that re-organizing the line had an effect on quality. By placing inspectors at the end of each group rather than at the end of the long line, earlier feedback of information was achieved offering chargehands the opportunity of controlling the quality of work in their areas. Statistical analyses of the relationship between quality and work rates also showed that the best quality was achieved by working at a medium, regular speed.

This rate of working was best facilitated using shorter lines with bufferstocks between adjacent workplaces. Moreover, the findings relating to both output and quality were further confirmed when the line was laid out with only half the number of workers, performing twice their original cycle, with storage between each workplace. In this case it was found that waiting time was reduced, any delays had less effect, and quality improved as a result of the more even rate of production.

Finally, concerning morale, where a questionnaire was used to assess this factor, the researchers again found benefits where the line was broken down into groups. In fact, even higher morale was discovered in groups assembling channel selectors, where the level of independence was still higher, and where a complete 'end product' was being produced.

In their final conclusions, the Philips' researchers stated that they were convinced that small groups with bufferstocks were most appropriate for the kind of work studied, despite requiring more space and materials. A proviso is added that the group should be able to obtain independent results, to set their own pace, have

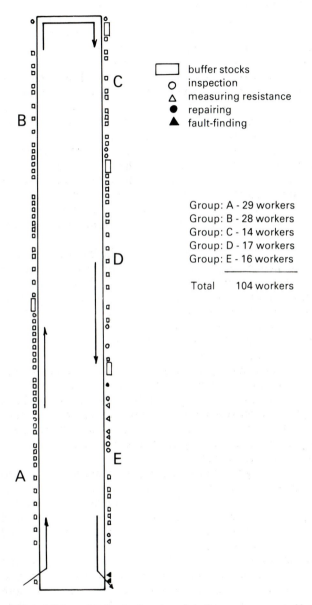

□ buffer stocks
○ inspection
△ measuring resistance
● repairing
▲ fault-finding

Group: A - 29 workers
Group: B - 28 workers
Group: C - 14 workers
Group: D - 17 workers
Group: E - 16 workers

Total   104 workers

Figure 1.3 Assembly line broken down into five groups separated by buffer stocks (from the Philips Experiments, Van Beek[10])

separate quality assessment, and be paid on a group basis. Although the size of the group will depend on production engineering factors and the duration of the cycle, at Philips it was found that sociological advantages gradually decreased if the size exceeded ten.

The problems of output, quality and morale experienced by Philips were by no means unusual among industrial companies during the 1960s. They are, however, better documented than most and the experiments which took place demonstrate a unique approach, the findings from which greatly influenced the design of more modern production systems in Europe particularly, but also elsewhere in the industrial world.

1.3 The framework of production systems design

The design of a production system is bound to be influenced and constrained by a number of factors. Resource arrangements (i.e. the layout of buildings and plant, together with work organization) are the most visually apparent of these but a number of other factors play an important part in determining the system's overall efficiency. These include motivational aspects, technology, environmental and legal considerations.

1.3.1 The organization of work

The historical perspective just described showed a number of examples of organizational alternatives, nearly all of which can today still be seen throughout the whole spectrum of manufacturing. Attention to the arrangement of resources featured highly as a means of determining the nature of production so it is appropriate to consider in more detail the available types of work organization, together with layouts which have traditionally facilitated each way of working.

Three types of organization can normally be identified, the first and perhaps oldest of which can be termed *product-orientated*. Based on the idea of a worker or team completing an entire end-product, this method of organization is illustrated in *Figure 1.4(a)*. In its strictest sense, product-orientated (or make complete) organization demands a wide range of skills on the part of the workers and a high degree of flexibility within the production system, requiring versatile facilities. Layout is traditionally *by fixed position* (i.e. there is no significant movement of the actual product) with materials, equipment and labour being

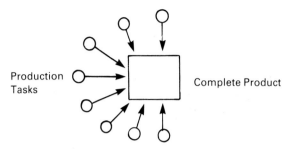

Figure 1.4(a) Product-orientated production organization

moved to the place of work as and when required. Although it is mainly a feature of job production, where single items or small orders are produced to customers' requirements, the product-orientated approach is gradually gaining acceptance for higher volume production.

The second type of organization emerged as a result of greater division of labour and the desire to improve the economy of scale; it can be called the *process-orientated* approach. Rather than using widely skilled workers and versatile facilities, more specialized labour and equipment are used so that similar operations can be performed repeatedly on a whole range of components and products. Volume levels are mainly higher than in product-orientated forms of organization so production is normally carried out in batches, with the entire batch being moved from one process to the next.

The layout in a process-orientated organization is usually *by function*, i.e. machines and equipment of the same type are grouped together so that batches are moved around from one department to another according to the operations which are required. In assembly work another feature of process-orientated organization is the widespread use of sub-assemblies which are again produced in batches and subsequently assembled together until, finally, a batch of finished products emerges (see *Figure 1.4(b)*).

The last type of work organization can be described as *task-orientated*. This, in essence, is the result of increasing the degree of specialization to its logical conclusion, which is the repeated performance of a short cycle time task on components and products which, by virtue of their demand, are produced continuously. This type of organization usually demands very little versatility on the part of either the operators or equipment since

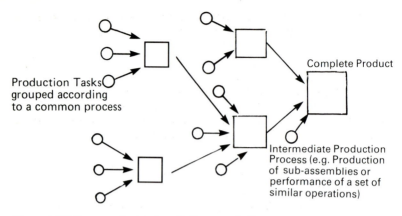

Figure 1.4(b) Process-orientated production organization

the degree of standardization is high with product variation being achieved by including a number of options where required.

One important feature of task-orientated organization is that material movement is minimized so layout *by product* (line layout) is widely used for this type of production. Facilities and work stations are arranged according to the sequence of operations required to produce the components or products and single items 'flow' or follow each other through from the beginning of the line to the end (hence the term 'flowline'). In assembly work it is feasible that every item or detail could be added separately at the various stations along the line (see *Figure 1.4(c)*). However, in practice it is common for some sub-assemblies to be produced off the line, either continuously or in batches, being fed into the final assembly at the required point.

The type of work organization used for production is important in determining the extent to which jobs are carried out by individuals or groups and the degree to which specialization can be adopted. Custom and practice has largely determined that job production uses a product-orientated organization with fixed

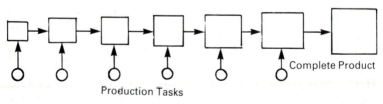

Figure 1.4(c) Task-orientated production organization

position layout, that batch production is process-orientated using functional layour and that continuous (or flow) production is task-orientated using a line layout.

However, these general 'rules' are increasingly being 'violated' as system designers recognize that benefits can often be derived by employing work organizations in circumstances where a different demand pattern is more usual. These newer ideas will be elaborated on in later chapters when the specific question of alternative forms of production system is dealt with.

1.3.2 Motivation, technology, environmental and legal considerations

Returning now to the other factors mentioned previously as shaping the overall design of production systems, the motivational aspects should next be considered. It was mentioned earlier that Taylor's 'scientific management' approach included the application of a financial incentive to jobs once they had been allocated to workers. A financial incentive was, he considered, the main motivator of direct labour, a thesis which he then attempted to demonstrate using a number of examples.

This approach to motivation, where an individual's pay is directly linked to output (piecework or payment by results), remains in common use today but is by no means the only form of motivation available nor is it without critics. One of the most vociferous of these was Wilfred Brown[11] who, as Chairman of the Glacier Metal Company in London, became a champion of the cause to replace piecework schemes with systems of payment based on daywork.

Brown was convinced that, rather than optimizing production and individual satisfaction in work, piecework schemes were hindering both. He based this thesis on experiments within his own company (the Glacier project) and also cited the experience of Vauxhall Motors, Lever Brothers and Perkins Diesels.

Brown concluded that each individual had his own norm of workpace and application and that, given a reasonable physical environment, a level of work reasonably consistent with his capacity and a regular level of pay consistent with such work, he will produce, on average, that quantity of work which is his own optimum contribution. At the Glacier Metal Company, piecework was substituted by a form of daywork known as 'hourly rated pay'. Here operators were simply paid at a predetermined rate per hour for the actual number of hours they worked, the rate being calculated to provide the same average pay per head employed in a department as before the change. Although the majority of managers and operators felt that output would drop sharply if incentive payments were abandoned, the result was that there could be judged no significant change in output. To quote Brown:

> 'The result demonstrated the falsity of the expectation that the type of wage payment system in use was a predominant variable in the situation'.

Taylor and Brown, therefore, represent opposite viewpoints regarding financial motivation, while other views range across the intermediate spectrum giving rise to a number of alternative forms of motivation and remuneration. Some of these will be discussed in Chapter 2.

Turning now to technological factors, these obviously can have a profound effect on the performance and capability of a production system. The best demonstration of this occurred during and after the Industrial Revolution[12] when British engineers, such as John Wilkinson, Henry Maudsley and James Nasmyth, developed machines for cutting and forming parts, so replacing the laborious and time-consuming methods previously used.

Of all the examples from this period one of the most graphic is probably the set of forty-four machines made by Maudsley to the designs of Marc Brunel for manufacturing pulley blocks for the Royal Navy. When commissioned, the machines produced 130 000 blocks per year using ten unskilled men doing the work of 110 skilled, saving £17 000 per annum for a capital outlay of £54 000. This example of Maudsley's and a similar plant set up in the USA by Eli Whitney for the manufacture of firearms, are among the first installations in the world where machines were used for 'mass production'. They established production engineering principles which, during the next 150 years, became standard practice for manufacturing a whole range of industrial and consumer products.

In fact, in some ways progress in terms of technological development was relatively slow after these initial advances had been made; and it is only recently (during the last twenty years) that technology is again becoming a prominent factor for system designers to take into account. The reason for this is that, despite there being little change in available processes, 'new technology' is enabling automatic, intelligent, versatile and flexible versions of machines to become available.

This finally brings us on to the remaining factors which shape production systems, namely the environmental and legal considerations. Unlike those previously mentioned, these 'external' factors are usually beyond the influence and control of the system designer, acting as constraints rather than offering choices which can be utilized in a constructive way.

By environmental factors we are referring to the set of prevailing conditions which allow a particular course to be followed when designing the system. They are not so much climatic conditions, though naturally these are sometimes important, but rather conditions relating to such matters as public opinion, ethics, religion and politics. In most cases, domestic manufacturers need not be too concerned with the detail of these considerations since custom and practice at home is well-known and long-established. However, when setting up an overseas operation it is essential to carefully examine in the greatest detail the local 'environment' in order to avoid the problems which often beset the unsuspecting company.

The same set of arguments holds true for the legal considerations except that they differ both by their mandatory nature and the more clearly defined penalties attached to them. The most important legal considerations for the production system designer relate to the working environment and to the safe and reliable operation of the goods produced (product liability).

As far as the first of these is concerned, the problem is largely a matter of adherence to the relevant prevailing legislation (in the UK this would be the Health and Safety at Work Act 1974), but in the case of the second, i.e. liability for defective products, it is a great deal less simple. Manufacturers are, in this case, in a position where they take a risk that their product might injure a user or a third party, sometimes with dire financial consequences. The production system must be designed to minimize that risk while, at the same time, remaining viable and efficient. The importance of this last point warrants greater coverage of the product liability issue so it will be taken up again in a later chapter.

1.4 Summary

In this introductory chapter the problem of designing production systems has been defined and the main issues of importance to personnel involved in this work have been highlighted. Design of the physical system, as opposed to the control system, is becoming increasingly important as firms discover that this is often the aspect which limits many achievements which could be made relating to smooth and efficient materials management. By looking at the historical development of production systems, the underlying rationale can be seen, together with the way it shapes the various organizational approaches taken.

Systems may be based on individual or group working, functional specialization or more generalized skills, and they may be process, product or task-orientated. Coupled with this, they may depend on a number of different motivational factors and their efficiency could be influenced by the type of technology involved. At the same time, environmental and legislative factors need to be recognized as constraining the designer and limiting the number of options that might be available.

This is the background to the subsequent chapters of the book. They seek in turn to deal with the range of issues which must be addressed when adopting a total approach to designing a production system. They do not provide every last detail, since only a specialized text on a particular topic can even attempt to do this. Their intention is rather to present the complete picture to the reader and thereby widen his or her view of the subject.

References

1. BURBIDGE, J. L. (1981), 'The Pseudo Economic Batch Quantity', *Production Management and Control*, **9**, No 1
2. SODAHL, L. O., DUBOIS, P. and LENERIUS, B. (1983) *Materials Management Efficiency – An International Comparison,* Chalmers University of Technology, Gothenburg, Sweden
3. SHINGO, S. (1981) *Study of 'Toyota' Production System from Industrial Engineering Viewpoint,* Japan Management Association
4. SASSER, W. E. (1978) *Management of Service Operations,* Allyn & Bacon, USA
5. BABBAGE, C. (Original pub. 1832), *On The Economy of Machining and Manufacturers*
6. SMITH, A., *The Wealth of Nations* (1776, Reprinted. Everyman's Library, London, 1970)
7. TAYLOR, F. W., *Principles of Scientific Management* (1911, Reprinted ed. Norton, 1967)
8. ROETHLISBERGER, F. J. and DICKSON, W. J. (1939) *Management and the Worker,* Harvard University Press, USA
9. TRIST, E. and BAMFORTH, K. W. (1951) 'Some Social and Psychological Consequences of the Longwall Method of Coalgetting', *Human Relations,* **4**, No 1
10. VAN BEEK, H. G. (1964) 'The Influence of Assembly Line Organisation on Output, Quality and Morale', *Occupational Psychology,* **38**
11. BROWN, W. B. D. (1962) Piecework or Daywork? *The Institution of Production Engineers,* E. W. Hancock Paper (25 September 1962)
12. COSSONS, N. (1975) *Industrial Archaeology,* David & Charles, Newton Abbot, Devon

Chapter 2

Human resource aspects

2.1 Motivation, incentives and remuneration

In Chapter 1 brief reference was made to motivation and the distinction was drawn between the use of financial incentives on the one hand and daywork payments on the other. These two simple generalized examples served to illustrate the opposing views which exist concerning motivation of the labour resource, but they only represent a couple of small corners in the total picture of motivation and payment.

In this section, the theme is taken up and extended. Firstly, the general issue of motivation is considered and then developed to consider the more formal means of providing an incentive. Lastly, attention is paid to the translation of work performance into some form of financial remuneration.

2.1.1 Theoretical aspects of motivation

No discussion of general motivation theory would be complete without a mention of the work of Abraham Maslow[1]. He recognized at least five sets of goals which he called 'basic needs', these being physiological, safety, love, esteem and self-actualization. Motivation, he claimed, derived from the desire to achieve or maintain the various conditions upon which these basic satisfactions rest and by other more intellectual aspirations. Maslow's 'needs' are arranged into a 'hierarchy' with the lowest being most dominant until it is fully satisfied, after which time the next lowest takes the dominant position. The order of need for most people studied by Maslow was as previously listed, but it is important to note that he found numerous exceptions. For instance, creativeness (a form of self-actualization) usually depends upon prior satisfaction of all the other basic needs, but some people could be innately creative despite a lack of basic satisfaction.

It is Maslow's recognition of the different needs, together with the fact that their order may differ, that is significant when viewed in connection with motivation at the workplace. Most importantly, it can be readily appreciated that only the lowest of basic needs can be satisfied completely by simply providing a financial reward. Moving further up the hierarchy it becomes increasingly difficult to rely on this form of remuneration since many of the more abstract needs cannot be acquired solely with money.

The idea of motivation being effected by more abstract factors was also the thesis of Douglas McGregor[2] who identified two views which could be taken towards the task of managing and motivating the labour resources. The first of these, the conventional conception, he called 'Theory X' which could be described in terms of three propositions

1. Management is responsible for organizing the elements of productive enterprise – money, materials, equipment, people – in the interest of economic ends.
2. With respect to people, this is a process of directing their efforts, motivating them, controlling their actions, modifying their behaviour to fit the needs of the organization
3. Without this active intervention by management, people would be passive – even resistant – to organizational needs. They must, therefore, be persuaded, rewarded, punished, controlled – their activities must be directed. This is management's task in managing subordinate managers or workers. It is often summed up by the phrase 'management consists of getting things done through other people'.

McGregor draws upon Maslow's work to demonstrate the inadequacy of the conventional approach and points out that there should be opportunities *at work* to satisfy the higher level needs. If such opportunities did not exist then people would feel deprived and any further focusing on physiological needs is bound to be ineffective. In recognition of this a second set of propositions, 'Theory Y', is put forward.

1. Management is responsible for organizing the elements of productive enterprise – money, materials, equipment, people – in the interest of economic ends.
2. People are *not* by nature passive or resistant to organizational needs. They have become so as a result of experience in organizations.
3. The motivation, the potential for development, the capacity for assuming responsibility, the readiness to direct behaviour towards

organizational goals are all present in people. Management does not put them there. It is a responsibility of management to make it possible for people to recognize and develop these human characteristics for themselves.
4. The essential task of management is to arrange organizational conditions and methods of operation so that people can achieve their own goals *best* by directing *their own* efforts towards organizational objectives.

McGregor's examples of some innovative (at that time) ideas consistent with 'Theory Y' include: decentralization and delegation, job enlargement, participation and consultative management, and performance appraisal techniques using self-evaluation and goal setting. His ideas have become increasingly popular among more progressive organizations and have also been endorsed by other management theorists such as Rensis Likert[3] and Frederick Herzberg[4,5].

Likert's contribution was to establish a *principle of supportive relationships* which stated that

> 'the leadership and other processes of the organization must be such as to ensure a maximum probability that in all interactions and all relationships with the organization each member will, in the light of his background, values and expectations, view the experience as supportive and one which builds and maintains his sense of personal wealth and importance'.

So, Likert argues, to be highly motivated, each member of the organization must feel that the organization's objectives are of significance and that his own particular task contributes in an indispensable manner to the organization's achievement of its objectives. He should see his role as difficult, important and meaningful. This is necessary if the individual is to maintain a sense of personal wealth and importance. When jobs do not meet this specification they should be re-organized so that they do. This is likely to require the participation of those involved in the work.

Herzberg's idea was that factors determining attitudes towards work could be clustered into those which relate to what a person does and those to the situation in which it is done. He found that, in general, the second cluster, which included company policy and administration, supervision, salary, interpersonal relations and working conditions (hygiene factors), served primarily to prevent job dissatisfaction. The first cluster, on the other hand, which included achievement, recognition, work itself, responsibility and advancement (the motivators), were all effective in promoting superior performance and effort.

One small but significant point on which Herzberg challenges McGregor's views is in the use of the term *job enlargement*. Job enlargement merely makes a job structurally bigger, he claims, by adding another meaningless task to the existing one (he called this *horizontal job loading*). His preferred idea is *job enrichment*, where motivator factors are added. Referring to this as *vertical job loading*, Herzberg proposes seven principles whereby this can be achieved. These principles, together with the motivators involved, are given in *Figure 2.1*.

Principle	Motivators involved
Removing some controls while retaining accountability	Responsibility and personal achievement
Increasing the accountability of individuals for own work	Responsibility and recognition
Giving a person a complete natural unit of work (module, division, area etc.)	Responsibility, achievement and recognition
Granting additional authority to an employee in his activity; job freedom	Responsibility, achievement and recognition
Making periodic reports directly available to the worker himself rather than to the supervisor	Internal recognition
Introducing new and more difficult tasks not previously handled	Growth and learning
Assigning individuals specific or specialized tasks, enabling them to experts	Responsibility, growth and advancement

Figure 2.1 Principles of vertical job loading (after Herzberg[5])

The few works relating to motivation that have been reviewed here represent only a small selection of the total contribution made by the psychologists and management theorists. They nevertheless give a clear indication of the considerable emphasis which academics and consultants alike have placed on non-financial forms of incentive.

Despite this apparent concensus on the part of the theorists as to the importance of such motivational factors, there still remains a gap between theory and practice relating to actual forms of incentive and pay system. This is evidenced by the results of a survey published by the UK Institution of Production Engineers[6] in which 85% of a sample of firms used a form of payment scheme based on performance (measured by output, profit or value added). What is also of significance is the fact that this type of scheme is not only commonly favoured by management – it is also often preferred by workers and unions. For instance, one shop steward is quoted as saying

> 'Piecework is our golden goose. We control our own earnings. Governments can come and go, with freezes, pauses and incomes policies and our earnings still increase by over 10% a year. And a method change gives us a chance for more pay'[7].

Such evident bias which exists in practice towards payment incentives necessitates that some of the various types of scheme which are currently in operation be considered, although as well as looking purely at the mechanics of each it is worthwhile relating their operation to the theoretical premise on which they and other forms of motivation are based.

2.1.2 Payment by results (PBR)

This is the traditional form of financial incentive scheme, otherwise known as piecework, in which pay is related directly to the output of the employee. The International Labour Office in Geneva documents over a dozen different types of PBR Scheme[8], classifying them under the following headings:

(i) Systems with workers' earnings varying in the same proportion as output;
(ii) Systems with workers' earnings varying proportionally less than output;
(iii) Systems with workers' earnings varying proportionally more than output;
(iv) Systems with workers' earnings varying in proportions which differ at different levels of output;
(v) Group systems;
(vi) Department or plant systems;
(vii) Systems for indirect workers.

To illustrate the operation of a PBR scheme is is appropriate to use, as an example the oldest most elementary but still probably the most common system – i.e. straight piecework. This simply operates on the basis of the worker's earnings varying in the same proportion as output (i.e. payment per piece).

Since workers in most industries are nowadays guaranteed a minimum wage this type of scheme is usually modified to pay a

Earnings
(as percentage
of time rate)

Figure 2.2(a) Payment by results scheme where pay is directly related to output, with guaranteed minimum

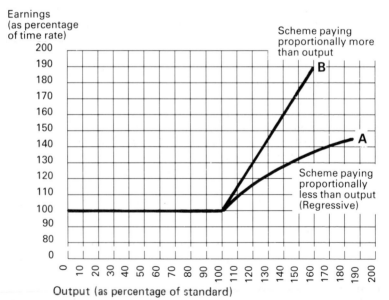

Figure 2.2(b) Payment by results scheme where pay does not increase at the same rate as output

fixed sum for any output up to a certain level, after which additional pay is related to further output, see *Figure 2.2(a)*. This modification protects the worker against unduly low earnings due to causes beyond his control. Cases where the scheme is not modified in this way might be where minimum wages are not guaranteed or where jobs are being done by outworkers, subcontractors, etc.

There are often reasons why under PBR, workers' earnings are chosen to vary proportionally less than output (e.g. where the worker can share with the employer the gains or losses resulting from changes in output). Conversely, but less commonly, it is sometimes the case that earnings are required to vary proportionally more than output (e.g. where the worker can share savings in overhead costs resulting from increased output).

Figure 2.2(b) shows two schemes which are designed to fulfil these two requirements. They both operate with a guaranteed minimum payment up to a certain level of output but thereafter Scheme A pays proportionally less than output while Scheme B pays proportionally more. The other feature of Scheme A is that the rate of increase in pay reduces as output increases, this is known as a regressive scheme (compared with a progressive scheme where the rate increases).

In order to evaluate PBR schemes it may be useful to note the comments made by the British Institute of Management[9] relating to these methods of payment:

(a) Advantages to management

1. A payment by results scheme enables the employer to vary his wage bill automatically as demand and output alter.
2. Fixing standards for payment by results automatically creates an incentive to improved management.
3. Payment by results provides a powerful incentive to increased output.
4. Greater output enables costs to be spread over a larger number of units of output, thus reducing total costs per unit.
5. Payment by results increases efficiency by indicating areas in which improvements may be effected when carrying out an analysis of methods and organization of production for rate fixing purposes.
6. It requires less supervision.
7. Piecework is easy to calculate both from the employer's and employees' point of view.

(b) Advantages to employees

1. Payment by results sets targets for employees by setting a standard for piecework.
2. It provides employees with an incentive value of increased pay for increased work.
3. It provides them with an opportunity to assert their importance and superiority.
4. Boredom is diminished and satisfaction in work increased.
5. A payment by results system allows more employee freedom from supervision.

(c) Shortcomings

1. In endeavouring to maximize bonus earnings, employees may allow the quality of work produced to suffer.
2. Rate fixing inevitably creates conflicting views between management and employees since the former wish to keep unit labour costs as low as possible whilst the latter wish to maximize earnings. This can easily lead to ill-feeling.
3. Employees may limit their output fearing that when new rates have to be set these will be 'tighter'.
4. Labour costs may become unduly high and the employer's competitive position in the market will be prejudiced.
5. When a new wage agreement is reached between employers' organizations and the unions involving a change in time rates of pay, a revision of all individual piecework prices in the plant is often necessary. Particularly in large manufacturing companies, this is a major task.
6. Productivity effects of payment by results are difficult to assess.
7. Employees act as sub-contractors and stop work when they have earned enough each day.

It is the weight of the claimed advantages over the shortcomings which has ensured PBR's continuance in popularity. However, many of the advantages listed are presumptions and are not supported by hard evidence; furthermore they conflict in many instances with the theories of motivation discussed earlier.

It is on examination of the prerequisites for PBR systems though that their appropriateness for modern production systems is called into question. These are listed as follows:

1. The work must be measurable, and directly attributable to an individual or group. In practice, this generally means that the work should be almost entirely manual, repetitive, and consist of fairly short-cycle operations.

2. The pace of work should be controlled to a significant degree by the worker, rather than by the machine or process he is tending.
3. The management should be capable of maintaining a steady flow of work, and of absorbing at least short-term fluctuations in demand or output.
4. The tasks involved should remain fairly constant through time, i.e. they should not be subject to very frequent changes in methods, materials or equipment.

Payment by Results schemes of the type described are, therefore, relevant in production systems where goods are mass-produced to a high and predictable demand using standardized, short-cycle tasks. However, by contrast, changes in the marketplace are demanding that systems are flexible and adaptable, can respond to the demand for wide variations in the finished product and, most importantly, can compete in terms of quality and delivery as well as cost.

Production systems having these characteristics are much more likely to employ groups with a wide range of interchangeable skills and whose members carry out a large amount of indirect as well as direct work. The associated system for payment and motivation needs, therefore, to be consistent with the special features exhibited by this different form of organization.

It was indicated earlier that PBR schemes can be designed for groups, departments or even for indirect work, but in essence they are similar in operation to those for individuals and suffer from many of the same deficiencies.

Other alternative schemes are also available where pay is linked much more loosely with performance (e.g. value-added schemes and profit sharing). These are in many ways more appropriate to the requirements described but unless sufficient control information is fed back to workers they cannot see the link between their own efforts and the basis on which they are remunerated.

2.1.3 Daywork and merit rating

Under both Daywork and Merit Rating systems there is no direct link between performance and pay. A system of Daywork has already been described in Chapter 1 called 'hourly rated pay' which was developed at the Glacier Metal Company. Today the term 'high day rate'[10] is usually attached to the form of payment system where fixed hourly rates are established for the total normal hourly earnings for each job or trade. These rates are paid for all normal hours of attendance, though there may be increments for overtime hours or shifts.

Under a time rate system workers are simply paid the standard rate for the job, the industry, or the area, whereas under high day rate working a basic rate is paid in excess of the standard rate. The fixing of hourly rates for high day rate working is usually done by job evaluation techniques, which will be described later, and they are generally accepted as containing a consolidated bonus payment.

The fundamental difference between these two types of daywork is that time rate workers have no financial incentive whatsoever to reach and sustain a reasonable level of work nor is there any financial motivation to improve working methods or procedures. Under high day rate, however, the responsibility for output and working practices should have been recognized in fixing the rate and the worker, theoretically, performs accordingly.

Both systems have their uses for different types of job; time rates are appropriate where output is not an important factor or where it is controlled by the process rather than the operator. High day rate is appropriate for more skilled work where quality and accuracy are important considerations.

The critics of these types of daywork system argue that, even under high day rate, there is insufficient motivation for workers to reach desired standards of performance and behaviour. The undue responsibility placed on management to secure acceptable levels of productivity and labour cost is also cited as a significant disadvantage.

For these reasons a modified version of this type of system, known as 'measured daywork', has recently gained considerable popularity. This offers a fixed rate of pay for a defined standard of motivated performance. The orthodox approach to developing such schemes involves the use of work study* to establish standard times for the various tasks and the use of negotiation to set the wage rate[11]. Each worker is then guaranteed a regular weekly wage on the understanding that he produces a weekly output at the performance level established as standard.

Thus measured daywork uses elements of both conventional incentives and straight time rates. The problem with measured

---

* Work study techniques are not described in this book since a knowledge of them is presumed. A basic account, however, may be found in most general production and operations management texts such as Wild, R. 'Production and Operations Management', Holt, Rinehart & Winston, 1984, or in more specialized works such as Currie, R. M. 'Work Study', Pitman, 1977.

daywork is that a progressive 'drift' in time standards is possible and sanctions must be agreed and available should work performance fall below the agreed standard. There is, therefore, a need for continuous attention to be paid to the work study function and for good labour relations to be revised whenever necessary.

It is, however, generally agreed that measured daywork schemes overcome many of the shortcomings associated with PBR and the other forms of daywork. A financial incentive is provided while, at the same time, it is relevant to production systems which are flexible and have long cycle-times (assuming appropriate work study techniques have been used). It is particularly applicable where group working is being employed, having much in common with earlier 'collective-bonus' systems.

All the schemes for payment described so far are based on attendance time, or (directly or indirectly) output, or a combination of the two. 'Merit Rating' by contrast is based on the systematic assessment of the abilities and/or behaviour of workers in their work. Merit Rating is rarely the sole basis on which pay is determined, being more usually a factor contained within a wider scheme such as high day rate or measured daywork. Periodic assessments are made of each employee or group of employees and a total points score used to determine that increment of pay which covers personal performance and behaviour. Points may be allocated for education and training, ability to do extra work, development of new methods, punctuality etc.

A problem with merit rating is that it is dependent to a large extent on subjective judgement. Like measured daywork, therefore, it depends on good industrial relations for its successful operation. It is also common for the score to be arrived at on a concensus basis, involving the use of some form of management/ union committee to reach agreement on the allocation of points to the various factors.

Given that a merit rating system is feasible and acceptable, its psychological benefits can be important to an organization wishing to develop the skills, productivity and loyalty of its workers. Unlike many of the financial incentive schemes previously described which almost regard employees as 'sub-contractors', merit rating reinforces the employees' commitment to the organization and can be used for all jobs at all levels. It is becoming increasingly commonplace in more enlightened organizations who place a premium on employee development when designing new production systems.

2.1.4 Job evaluation

The merit rating system just described assesses *workers* in their work. Whatever system of remuneration is used, however, a *rate for the job* must also be determined. This could be arrived at by negotiation, custom and practice, or as a result of some industry-wide agreement, but there are many occasions when the job is assessed in order to rate its value.

Job Evaluation[12] seeks to highlight significant disparities between units of work on a comparative basis, and so produce a more equitable distribution of income within an organization than might be obtained by more arbitrary methods. Any system of evaluation commences with a job description being drawn up and agreed. This sets out the job requirements, the conditions under which it is to be performed and how it relates to other jobs. In order to then evaluate the job, there are a number of quantitative and non-quantitative techniques available.

Most of the quantitative techniques involve some form of points allocation, in a similar way to merit rating except that the job is being evaluated – not the person doing it. Points might be allocated for training requirements, responsibility, monotony, physical requirements, etc. until a total score has been awarded to the job. This score can then be used to compare jobs and can be translated into a rate for payment purposes. Non-quantitative techniques of job evaluation require subjective measures to be taken such as comparisons of jobs with a 'bench mark job' or using 'paired comparisons' to produce a ranking of all jobs being evaluated.

Whatever the technique used, great care must be taken and only experienced personnel should be engaged on a job evaluation exercise. There are many pitfalls awaiting the unsuspecting and inexperienced 'job evaluator', and an often embarrassing outcome is to rate a worker's job higher than that of his manager!

2.2 Job design

The emphasis in the previous section was placed on methods of motivation directed specifically at the workers, be they in the form of a direct financial incentive or a method of remuneration more loosely connected with performance. However, none of the methods described are completely consistent with the motivation theories described earlier – providing little to satisfy McGregor's Theory Y nor supplying the opportunity to satisfy Herzberg's idea of vertical job loading. In the last analysis it is unlikely that any signficant achievements can be made by directing attention at the worker alone, it being the work or job itself that must be examined and changed.

Job Design is described by Davis[13] as meaning 'specification of the contents, methods and relationships of jobs in order to satisfy technological and organizational requirements as well as the social and personal requirements of the job-holder'. This description can be widely interpreted and indeed the scope and many diverse aspects of job design can readily be seen from the literature. At one extreme there is the rather mechanistic approach which focuses on the design of equipment and the physical environment[14], while at the other there is the approach which analyses the socio-technical system and concentrates on organizational change[15].

Davis (*op cit*) states that the specification of job contents can be divided into two categories:

(a) physical environment and physiological requirements;
(b) organisation, social and personal requirements.

Although his work does not consider the former category, this is because he considers that an extensive body of knowledge already exists and is assiduously applied. It is appropriate for the purposes of this discussion, however, to consider both these aspects of job design since they can be regarded as being of equal value to the manager.

2.2.1 Ergonomic considerations

Ergonomics has been defined as the scientific study of the relationship between man and his working environment[16]. The work *ergonomics* was created in 1949 to distinguish this interdisciplinary new field from other more traditional fields of study; its roots are the Greek *ergos* (work) and *nomos* (natural laws). Many of the early contributions to the subject had military applications – the reason being that the rapid development of hardware during World War II had resulted in a situation where personnel were often unable to obtain the best from complex, high performance equipment.

Today ergonomics has universal applicability, being used for such diverse purposes as designing household items (cookers, furniture etc) through to arranging the equipment and controls of spacecraft. It is of particular relevance to the design of production systems where both the working environment and the design of machines, tools and equipment can be an important factor in achieving the best results from the labour resource.

When applied to production systems design, ergonomic criteria can be considered in relation to machine displays and controls, the design of hand tools and equipment, methods of communication, air pollution, lighting, noise, posture etc. *Figure 2.3* shows in a structured way the breakdown of this total field into its various component topics.

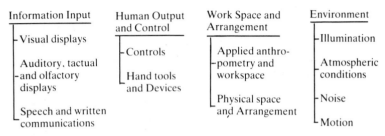

Figure 2.3 The components of ergonomics in relation to production systems design (adapted from McCormick and Sanders[17])

It is not only relevant to recognize the components of ergonomics in order to appreciate its application as a management tool. The two stage approach to the subject is another important factor meriting some discussion.

The first of these is *ergonomics research* – the basis by which relevant information is gathered and the data subsequently collated. Most of the data used in connection with the design of jobs and work is based on experimentation and observation. This experimentation may be carried out either in the laboratory or in the field (i.e. using actual working situations). The laboratory obviously has the advantage of providing a controlled environment in which experiments can take place but field research is often preferable since the real conditions can rarely be reproduced exactly.

There are many institutions and organizations carrying out ergonomics research including universities, government laboratories, international agencies and both private and publicly owned companies. The data resulting from their work can occasionally only be applied within a limited context, but commonly they are made widely available in the form of diagrams, graphs, tables, charts etc.

The data will then be put to use in the second stage, that of *applied ergonomics.* There may be a number of different personnel

who will use ergonomic data in connection with the design of
production systems; these might include machine and equipment
designers, method study staff and plant engineers as well as
ergonomics specialists and industrial psychologists.

The following comments and examples are intended to provide
an appreciation of the type of information available within the
various categories outlined previously.

2.2.2 Information input

The way in which information can be transmitted to workers is in
the form of displays or by some form of speech or written
communication. Displays are 'read' by the senses and they can
take visual, auditory, tactual and olfactory form. By far the most
common method of relaying routine information is visually and
Figures 2.4(a) and *(b)* show the features of a number of different
visual displays for transmitting numerical information. Displays
which depend on the other senses are usually warning devices.

There are some data available concerning speech and written
communications, though not in proportion to their widespread
usage. The need for research in this area is becoming more
apparent as speech displays are increasingly being used to
communicate information to operators of machines and vehicles,
and the need for unambiguous equipment operating and
maintenance instructions is being demanded by health and safety
legislation.

Type of dial	Movable pointer	Movable dial	Counter
Reading absolute values	Fair	Fair	Very good
Observing rates of change	Very good	Fair	Useless
Setting a definite value. Directing a process	Very good	Fair	Fair

Figure 2.4(a) Common display instruments and their utility (Grandjean[18])

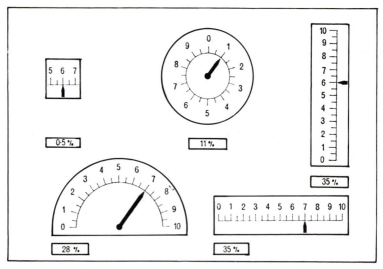

Figure 2.4(b) Effects of different types of information display on reading precision
(Grandjean[18])

2.2.3 Human output and control

There is a wealth of information and data available under this heading. A great deal of research effort has been directed at studying the effectiveness of various controls for specific purposes and published details are available concerning the features of switches, buttons, cranks, levers, wheels, pedals and knobs; see for example *Figure 2.5*.

Similar principles may be applied to hand tools and other devices where alternative types of handle, trigger, etc. have been developed which are anatomically more correct, thereby enabling safer and more efficient operation.

2.2.4 Workspace and arrangement

The relationship between the worker and his or her immediate workspace is becoming an important aspect in the design of machines and equipment. There are many everyday examples of machinery, vehicles, control panels, etc. which have been constructed without any regard for the people who are going to operate them.

As a result of this omission excessive body and eye movement is often incurred and poor posture results in discomfort and fatigue.

Type of control	Speed	Accuracy	Energy expenditure	Range	Load
Horizontal lever 	good	poor	poor	poor	up to ca. 9 kg
 Vertical lever	good	moderate	good	poor	up to ca. 13 kg
Joy-stick (small) 	good	moderate	poor	poor	ca. 1 kg
(large)	good	poor	good	poor	ca. 2-9 kg
Gear lever 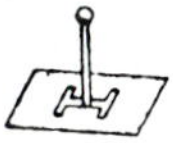	good	good	poor	very poor	up to ca. 9 kg
Crank (small) 	good	poor	very poor	good	0·9-2·5 lever arm: up to 120 mm
(large)	poor	very poor	good	good	over 3·5 kg lever arm: 150-220 mm
Handwheel 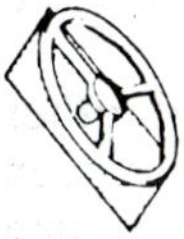	poor	good	moderate	moderate	2-25 kg diameter 180-500 mm
Continuous Control Knob (small) 	poor	good	very poor	moderate	up to 450 cmg diameter 10-30 mm
(large)	very poor	moderate	poor	moderate	up to 2500 cmg diameter 35-75 mm
Knob with step functions 	good	good	very poor	very poor	350-1500 g diameter 25-100 mm

Figure 2.5 The principal features of common controls (Grandjean[18])

Average body heights of 1008 employees in a Swiss engineering works

	Body height in cm	Standard deviation S	95% of value	99% of value
Women	159	±10·5	±21	±27
Men	169	± 9·5	±19	±25

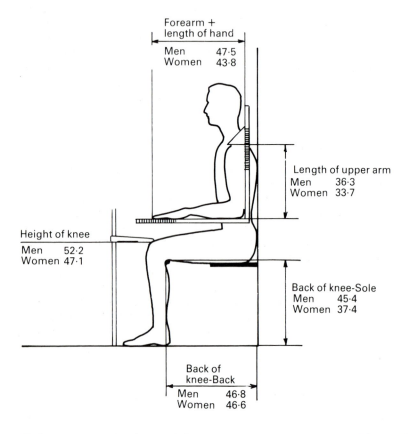

Body measurements when seated   cm

Figure 2.6 Typical anthropometric data (Grandjean[18])

As well as leading to inefficient working, a potentially hazardous work situation may also be created. Either or both of these conditions may lead to financial losses.

Anthropometry is the scientific measurement of the human body. The collection of anthropometric data is another aspect of ergonomic research. Care should be taken when using such information since the samples taken are usually from specific ethnic groups and measurements are obviously subject to some variation. *Figure 2.6* relates to the average measurements of a sample of 500 males and 508 females, most of whom were of Swiss nationality.

Designing the physical space and arranging equipment, places the emphasis less on the immediate workspace and rather more on the total work area within which the operator is free to move. Although anthropometry is again important, the layout of equipment is an additional factor in ensuring that movement of both people and materials are minimized. Other factors which might be taken into account include operational importance, frequency of use, sequence of use, and functional grouping of components.

2.2.5 Environment

The working environment has long been regarded as affecting the performance of personnel in industry. For instance, the Hawthorne research conducted in the 1920s, and described in Chapter 1, started out by being a study into the effect of different lighting levels on output. Experiments have also been conducted on military personnel over the years to test their abilities in extremes of pressure, temperature, and other climatic conditions.

So today there are data relating to illumination, temperature, humidity, air pollution, noise, vibration, etc. The effect of such data being available is that the environment in many factories bears little resemblance to that of fifty years ago. A modern plant is often clean, well-lit, quiet and air-conditioned, creating working conditions which are both physiologically and psychologically beneficial to the workforce.

2.2.6 Organizational aspects of job design

Most of what has so far been described as job design has come within the 'hygiene factor' category described by Herzberg. It is only through making organizational changes that the possibility of providing 'motivators' begins to emerge.

It is appropriate to look at this aspect of job design at two levels:

1. At the level of the work required to produce the product (the Company level).
2. At the level of the industry or country in which the work is taking place.

The first of these is concerned with the arrangement or re-arrangement of tasks and responsibilities, within the constraints of currently agreed practices and legislation. The second relates to changes made in the field of industrial democracy, trade union legislation etc.

Much research has been carried out and numerous books and papers have been written about the first level[19,20,21] and an example of some of this work, at Philips, has already been described in Chapter 1. Many of the organizational changes which are proposed can be seen as having much in common and all are in agreement as to what are desirable features (as far as the labour force is concerned) of the work organization. These can be summarized as follows: autonomy, responsibility, freedom from the technical system, involvement, and self-development.

The main differences in practice relate more to the technicalities of how the desired features of work are achieved rather than to the underlying principles, and this will always depend on the product, its demand pattern, available processes and other pre-conditions. Lindholm[22], however, identifies four criteria which are most prominent in the development of new forms of production organization in Sweden:

(a) *Small autonomous production units*

It is increasingly the practice to break down large, complex production systems into smaller units which make finished products or finished components, and which have their own services and administrative resources. Such production units can thus function as small companies within companies. Administration is simplified, the need for co-ordination is reduced, and the employees obtain conditions in which they can understand the context of their work and become more involved in how the production process is to function.

(b) *People less bound to machines*

Nowadays, greater efforts are being made than previously to free people from being bound by their work to the production rate of individual machines or to operations alongside the conveyor belt.

Increasingly, short-cycle feed and handling operations have been automated. Productivity improves and the operative obtains a freer job in which he or she can control several machines or a more extensive process.

(c) *Jobs with more involvement*

Attractive, interesting jobs are another clear aim in the design of modern factories. The work is arranged so that the individual or the team can function more independently. Work roles and the organization should be built up on team spirit and team work with joint objectives. The individual employee should be aware of the whole and understand the importance of his own work for the end-product. But people differ, so the tasks performed should not merely be extended; those who want simpler tasks should also get them.

(d) *Reliable, fast production systems*

A clear feature of the new production systems is the attempt to create simple and reliable production flows. In bath production, for example, attempts are made to assemble the manufacture of a particular product to one workshop and the machining or processing of a specific family of components to one product group. In this way the number of planning points is reduced and it is easier to monitor the production process. Throughput times for products are shorter and delivery times more reliable.

These criteria identified by Lindholm are now reflected in numerous examples of factories and production systems where the organization of work and material flow has been changed to allow the adoption of new job design principles. Specific cases will not be mentioned here, although many are well-known, since alternative forms of production system will be considered later when detailed examples will also be provided.

Whatever re-organization can take place within the first level of job design must depend to some extent on second level aspects. Lindholm himself considers the new issues relating to company democracy and points out that a number of fundamental principles have been settled in Sweden which can be taken as a basis for the development or organizations and work forms.

In many countries and within specific industries, recent agreements and legislation have eased and facilitated the introduction of novel forms of organization and working practice which hitherto have been considered impractical.

The Swedish examples are the Act of 1972 introducing mandatory labour representation on the Boards of Directors of corporations and the 1977 Act on Co-determination. The Co-determination Act granted employees the right to be given extensive information, through their unions, about all the activities of the company, and employers were compelled to consult the unions before making decisions involving major changes. In 1982 the legislation was supplemented by an industry-wide development agreement laying down the procedures by which the legally established principles could be upheld[23].

A similar situation exists in the Federal Republic of Germany where for several years worker representatives have had participation rights. Here an Act of 1972 extended works councils' rights to information and consultation to include job design, work operations and the working environment. Again, as in Sweden, the legislation has been supplemented by collective agreements on co-determination and 'work humanization'[24].

The Swedish and West German examples provide an indication of the changes which have taken place and are taking place throughout the industrial world in relation to industrial democracy and trade union relations. They demonstrate a growing and important trend which, from one country to another, only differs in terms of its rate of advance and the extent to which governments seek to influence and legislate for the changes. The governments of the USA and the UK, for instance, have deliberately sought not to control directly the course of industrial democracy, preferring rather to encourage agreements at a local level.

What is important, however, is that ultimately it will become the norm for workers to be involved in designing their own jobs as well as participating in company-wide decision-making. This is bound to influence, almost more than anything, the form which work organizations take in the future and what is more, will provide a so far untapped source of 'grass roots' knowledge which can be applied constructively in conjunction with job design activities.

2.3 Summary

In Chapter 1 the labour force was described as being one of the components or resources used by a production system for converting input into outputs. In these two sections the objective has been to present the human resource as an 'active' rather than 'passive' one.

The term 'rational economic man' is often used to describe the view taken by Taylor (*op cit*) towards the labour resource. This view is essentially one which supports the idea of labour being passive as may be demonstrated by Taylor's own words.

'The work of every workman is fully planned out by management at least one day in advance, and each man receives in most cases complete written instructions, describing in detail the task which he is to accomplish, as well as the means to be used in doing the work . . . This task specifies not only what is to be done but how it is to be done and the exact time allowed for doing it. And whenever the workman succeeds in doing his task right, and within the time-limit specified, he receives an addition of from 30% to 100% to his ordinary wages'.

This view of the worker can no longer be supported given the weight of evidence provided by industrial psychologists and behavioural theorists, neither is it one which even its originators could find easy to defend in today's economic and social conditions. The modern view is that the workforce should not be controlled and directed in the way Taylor describes, nor is the direct financial incentive by any means the prime motivator for achieving the best levels of performance.

The response to the currently held theory can be seen in both the methods now in use for providing remuneration and incentive, and in the design of jobs and organization of work. Alternative systems for remuneration which have been developed are far less linked to output than were their predecessors, providing recognition for initiative, responsibility, quality of work and adaptability. Some schemes, even for productive work, are not related to output at all.

As well as those factors relating to the industrial worker, the design of jobs is today considered an important aspect of workforce management. Ergonomics concentrates on the physical environment and physiological requirements. Organizational aspects of job design are concerned with making jobs which are more enriched and contain the 'motivating' factors.

Many managers and engineers think of production systems as comprizing hardware and ignore the vital role played by both direct and indirect workers. No system, however automated, can run uninterrupted without the human element (as, for instance, the printing industry has discovered to its cost) and organizations which appreciate this fact operate more smoothly and efficiently than those which do not.

References

1. MASLOW, A. H. (1943) 'A Theory of Human Motivation', *Psychological Review*, **50**
2. McGREGOR, D. M. (1960) *The Human Side of Enterprise*, McGraw-Hill, New York
3. LIKERT, R. (1961) *New Patterns of Management*, McGraw-Hill, New York
4. HERZBERG, F. (1966) *Work and the Nature of Man*, World Publishing Company
5. HERZBERG, F. (1968) 'One More Time: How Do You Motivate Employees?', *Harvard Business Review*, **46**
6. THE INSTITUTION OF PRODUCTION ENGINEERS (1981) *A Management Guide to Incentive Payment Schemes*, Inst. Prod. E, London
7. SCOTT, R. (1973) 'How to Structure Pay', *Management Today*, (April)
8. INTERNATIONAL LABOUR OFFICE (1951) *Payment by Results*, International Labour Office, Geneva
9. BRITISH INSTITUTE OF MANAGEMENT (1970) *Financial Motivation – An Outline of Some Current Incentive Schemes*, British Institute of Management, Information Note 81 (September)
10. BEACHAM, R. H. S. (1979) *Pay Systems*, Heinemann, London
11. HUSBAND, T. M. (1976) *Work Analysis and Pay Structure*, McGraw-Hill, Chichester
12. LIVY, B. (1975) *Job Evaluation – A Critical Review*, George Allen & Unwin Ltd, London
13. DAVIS, L. E. (1966) 'The Design of Jobs', *Industrial Relations*, **6**
14. KONZ, S. (1979) *Work Design*, Grid Publishing Inc
15. KLEIN, L. (1976) *New Forms of Work Organisation*, Cambridge University Press, Cambridge
16. MURRELL, K. F. H. (1965) *Ergonomics*, Chapman and Hall, London
17. McCORMICK, E. J. and SANDERS, M. S. (1982) *Human Factors in Engineering and Design*, McGraw-Hill, New York
18. GRANDJEAN, E. (1975) *Fitting the Task to the Man*, Taylor & Francis, London
19. BIRCHALL, D. (1975) *Job Design – A Planning and Implementation Guide for Managers*, Gower Press, London
20. CARBY, K. (1976) *Job Redesign in Practice*, Institute of Personnel Management, London
21. BAILEY, J. (1983) *Job Design and Work Organisation*, Prentice Hall, Hemel Hempstead, UK
22. LINDHOLM, R. (1979) 'Towards a New World of Work – Swedish Development of Work Organizations, Production Engineering and Co-determination', *International Journal of Production Research*, **17**, No 5
23. SAF-LO/PTK (1982) *Agreement on Efficiency and Participation*, Swedish Employers' Confederation, Stockholm
24. SPIEKER, W. (1979) 'Trade Unions' Attitudes in Relation to Work Humanization' in *Humanization of Work in Western Europe*, European Association for Personnel Management

Chapter 3

Established concepts for production organization

3.1 Categories of production system and layout conventions

In Chapter 1 some of the types of work organization available for production were described in terms of the manner in which they focused on products, processes or tasks. The more commonly adopted means of categorizing the production system itself (or its constituent sub-systems) tends on the other hand to use as a basis the demand pattern for the finished products or component parts and subassemblies. This is the basis of the more traditional classification which places production systems into the categories of job batch and flow*, each of which can be described as follows[1]:

The **Job** system is where a complete product is manufactured by individuals or a group of workers and facilities. In this way a variety of different products can be completed in parallel. This is the most general and versatile type of system but does not usually make the most efficient use of resources so is, in most circumstances, considered a relatively costly alternative. As a result its use is generally limited to purpose-built items made entirely to customer specification such as power stations, large passenger ships, and certain one-off factories and office buildings.

---

* There are variations on this basic classification which are sometimes identified. For instance, one author[2] identified five categories, viz: project, jobbing, batch, line and continuous process, while another[3] identifies: unit and small batch, large batch and mass, and process. Furthermore, in the USA, the category called 'job' is often referred to as the 'project system' and 'batch' as the 'job shop system'[4].

Notwithstanding these differences in terminology and number of categories identified, the basic concept behind them remains the same, i.e. they are based on sections of a scale which ranges from 'one off' production of an item which is never repeated to continuous production of discrete or bulk items which never stops (both these extremes being rarely encountered in practice).

The **Batch** system is where a number of products are processed in batches (or lots) in order that some of the recurring fixed items of expenditure may be shared between each individual in the batch. This lacks some of the versatility of the job system and, because of variations in production and consumption rates, inevitably leads to storage or queueing of materials at some stage within the system. Examples of products which might be batch produced include machine tools, furniture and glassware.

Lastly, the **Flow** (or continuous) system is where products are processed continuously, being passed successively through the required sequence of facilities. Flow systems are the least flexible and least versatile of the three types, changes to the product being made infrequently. Continuity of demand is necessary in order that the rate of production can match that of consumption. Obvious examples of goods which are normally flow produced include household items such as washing machines, radios, light bulbs etc.

Putting production systems into categories is in itself a rather academic exercise unless an in-depth examination is made of the characteristics of each type. It then becomes easier to understand the rationale behind using a particular production system and the associated advantages and disadvantages. Most importantly, it becomes possible to analyse critically those features of the system which are seen as creating problems and inefficiencies, and to identify possible alternative approaches.

The characteristics of a production system can be grouped under three broad headings, namely:

1. Physical characteristics (i.e. layout of facilities and type of machinery, tooling and material handling equipment).
2. Control characteristics (i.e. routing of material, queueing and work-in-progress, and throughput time).
3. Labour and organizational characteristics (i.e. proportion of managers, type of hierarchy, and proportion of skilled workers).

It can be seen that these three headings relate closely to the three types of tangible resource identified in Chapter 1 (i.e. physical facilities, materials and labour). It will also be remembered that the control of materials was not an issue that this book intended dealing with in depth. However, control characteristics justify some discussion here, not because of a change in this intention, but because many of the characteristics identified under the heading of control are themselves determined by other features, particularly the physical layout of facilities.

3.1.1 Conventional layouts and their rationale

Looking now at the various characteristics, an appropriate start is to reiterate and develop some of the points made earlier about facility layout. In the previous discussion, layout was described as being by one of three types fixed position, function, or product. Some further detail is now provided about each of these.

Fixed Position Layout is where the product remains (more or less) stationary and materials, equipment and labour are brought to the place of work – see *Figure 3.1*. Its use in connection with production is evident from examples such as the building of oil rigs, the construction industry, and the manufacture of other purpose-built engineering items such as steam turbines for power stations.

It is sometimes argued that the use of a fixed position layout is attributed to the size and bulk of the product being manufactured. Although this sometimes might be the case, it is by no means the best and only explanation. Moreover, some extremely large items such as ships and aircraft are often moved very large distances during their manufacture while, conversely, some relatively small products such as electrical control panels are manufactured using fixed position layouts.

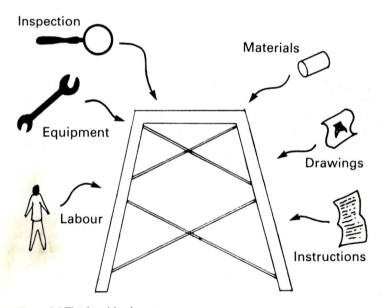

Figure 3.1 Fixed position layout

The most logical rationale for using a fixed position layout is its suitability for product-orientated work organization, which itself is a feature of job production. The fact that a worker or group of workers is producing a single complete item means that this particular type of organization is the most appropriate, with its emphasis on wide-ranging skills and flexibility. Any attempt to try and apply the principles of strict division of labour and specialization of skills would probably lead to grossly under-utilized manpower and a massive problem of co-ordinating the whole set of productive activities.

Layout by Function is where machines, processes and equipment of the same type are grouped together in one department or area. A further feature of this type of layout is that the skills required for setting and operating a particular type of machine or process are kept together and put under specialized supervision. This type of layout has become common in the engineering industries as a way of realizing the benefits to be gained from skill specialization and the division of labour.

Under these principles factories have evolved where separate departments engage in such activities as milling, drilling, grinding, turning, painting, sub-assembly work and final assembly, see *Figure 3.2*. Each of these departments will have groups of setters and operators who are familiar with a particular process or machine type and who carry out a common operation on the entire range of components and products which are routed through the department.

Even outside the engineering industry, layout by function has gained widespread acceptance. For example, shoe manufacture is traditionally organized so that production is carried out in a number of 'rooms' (clicking, closing, making, finishing etc) while made-up textiles, fasteners, tyres and toys are all examples of the wide range of products which often rely on this form of layout for their manufacture. The one thing these products have in common is (relatively) high demand but, at the same time, there will be reasons for not using continuous (flow) production methods. These reasons may include: erratic or seasonal demand patterns, much higher production rates compared with consumption or a large number of product variants. Each of these reasons would justify manufacture in discrete batches in order to overcome the problems otherwise associated with continuous production methods.

Functional layout thus enables batch production to take place whereby a single operation or set of operations is performed within a processing department on the entire batch. Batches are

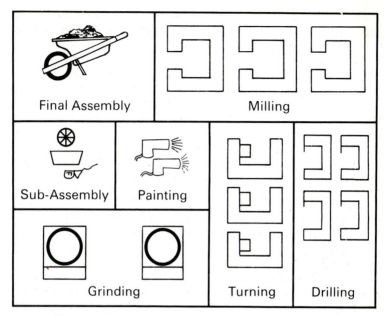

Figure 3.2 Layout by function

routed from one department to another, as necessary, according to the sequence of operations required for their completion. It is feasible to even use a functional layout for job or continuous production; in fact, it is sometimes the case that organizations send occasional orders for one or two 'specials' (or spares) through their factory along with the more routine orders for batches of standard products.

The problem here is that machines and processes need resetting and schedules made out just for one or two components or products, thereby incurring effort and expense out of all proportion to the size of the order. In such cases a 'specials' department is often created in order that this type of activity does not disturb normal production. The other possibility, that of using functional layout for continuous production, is (though feasible) rather illogical since unnecessary movement of materials would be incurred and uniform flow could not be achieved.

The use of functional layout is, therefore, rationalized in circumstances where a process-orientated form of work organization is favoured. Some economy of scale can be achieved by adopting production engineering principles and by sharing some of the recurring fixed costs among each of the items in the batch.

Such a layout enables these benefits to be derived without the need to manufacture continuously and without the adoption of a layout designed for continuous flow production methods.

Product Layout is the result of arranging machines, equipment and workplaces according to the sequence of operations required to produce a complete component, product or sub-assembly. This often takes the form of a line, hence the term 'line layout' which is often given to this type of arrangement, see *Figure 3.3*. A product

Figure 3.3 Product (line) layout

layout does not have to be of the line type however; it could be a group or 'cell' of facilities comprising all the machines and processes necessary to perform the required set of operations to complete an item. This alternative arrangement provides greater flexibility since operations can easily be performed in different sequences and 'backtracking' of material is possible. The cost of such flexibility, however, would be the need for greater versatility of the handling equipment compared with the simple transfer devices usually found on unidirectional lines.

The type of work organization commonly used with product layouts is the one described earlier as being task-orientated. This is particularly true in the case of lines, the reason being that they are traditionally used where production is of the continuous or flow type. In this way the same task can be repeated over and over on the same product and a high degree of specialization can be achieved.

The use of product layouts involves such a high degree of repetition and the product is often so standardized that it frequently lends itself to the application of automation. This has long been the case with machining (rather than assembly) work where 'transfer lines' are employed in the manufacture of such items as vehicle engine blocks, cylinder heads, and parts for use in domestic appliances.

Not all types of product layout have been considered suitable for automation though; where they take the form of cells or where assembly work is involved, automation has traditionally been more difficult. A lack of standardization has also been regarded as an impediment to automation, i.e. where a number of different variants of the product need to be manufactured.

In these situations the need for complex and versatile material handling and the variety of possible operations have in the past placed them outside the capabilities of available automatic equipment. However, rapid progress is being made in this area and a whole new field called 'advanced manufacturing technology' is being developed which is aimed at producing automated systems capable of performing the type of work described. Chapter 7 will be devoted to this topic.

Before leaving the issue of product layout, the question must be asked whether it is a suitable arrangement for production systems other than the continuous or flow type. Product layouts have considerable benefits which will be discussed later and which make them attractive for batch production in particular. The problem which must be faced, however, is how to reconcile the idea of producing a wide variety of components and products on a system which was conceived on the presumption of more or less complete standardization. This conflict will be examined before describing some more novel concepts which seek to overcome the obstacles that seemingly stand in the way of putting product layouts into more widespread use.

3.2 Further characteristics of production systems

In the last section the three basic types of layout were described together with their application in providing for different kinds of work organization. Layout is just one of the physical characteristics identified but it is probably the more important, thereby justifying a detailed examination. The reason why layout is so important is that, apart from being one of the most visible characteristics, it has the most significant influence on the other system features. In particular, it often determines the type of equipment used, the flow of materials and the labour and organizational requirements.

These further characteristics can be described and explained as follows:

Machinery, tools and material handling equipment may be broadly described as (i) general purpose, (ii) specially adapted general purpose, and (iii) special purpose.

Although general purpose items are flexible, relatively inexpensive and available 'off the shelf' they have the disadvantage of being comparatively inefficient and requiring a higher degree of operator skill. Adapting such items (for example, by fitting automatic feeding or control devices) overcomes some of these disadvantages, but obviously reduces the flexibility and increases the expense. Therefore, although general purpose equipment might be found in all types of production system, adapted variants are a feature of large batch or flow systems where they can be justified by higher volume levels or by continuity of demand. Special purpose items of equipment are purpose-built and, consequently, least flexible and most expensive. They are, therefore, almost exclusively used in flow systems where economies of scale can justify the heavy investment involved.

Routing of material, like all the control characteristics, is to a large extent determined by the layout of facilities. Job systems using fixed position layout involve very little movement since most of the facilities and labour are brought to the workplace. By comparison, functional layout involves extensive movement of materials (usually in batches) between each facility where an operation is carried out. In the case of product layout, this interfacility movement is minimized due to the close proximity of each of the machines or work stations.

Queueing and the amount of work in progress generated is also affected by layout. With fixed position layouts, queues and work in progress are dependent on the overall project time scale which, in turn, depends on the amount of resources allocated. Functional layout involves extensive queueing due to the more or less random arrival of jobs at facilities and a considerable amount of work in progress is generated as a result. The queueing and work in progress occurring in product layout situations is very much reduced due to the minimum of partly finished work being held between processes.

The throughput time is largely dependent on the amount of queueing and work in progress, so it follows that, when functional layout is used, this time could be of a high order compared with the sum of the individual operation times. In some industries planning is sometimes even done on the basis of 'one week per operation' making a throughput time of several weeks (or even months) quite common. Conversely, where a product layout is used, the time the job spends in the system may be little more than the sum of the individual operation times, a matter of only hours for even the most complex of products. The time-span for job systems is largely a function of project management effectiveness and resource availability.

The proportion of managers compared to other grades of employee, when studied in a survey[3], was found in job type industries to be small (1 manager to 23 total personnel), in batch industries it was higher (1 to 16), while in flow type industries the highest proportion of managers was observed (1 to 8)*.

This situation is due to the fact that workers in job systems are often able to plan the work for themselves and, therefore, require the minimum of supervision whereas with batch production (using functional specialization) the autonomy of the workforce is reduced. In flow production, workers are not free to control their own work and must stick rigidly to the production cycle, therefore requiring the greatest level of supervision.

The number of management levels, as may be expected, is similarly affected. Consequently job production has the least (three in the survey just mentioned), batch production slightly more (four), while flow systems have the most (six).

Lastly, **the ratio of skilled to semi-skilled workers** can be demonstrated by looking at shipbuilding (an example of a job system) which has, in the UK, 67% skilled and 14% semi-skilled, and domestic appliance manufacture (an example of a flow system) which has 18% skilled and 55% semi-skilled workers. This clearly illustrates the dependency of job production on large amounts of skilled labour compared with flow systems, while batch systems fall somewhere in between. Although flow systems employ a smaller percentage of skilled labour it should, however, still be stressed that the skills in this type of system are used in the important areas of machine setting, maintenance etc.

Figure 3.4 summarizes the various characteristics of production systems together with their overall determinant factors.

3.2.1 The cost justification for using a particular production system

In the final analysis the choice of production system is usually based on a cost justification, the objective being to find that system which will result in the lowest unit production cost. A simple translation of the various characteristics into elements of cost normally yields the breakeven analysis illustrated in *Figure 3.5*.

* In the survey of South Essex firms conducted by Woodward different categories of production system were defined. Their configuration, however, made them broadly equivalent to job, batch and flow.

Overall Determinant Factor	Increasing volume and continuity of demand → ← Increasing variety of products and intermittent demand pattern		
System Type \ Characteristic	**Job**	**Batch**	**Flow**
Layout	Mostly fixed position	Mostly functional	Mostly product
Machines, tools and material handling	General purpose	General purpose + Adapted	General purpose + Adapted + Special purpose
Routing	Negligible movement of product	Extensive routing of materials and components	Short distances moved
Queues and work in progress	Depends on amount of resources allocated to production activities	Long waiting times and large amounts of work in progress	Minimal queuing between operations and low work in progress levels
Time in system	Processing time depends on project management and resource availability	Long overall processing time	Short overall processing time
Ratio of managers to other grades	Small proportion of managers (1 to 23)	Higher proportion of managers (1 to 16)	Highest proportion of managers (1 to 8)
Number of management levels	Few levels (3)	More levels (4)	Most levels (6)
Ratio of skilled to semi-skilled workers	Highest proportion of skilled operators	Moderate proportion of skilled operators	Lowest proportion of skilled operators

Figure 3.4 Categories of production system – determinant factors and characteristics

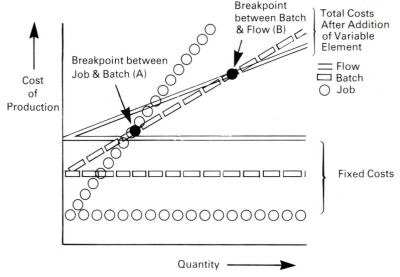

Figure 3.5 Breakeven analysis for different types of production

On the basis of this elementary economic analysis, job systems with their low fixed costs are seen as theoretically suitable for low volumes (i.e. below point A), whereas for higher volumes they are normally regarded as unsuitable due to what are seen as disadvantageous variable costs. In such cases flow production is considered appropriate (i.e. for volume levels above point B) since variable costs are lower and the high fixed costs can be more easily absorbed. For intermediate volume levels (i.e. between A and B) batch systems are normally regarded as most suitable.

This rather theoretical argument is based on the assumption that the cost profile of a particular production system is completely bound by the various characteristics just described. However, it was pointed out earlier that most of the systems' characteristics are influenced by facility layout and that alternative forms of layout might be feasible in situations where traditional practice has normally been adhered to.

A further important point to be made here is that the majority of the costs included in the above analysis are tangible. The intangible costs associated with labour relations, competitiveness, etc. cannot be readily calculated and are, therefore, often excluded from the argument. If they are taken into consideration, however, then extra weight might be added to the case for considering an alternative approach.

The next logical step, therefore, is to summarize briefly the fundamental attributes of the three traditional systems and then to identify their favourable and unfavourable features. A rational approach can then be taken to seeking out more novel alternatives.

3.3 An appraisal of job, batch and flow systems

In an earlier part of this chapter, job production was described as being where individuals or groups produce a complete product and where several different products can be made in parallel, with fixed position layouts being most commonly used. Batch production on the other hand is where individuals are employed in performing a repetitive operation on a complete batch of items, working within a functional department or area.

Lastly, flow production was the continuous processing of items, at a rate more-or-less equal to that of consumption, using facilities laid out by product. An additional point to mention at this stage is the common use of batch production techniques for component manufacture against the more frequent use of flow production for assembly work.

3.3.1 Favourable features of the production systems

One of the main advantages of job production is its flexibility in terms of its ability to handle a wide variety of work, with financial benefits arising from the lower fixed cost component when compared with producing the same product on a different system. From the worker's point of view, job production provides enlarged work elements requiring a range of skills and giving individuals greater responsibility for both quality and output. Relatively simple production control systems can often be used with much of the planning being done by the workers themselves.

Batch production also provides a degree of flexibility together with the opportunity for some task specialization (presumed here to be desirable). Specialized supervision can also be used and production usually takes place on standard equipment. The use of functional layout means the isolation of unpleasant and unsafe processes without special measures needing to be taken. The production control system can usually accommodate sudden changes in priority and demand.

Flow production has a number of favourable features, arising in the main from the associated material flow. These include the minimum of resetting, low work-in-progress levels and short distances moved by materials. Lower skills are required and a high degree of specialization is possible (presuming again that these are desirable features), both these features being reflected in the fact that less operator training is required. Of all the favourable features of flow production which make it an attractive proposition today, the most significant in terms of raising efficiency and lowering costs still further is the possibility offered for automation. Indeed, many of the unfavourable features of flow production, described later, which are concerned with the problems of labour can, it is claimed, be 'automated out' – an approach now taken by a large number of major organizations.

3.3.2 Unfavourable features of the production systems

Most of the disadvantages associated with job production are economic in nature and result from the system's inefficient use of resources. Long setting times and the need to duplicate equipment adversely affect the capital costs while the greater skill require-ments demand longer training periods. It is, therefore, the resultant poor economy of scale which more often than not outweighs the advantages mentioned previously and limits the job system to relatively few examples.

Despite the popularity of batch production (it is by far the most common system), there are a number of inherent problems. Very high work-in-progress levels demand that large quantities of working capital are tied up in inventory and heavy costs are incurred in moving batches of material between machines and departments. Frequent and time-consuming resetting is not only costly but interferes with the smooth running of production. This in turn results in the need for complex production control systems to monitor and progress the productive activities. Lastly, throughput times are long when compared with the actual operation times, a factor which affects customer service and the ability to make accurate forecasts of demand in advance of production.

The features of flow production which are disadvantageous can be divided into those relating to the physical system and those relating to labour (human problems). In the first category can be put the following: high capital cost, susceptibility to breakdown, rigidity and inflexibility, inability to respond to sudden variations in demand, and the need for product standardization. Balancing losses, system losses and the problem of dealing with product variants are also unfavourable features (these will be explained in

Chapter 5), as is the fact that an additional 'pool' of labour is required to replace workers who are absent or need to leave the production area for short periods.

Human problems associated with flowline work have been the subject of debate since the system of production was first conceived. Most readers will be familiar with the 1936 Charlie Chaplin film *Modern Times* in which the star spends much of his time performing an inane 'nut tightening' task on a relentless assembly line. Chaplin's message, as he was driven progressively crazy, was regarded as serious even then and, offscreen, he was approached by those who wanted to re-organize and humanize the system he portrayed.

But the attractiveness of such an apparently efficient production system meant that little was done to change the routine and even years later Chaplin's image of the system remained.

> 'The job gets so sickening, day in day out, plugging in ignition wires. I get through with one motor, turn around and there's another staring me in the face. It's sickening. The assembly line is no place to work I can tell you. There's nothing more discouraging than having a barrel beside you with ten thousand bolts in it and using them all up. Then you get a barrel with another ten thousand bolts and you know every one of those bolts has to be picked up and put in exactly the same place as the last ten thousand bolts'[6].

It was only when the underlying discontent of the workforce manifested itself in ways which adversely affected their efficiency that many organizations started taking serious note of the human problems associated with flow lines. Philips in Holland, for instance, experienced a deterioration in output and quality which led to the experiments described in Chapter 1.

In the USA the Lordstown plant of General Motors suffered a twenty day strike with a loss of 70 000 vehicles following a long period of unrest during which both cars and equipment were sabotaged[7]. Though the reasons for the strike and unrest at Lordstown were various, they were thought to be a direct result of the speed of the line and monotony of the work. Cycle times approaching thirty six seconds were being sought while, at the same time, a younger than average workforce (average age 24 years) created the need for more interesting work.

In Sweden the annual rate of labour turnover at Volvo reached 52% in 1969 and deteriorating quality levels at around this time were severely damaging one of the most important aspects of its corporate image[8]. In fact, Volvo's crisis led to one of the most dramatic programmes yet of work restructuring, resulting in a complete change in attitudes and a major turnround in the company's fortunes.

In summarizing the various symptoms of discontent which can exist as a result of flowline working, the following six points emerge as being relevant. They all have significant cost implications which should cause organizations to look again at the merits of using conventional flow production techniques and to seek possible alternatives whereby the benefits can be maintained and the unfavourable features avoided:

1. More frequent occurrences of strikes and other forms of industrial action.
2. Deterioration of quality.
3. Sabotage of products and equipment.
4. High labour turnover rate.
5. Recruitment difficulties.
6. High levels of absenteeism.

The approach which might be taken when seeking alternatives to conventional methods of production can be illustrated by reference to *Figure 3.6*. Here two alternative approaches are identified, namely 'group technology' and 'autonomous working'. Both will be described in detail in later chapters but the fundamental logic on which they are based can readily be seen in the diagram.

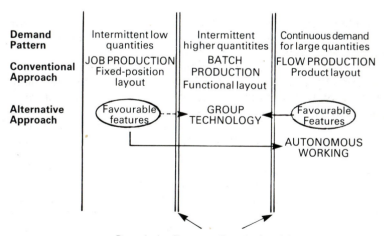

Figure 3.6 The development of alternatives to conventional methods of production

The first of these, group technology, is based on an approach which attempts to overcome many of the difficulties normally associated with batch production when using conventional techniques. It is based on the idea that considerable benefit can be gained by creating a system which will exhibit the favourable features of flow production, but in a batch production environment, thereby gaining the 'best of both worlds'. Moreover in some respects group technology can also be said to exhibit some of the features of job production, hence the dotted line in *Figure 3.6*.

The approach that autonomous working takes is similar except that it applies to continuous production situations and attempts to overcome the difficulties normally associated with flow systems. It does this by identifying the favourable features of job production and transplanting them into the flow production environment, again with the intention of creating a system in which the worst features of one have been substituted by the best features of another.

3.4 Summary

Designers of production systems normally tend to adhere to a limited set of conventions when making choices relating to the system's configuration and facility layout. This has led to one of three options being most commonly selected with the particular choice largely depending on the pattern of demand.

The three common options in questions are: job production using fixed position layout, batch production using layout by function, and flow production using a product layout. Each has its own justification for a specific case but, at the same time, there are a number of unfavourable features associated with all of them which prevent the achievement of the best possible results.

If system designers free themselves from the established conventions then it should be possible to develop new practices which can benefit from advantages normally outside the reach of a particular system. Two alternative approaches that have been developed are 'group technology' and 'autonomous working'. The first seeks to take some of the characteristics of flow production and transfer them to a batch production environment; while the second tries, within flow production, to create some of the favourable features of the job system.

The successes achieved have shown that it is possible to design systems which, by deviating from accepted practice, can achieve high levels of output, quality and efficiency without being burdened with many of the technical, control and human problems associated with more conventional approaches.

References

1. BENNETT, D. J. (1981) 'An Introduction to Operations Management', in *Operations Management in Practice* (edited by C. D. Lewis), Philip Allan, London

2. HILL, T. J. (1983) *Production/Operations Management,* Prentice-Hall, Hemel Hempstead, UK

3. WOODWARD, J. (1965) *Industrial Organization: Theory and Practice,* Oxford University Press, Oxford

4. STARR, M. K. (1971) *Systems Management of Operations,* Prentice-Hall, Hemel Hempstead, UK

5. BENNETT, D. J. (1981) *Training Manual for Industrial and Production Management,* INTAN, Kuala Lumpur, Malaysia

6. WALKER, C. R. and GUEST, R. H. (1952) *The Man on the Assembly Line,* Harvard University Press, Harvard, USA

7. WILD, R. (1975) *Work Organisation,* Wiley, Chichester, UK

8. WILLATT, N. (1973), Volvo Versus Ford, *Management Today* (January)

Chapter 4

Grouping methods for batch production

4.1 The development of group technology and its rationale

The various grouping methods which have been developed as alternatives to the conventional approach to batch production have become known collectively as Group Technology. The ideas on which Group Technology are based go back many years and have been refined and developed so that today it has become a complete philosophy rather than a single technique, embracing a number of similar but individual concepts.

The common thread running through the Group Technology philosophy is that it attempts to find alternative methods to those used in conventional batch production which are based on the idea of grouping. This grouping can be of component parts, machines, equipment and people. The purpose of grouping is to seek to overcome some of the problems of batch production, as outlined in Chapter 3, by attempting to apply principles and methods which traditionally have been associated with other types of production. For the main part this involves applying flow production principles to a batch production environment but it can also, to some extent, include borrowing ideas from job production.

Standing in the way of this approach is the fact that the demand pattern associated with batch production does not normally exhibit the characteristics which enable other forms of production system to be used. Demand is not large and continuous and products and components lack standardization, so flow production based on layout by product would normally be regarded as impractical. Neither, conversely, has demand been considered small enough to warrant an approach based on product-orientated work organization so job production principles have also traditionally been ruled out.

These obstacles have meant that the development of the Group Technology philosophy has been slow and cautious with an incremental approach being taken throughout. In fact, the first of the obstacles to be tackled was the problem of time taken to reset machines and processes when changing over from one batch of items to another.

4.1.1 Component families

It is well known that if batches of work arrive *in random order* at a machine, an abnormally high proportion of the available time can inevitably be spent on re-setting and re-tooling between batches. Conservative estimates are that this sometimes might be around 20–25% of the available time, being one of the reasons for poor overall utilization of batch production systems[1].

One explanation for such long re-setting times is that they are due to the dissimilar shapes and sizes of the various items which are to be produced and the different operations which need to be performed. However, an intelligent machine setter, if given sufficient notice and information about future work, can reduce the total setting time required by sequencing the batches in such an order that each item follows another which is similar in some way. It was this basic idea, which of course is just good planning practice, that was extended and formalized to become the first step taken in the development of group technology.

A Russian engineer, S. P. Mitrofanov, who worked in the Leningrad Optical-Mechanical Association, is generally given the credit for developing this first phase of group technology although, as with most such breakthroughs, his work was to some extent paralleled and, some would argue, preceded by others. In 1959 Mitrofanov published his book *The Scientific Principles of Group Technology*[2] wherein he advocated the grouping together of component parts into *families* based on their having common features which would enable re-setting time between them to be minimized.

Figure 4.1 illustrates such a group of parts which were identified for manufacture on a single machine, in this case a 'capstan lathe'. If careful thought is given to tooling requirements, tool design and machine settings, then changeover times between components within the family, can be reduced to only a fraction of those which existed under the old system. For instance, cases are recorded of lathe changeovers being cut from 40 minutes to 5 minutes[4], while for power presses changeover times of 15 seconds have even been achieved[5].

Part of the thinking behind the reduction in setting times involves the creation of a *composite component*. The composite component, formed from all the different components in the

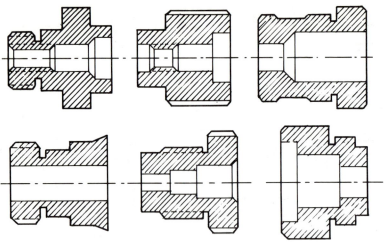

Figure 4.1 A group of parts identified for manufacture on a capstan lathe (Ivanov[3])

previously identified family, is simply one which incorporates all or most of the features exhibited by the individual component designs. Although, in theory, the composite component may be either 'real' or 'hypothetical', real composites are rarely encountered in practice.

Once the design of a composite component has been established then it becomes a matter of equipping the chosen machine with all the tools and sequences necessary to manufacture it, rather than any one of the constituent parts of the family. In the case of hypothetical composites, they will of course never actually be produced, but what will have been achieved is the possibility – by making only small adjustments – of quickly changing from the manufacture of one part of the family to another.

4.1.2 Machine groups

The idea of producing a group of parts on an appropriately equipped machine is known as the 'single machine' case of group technology and is normally recognized as the first important step towards tackling the problems of batch production. It is, on its own, only of limited value since in practice most parts require processing on a number of different machines (for example, having been on the lathe a component may then need to be milled, drilled and ground).

If layout by function were used, therefore, the manufacture of such parts would still involve extensive movement between

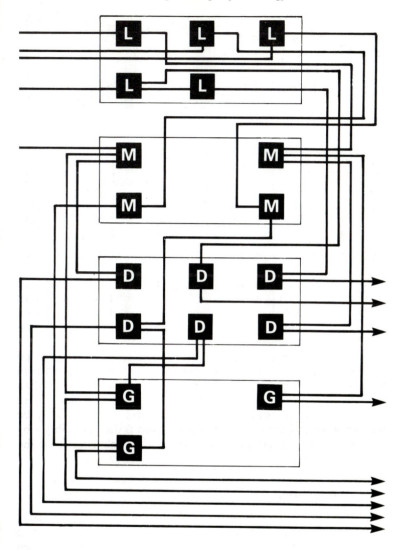

L = lathe section M = milling section D = drilling section G = grinding section

Figure 4.2(a) Typical 'functional layout' and work flow (NEDO°)

departments, waiting in queues and as work in progress – resulting in high investment costs, long throughput times and requiring a complex planning and control system. These problems can be regarded as the next set of obstacles which needed to be tackled in

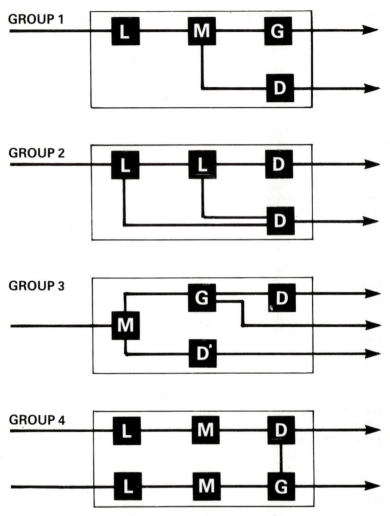

Figure 4.2(b) Typical 'group layout' and work flow (NEDO[6])

the development of group technology. The approach taken this time was to group not just components into families but also to group machines into 'cells'.

Figure 4.2(a) shows a typical pattern of workflow in conventional batch production using functional layout. Although this is a rather simplified example of only four functional departments and eighteen machines, it still serves to illustrate the complex nature of the various routings involved. The alternative approach is to arrange the eighteen machines into four groups on the basis of their ability to manufacture a complete family of components. For instance, the machines in the example could be rearranged as shown in *Figure 4.2(b)* so that all the routings remain the same but they are retained within a single cell of machines rather than crossing between the functional departments.

Such an arrangement can still retain the features and advantages of the single machine case but also goes much further in terms of the additional benefits achieved. In summary the benefits derived from this approach to Group Technology are:

1. Reduced setting times due to the similar nature and sequence of machining operations.
2. Reduced material handling due to shorter routings between machines.
3. Shorter throughput times due to rapid flow of parts through the cell.
4. Reduced levels of work in progress because large batches of part-completed components are not waiting between operations.

This last point merits some further explanation since it represents a good example of how changing the design of a production system can negate the application of operational research techniques to production control problems. One of the benefits of reducing setting times, apart from its effect on the cost of this activity, is that batch sizes can consequentially be reduced.

One of the main reasons that batches are often so large is that they are thought to be economic (i.e. the total cost associated with setting and stockholding is theoretically minimized). Reducing setting times has the result of decreasing the size of the 'economic' batch to the point where eventually other considerations can take precedence over theoretical economic arguments.

Parts can be produced in quantities required only for immediate use and even batch sizes approaching one can be contemplated. In this case the characteristics of a group technology cell are almost the same as those of continuous flow production using a line layout.

4.2 Designing a group technology system – the formation of component families and machine groups

The group technology ideas just outlined might seem at first sight to be so obvious and potentially effective that, if put into widespread use, they would be the panacea for all the problems of conventional batch production. Of course, ideas are never as simple to implement as they first seem and this is no less the case with group technology. The main problem which is encountered when putting group technology into practice is that of forming component families and the cells in which to process them.

Numerous organizations have attempted to implement group technology. Their success, or failure, has often resulted from the choice of method for identifying component families and, in the case of more than one machine being used, the means of then creating an appropriate group of production facilities. There are five basic approaches to this that might be taken:

1. Family formation 'by eye' or 'rule of thumb' using local product knowledge.
2. Formation based on coding and classification of parts using a universal system.
3. Using a tailor-made component classification system.
4. Using production flow analysis.
5. Designing products for group technology manufacture.

The idea of identifying families by eye would seem attractive and is often regarded as an inexpensive way of quickly achieving the benefits associated with group technology. Indeed, in a few cases it is probably quite feasible to form a family of gears, shafts, bearings, etc. since they can readily be seen as being of similar shape, produced from the same material, and requiring common machining operations.

However, if an attempt is made to extend the idea across an organization's entire product range, its limitations quickly become apparent for a number of reasons. Among these is the fact that, in reality, thousands of different parts could be produced by the firm, not just a few gears and shafts, many of which may only be drawings and their existence may not immediately occur to the planner. There is also the fact that identification need not only be on the basis of physical shape or material, but also on the sequence and nature of manufacturing operations, making visual grouping extremely difficult.

4.2.1 Coding and classification

In view of these limitations the next alternative might be the use of some system of coding and classification based on a proprietary universal part numbering system. Typical examples of these generally available systems are OPITZ (from West Germany), VUOSO (from Czechoslovakia), KCI (from Japan) and PGM (from Sweden). Although they differ in various ways, they are all basically trying to achieve the same thing – that is to assign a number (or alpha numeric code) to a part which describes some of its salient features.

Their main differences are in the degree of detail to which they go and, as a general rule, the greater the number of digits used the more information that can be included. VUOSO, for example, uses only four digits and can be summarized on one side of paper, as shown in *Figure 4.3*, so there is only a limited amount of information that this code can contain. Nevertheless some successes have been claimed in using VUOSO and other simple coding systems in connection with identifying suitable families for group technology production. In contrast to the simpler codes others, such as OPITZ and PGM, can contain up to nine or ten digits so they are able to describe in much greater detail such features as dimensional accuracy and form of raw material. This enables a greater range of variables to be used when forming families.

Once a particular coding system has been decided upon, the next step is to assign a code number to all 'live' components (i.e. those which are produced regularly), either entering this number onto some form of document prior to data processing or using direct data entry. Identification and formation of families is then a matter of sorting the data using one or more of the digits and thereby classifying components into the required categories according to shape, size or other relevant feature.

In the early days of group technology the methods employed involved the use of coding forms and punched cards followed by long data processing runs on early generation tabulation machines. Today the task is very different since computers and programs are available which greatly shorten and simplify the problem of sorting and classification.

However, despite these developments, the job of assigning part numbers to components using the coding system still remains which, it is estimated, can be done at the rate of 100 to 200 parts per man-day.

The methods of component family formation which use a universal coding system can often suffer from the inadequacies associated with the fact that such systems were intended for general use. In particular, they will have been designed to suit an *average* mix of component shapes (i.e. fixed proportions of rotational and prismatic parts, etc.), so for a specific application part of the code may be under-utilized while in another part insufficient detail may be available.

Vúoso-Praha   Workpiece classification system

Kind of workpiece						Rotational workpieces					Flat and irregular		Box-like		Other mainly non-machined	Materials

Rotational workpieces

		Hole in axis			Geared and splined				Flat and irregular		Box-like		Other mainly non-machined	Materials
		None 1	Blind 2	Trough 3	None 4	Trough 5			6		7		8	Plain steel STL

	D	L/D	Rough form	Rough form	Lmax	Rough weight	Made of	
0		~1		Gib-like L/B>5	mm 0-200	0-30 kg	Extruded forms	
1	0-40	1-6			mm 200-	30-200 kg	Bars	
2		>6		Platforms L/B<5	mm 0-200	200-500 kg	Tubes	
3		~1			mm 200-	500-1000 kg	Sheets	
4	40-80	1-4		Lever-like	mm 0-200	1000- kg	Wires	
5		>4			mm 200-			
6	80-200	<3		Irregular	mm 0-200			
7	80-	>3			mm 200-			
8	200-	<3		Prism-like	mm 0-200			
9	Various	>30			mm 200-			

	Group of workpiece													
0	Smooth		Spur geared	Splined	Other		Flat Parallel		Boxes Spindlestocks Frames	Non mach	Example of a class number
1	Thread in axis			Other			Flat Other		Columns	Part mach	
2	Holes not in axis		Taper geared	Splined	Other		Rotat. Parallel		Beds Bridges	Non mach	
3	Splines or grooves			Other			Rotat. Other		Outriggers Knees	Part mach	
4	Comb. 1+2		Wormgeared	Splined	Other		Flat Parallel Rotat. Parallel		Tables Slides	Non mach	
5	Comb. 1+3			Other			Flat Parallel Rotat. Other		Lids	Part mach	
6	Comb. 2+3		Multiple gears	Splined	Other		Flat Other Rotat. Parallel		Basins Containers	Non mach	
7	Comb. 1+2+3			Other			Flat Other Rotat. Other			Part mach	
8	Taper		Other	Splined			Geared				
9	Unround			Other					Counterweights		

Example of a class number: **3 3 7 2**

Kind — Class — Group — Material

3 - rotational trough hole

3 - max. φ 40-80 L/D ~1

7 - threaded, holes not in axis, splines

2 - alloy steel

Figure 4.3 VUOSO parts classification system (Gallagher and Knight[7])

It was to overcome this problem that the tailor-made codes were developed. These include BRISCH (from the UK), MICLASS (from the Netherlands), and CODE (from the USA). Whereas the use of universal codes can quickly be learned by a company's own staff, these tailor-made systems often require installation by qualified consultants, at an appropriate fee, or at least the provision of training in their use by the consultants. In such cases it may take between six months and a year to complete the coding of components, and then must start the classification phase and the implementation of group technology.

However, in spite of their cost and the time required to install them, there are substantial benefits in adopting tailor-made coding systems. In general, they are far more useful and robust than universal systems and they can be adapted to suit the particular requirements of a particular organization. Indeed, the best testimonial to these particular types of coding system is the fact that they have been used in a number of the more successful group technology applications.

4.2.2 Production flow analysis

Production flow analysis (PFA) is an alternative approach to group formation which does not rely on coding and classifying parts. The technique assumes that physical shape is less important than the route which a component follows during its manufacture. This is undoubtedly true where several different machining processes are involved, in which case a coding system based largely on component geometry is of little value in identifying the relevant machine group.

Production flow analysis[8] is concerned solely with methods of manufacture and does not consider the design features or shape of components. More than this, it does not attempt to change the established processing methods, employing only those methods, plant and tooling which are at present being used. This contrasts with the previous methods described since they place more emphasis on the formation of component families than on finding an appropriate machine group, which often means the creation of groups requiring some new investment. Where production flow analysis also differs is that it simultaneously groups both parts and machines, thereby attaching equal emphasis to the two activities.

The data required for production flow analysis is contained in the process route cards and the plant list, and manual methods of analysis have proved possible for up to 2000 parts. Three main levels of planning are employed, namely: 'factory flow analysis', 'group analysis', and 'line analysis'. The aim of factory flow analysis is to find the division into departments, and the allocation of plant and components to these departments, which will give the simplest possible material flow system.

Group analysis then divides the components allocated to each department into families and divides the plant allocated to each department into groups in such a way that each family is completely processed by one group only. The third planning level – line analysis – then seeks to find the sequence of layout for machines which will give the nearest approximation to line flow.

Factory flow analysis and line analysis both employ networks in their solution procedures while group analysis depends on the use of matrices. A fourth planning stage – 'tooling analysis' – is also possible where component families are further sub-divided into 'tooling families' which use common tools; this stage also relies on matrix techniques[9]. *Figure 4.4(a)* gives a matrix of components and machines used in group analysis, while *Figure 4.4(b)* shows the matrix after being re-arranged to put both parts and machines into their appropriate groups.

Although manual procedures were originally proposed for processing the data in production flow analysis (involving the sorting of cards, etc.), a number of computerized procedures have

	K48251A	L48388	L48267B	M44276E	M47693F	L48388M	M48195C	M44276D	E41795	E48596	E34267	E12204	E12288	K47697	E47782	E48586	K34596	E33494	M48265D	K44276C	M45691D	M45691D	M48386H	K34098A	E7392	E46384	E33295	K45199	K43390	M61592	E18694
DMT (3)	✓								✓		✓	✓	✓											✓		✓		✓	✓	✓	✓
DM (3)		✓	✓				✓			✓		✓				✓	✓	✓							✓			✓	✓	✓	✓
PG			✓			✓										✓	✓	✓	✓												
OXY (3)	✓	✓	✓													✓									✓			✓	✓	✓	
P&GR					✓																										
PGR													✓													✓					
PGH																															
PGG																				✓	✓					✓					
P&G							✓	✓	✓	✓	✓	✓												✓	✓		✓	✓	✓	✓	✓
RP																							✓								
PGB			✓											✓	✓					✓	✓					✓					
W&P	✓					✓																			✓			✓	✓		
WG (3)										✓																					

Figure 4.4(a) Production flow analysis – a matrix of components and machines used in group analysis (Burbidge[8])

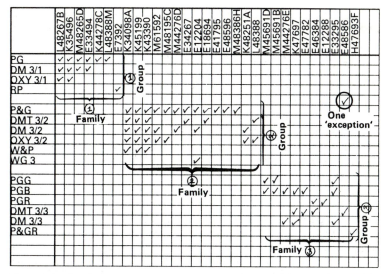

Figure 4.4(b) Production flow analysis – matrix of components and machines after arrangement into families and groups (Burbidge[8])

been developed in more recent years. Some of these are merely 'automated' variations of the original methods of analysis, but some use the type of technique which can readily be programmed into a computer[10].

All four approaches to designing a group technology system which have been described so far have relied on taking existing components and trying to find a way in which they can be manufactured using group technology principles. In many cases this is probably the only option available since product designs are already in existence. However, perhaps the most creative approach to designing a group technology system is to start one step further back, to before the product has reached the drawing board.

4.2.3 Designing for group technology

Examples of products which have been specifically designed with group technology manufacture in mind are fairly rare but there are still some notable examples. One of these is the 'Trantor' (meaning literally 'transport tractor'), which was originally conceived as part of a university research project at Manchester in the UK[11].

As with every good product innovation, Trantor was based on a simple idea which, in this case, was to produce a single vehicle that could haul heavy loads at truck speeds, carry several people in comfort, and perform conventional agricultural tasks. Therefore, the Trantor was designed to replace a tractor, a rough terrain vehicle and a medium-size truck while still fulfilling the purposes of all three.

The novel thinking that went into the design of the product was also applied to the method of production. It was decided from the start that group technology would be used so the design work took place with this in mind[12]. One of the reasons for group technology manufacture being selected was that the vehicle was intended for production worldwide – not just in industrialized countries but also in developing economies. The product and production system were, therefore, designed in parallel with the intention that manufacture should take place in factories of just over $3000\,m^2$, employing one-hundred-and-fifty people, with an output of 1000 units per year. If demand was greater, then factories would simply be replicated (so defending an additional principle that 'smaller is better' when using this type of production); if demand was less, the operation could be scaled down accordingly.

Figure 4.5 Parts designed as a family for group technology manufacture (Marklew[12])

As far as materials were concerned, the Trantor was designed so that many of the constituent parts were themselves proprietary products which could be obtained throughout the world. On the other hand, the unique parts which required in-house manufacturing were designed where possible as families, enabling them to be produced on one machine group, see *Figure 4.5*.

The Trantor project represents a novel departure from custom and practice, not just in terms of the uniqueness of the product, but also as an example of how a group technology production system can be designed along with the items it is going to produce. It illustrates that by deliberately designing families of parts with group production in mind from the start, the need to later 'rectify' a deficient system can be eliminated.

4.3 Further benefits of group technology

So far most of the described benefits to be derived from using group technology have been largely 'technical' in nature in the sense that they relate to such matters as machine re-setting, material flow, work-in-progress levels, etc. Indeed, the original ideas relating simply to the grouping of parts into families were engineering answers to engineering problems and only later, when these ideas were refined and developed, was consideration given to other factors.

It was stated earlier that group technology used alternative methods to those of conventional batch production which involved the grouping of component parts, machines, equipment and people. It is by grouping people that most of the further benefits are derived, since in so doing the organizational characteristics are changed as well as the physical ones.

In one of the first complete applications of group technology, at Serck Audco Valves in the UK[13], a number of organizational-related issues were addressed along with those relating to the engineering function. Most notable among these concerned the management structure, where it was recognized that group technology would call for complete company restructuring. This restructuring involved a radical departure from the accepted practice of having the production function include production control and buying (purchasing or procurement), the belief being that production should produce and sales should sell with a unit between them interpreting the needs of sales and instructing production when and what to manufacture.

Thus, *Figure 4.6* shows the new structure with the finance function, rather unusually, including production control and buying. The reason that such a structure was considered appropriate in connection with group technology is that clearer goals can then be set for the groups of people who are manning the cells and making the families of components. They have well-defined responsibilities for the production of complete components rather than for just a single operation and can see their processing through from start to finish.

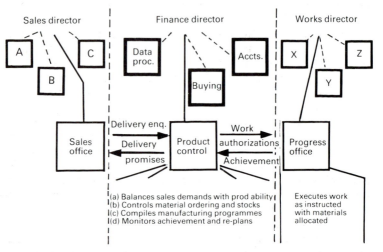

Figure 4.6 A new company structure after the introduction of group technology (Ranson[13])

At Serck Audco it was felt that the new structure enabled those involved in production to carry out their jobs without interruption, whereas previously their involvement in such matters as stocks and buying were a distraction and not subject to control by the right disciplines. The sales function similarly could concentrate on the job of selling, improving customer service and marketing research, while not being distracted by the problems of progressing or expediting orders (now firmly the responsibility of production). The benefit to the accountants, despite their being burdened with extra responsibilities, was that being involved in the total operation enabled them to make decisions based on logic rather than sticking rigidly to accountancy and costing rules.

Apart from the effect of restructuring on the efficiency of the business functions, a further issue arising from applying the group technology philosophy is the effect it can have on labour relations.

In Chapter 2 the idea of job design being an important motivational factor was introduced and some criteria were listed as being prominent in the development of new forms of production organization. Two of these criteria were:

(i) small, autonomous production units, and
(ii) jobs with more involvement.

Group technology can provide for both of these within a batch production environment. Much of the more recent work which has been carried out related to how the work groups can be organized and what are the motivational benefits.

To consider how the above criteria can be satisfied, a further examination of the characteristics of group technology production is required. The question of autonomy has already been mentioned briefly in connection with organization structure when it was pointed out that cells or groups are responsible for the production of complete components.

One factor contributing to the group's autonomy, therefore, is that they are not dependent on other departments for the completion of previous operations, nor will they need to take account of any subsequent processing operations (save for assembly). The groups can, therefore, determine when to carry out the necessary operations, in what order, and on what quantity of parts, subject to the overall delivery and quantity requirements laid down by production control.

Other factors contributing to the groups' autonomy will include complete responsibility for the quality of parts and, in many cases, responsibility for, or at least an involvement in, methods and production engineering. The other aspect of the autonomy criterion, that of size, is also satisfied with the introduction of group technology since average size is approximately nine persons and rarely more than twenty[14].

The question of jobs with more involvement is one which has been the subject of controversy among writers, some of whom argue that job satisfaction can actually decrease with group technology. This will be taken up later under the 'Group Technology Debate'.

Looking at the formation of groups, it can be seen that in order for them to work efficiently, a certain degree of flexibility is required on the part of the operators, particularly when there are several occasionally-used machines in a cell and the operations require semi-skilled labour. It is also a factor for dealing with the effects of absenteeism or changes in schedule[15]. Although the need to be flexible does not in itself provide the type of work which has a high 'motivator' content, with proper training and employee development it can form part of a total package of factors that together enrich the job.

Some of the other factors in the package have already been mentioned in the context of autonomy and these include responsibility for output and quality. Another which may be added relates simply to the beneficial effects on morale of working in a small unit[16].

The fact that group technology is considered as providing positive attributes in connection with the quality of work is witnessed by the number of cases where its application has been cited for reasons other than economic ones[17]. So although the controversy will continue, there remains the strong conviction in many circles that group organization points the way forward for future batch production systems.

4.4 The group technology debate

The preceding sections of this chapter have described a philosophy which, if all its claimed benefits immediately came to fruition, would seem to be the antidote to all that is wrong with conventional batch production. The question then arises as to why, given all that is promised, group technology has not been adopted by each and every manufacturer using batch production techniques. In fact, the reality is that out of several thousand organizations using batch production, only a hundred or so have adopted group technology on a large scale; hardly an enormous take-up rate considering all that has been said and written over thirty years.

The advocates of group technology have tried themselves to answer the question of its limited application by citing a number of imaginary barriers which are often put up to prevent or impede its implementation; among these are:

(i) that senior management will not sanction its introduction because they do not comprehend the technical issues involved: or
(ii) that too much organizational change is required compared with the benefits to be accrued; or
(iii) that it will never be accepted by trades unions.

Of course, these are opinions only but the possibility of needing to overcome such perceived barriers will often lead an organization to maintain the status quo, rationalizing its actions by saying

'We've always managed to get by up to now and cannot be bothered with putting in difficult changes'.

The other angle on the question of group technology's lack of widespread adoption is the fact that it has its critics as well as its advocates, who, though small in number, put their arguments in vociferous terms[18,19].

Drawing on their own research, these critics make the following points in support of their own thesis that effectively managed batch production using functional layout is superior to the group technology approach:

(i) it is claimed, job satisfaction can fall with group technology due in part to the reduced variety of parts being processed in a cell;
(ii) it is contended that work-in-progress levels will remain high since machines in a cell will each require their own pool of work rather than sharing a pool in a functional department;
(iii) utilization will be lower in group technology due, among other things, to duplication of machines, and this has cost implications which adversely effect competitiveness;
(iv) production control is more complicated, rather than being simpler, since it is difficult to balance load against capacity;
(v) once cells have been designed on the basis of a particular level of demand and product mix, they are highly vulnerable to any changes which subsequently take place.

While the ideas of group technology are not completely dismissed by the critics, its widespread use is looked upon with scepticism. Situations where it can be used effectively, they say, are where single machines rather than cells are employed and where mix and demand are stable.

The group technology debate has become one of the most heated arguments relating to production system design, causing both academics and practitioners to express a number of conflicting views concerning the issues just discussed. However, rather than subscribe to the opinions of one particular side, it is more appropriate here to present only the arguments and the facts. Although one point is worth mentioning where a degree of consistency exists regardless of source. This concerns the relationship between group technology and automation. Here most of the critics do concur by finding that numerically controlled (NC) machines might be found a useful place within machine cells, while the advocates[20] see a change to groups as an essential first step towards the much more important automation of complete component production in multi-product batch manufacturing.

4.5 Summary

The intention of this chapter has been to provide an account of the alternative approaches to batch production which are based on the idea of grouping. The original idea of grouping similar components into families was termed group technology, the expression later being widened to include a number of different but closely connected procedures involving the additional grouping of machines, equipment and people.

Grouping components into families, and machines and equipment into cells can, it has been demonstrated, lead to reductions in setting time, throughput time, handling of materials and work-in-progress, while batch sizes can be kept to a minimum. In this respect, group technology tries to achieve for batch production some of the advantages of flow systems while still maintaining the required degree of flexibility.

The 'human' advantages claimed to arise from using group technology do not result from flowline principles being adopted but rather more from its similarity to job production. The reason for this is that the operator groups need a wider range of skills and are additionally responsible for such matters as control of orders through the group, quality and sometimes maintenance, method study etc.

Considering its claimed advantages, group technology has not gained wide acceptance in the engineering industries, due in part to the perceived difficulties encountered in putting the theory into practice. In any case, critics of group technology argue that many of its claimed advantages are spurious and that greater benefits can be derived from using functional layouts more effectively.

However, group technology does not appear to lend itself better to automation since more closely linked machines and processes must be preferable to machines which are isolated within a functional department. The group technology ideas will not be terminated here therefore; in a later chapter the theme will be taken up and explored further, but within the context of new technology and automated systems.

References

1. WILLIAMSON, D. T. N. (1968) 'The Pattern of Batch Manufacture and its Effect on Machine Tool Design', *Institution of Mechnical Engineers,* James Clayton Lecture (27 March)
2. MITROFANOV, S. P. (1959) *Scientific Principles of Group Technology.* Leningrad, English translation by the National Library (1966)

3. IVANOV, E. K. (1963) *Group Production Organisation and Technology.* USSR. English translation by Business Publications Ltd, London
4. EDWARDS, G. A. B. (1971) *Readings in Group Technology.* Machinery Publishing Co, London
5. BURBIDGE, J. L. (1973) 'Group Technology – The State of the Art', *The Chartered Mechanical Engineer* (February)
6. NEDO (1975) 'Why Group Technology?', *National Economic Development Office,* London
7. GALLAGHER, C. C. and KNIGHT, W. A. (1973), *Group Technology,* Butterworths, London
8. BURBIDGE, J. L. (1971) 'Production Flow Analysis', *The Production Engineer* (April/May)
9. BURBIDGE, J. L. (1975) *The Introduction of Group Technology,* Heinemann, London
10. KING, J. L. (1979) 'Machine–Component Group Formation in Group Technology', in *Proceedings of Vth International Conference on Production Research,* Amsterdam (August)
11. BUTTERWORTH, W. (1976) Trantor, the Transport Tractor, *Livestock Farming*
12. MARKLEW, J. J. (1976) 'Not Just A Trantor', *Machinery and Production Engineering* (April)
13. RANSON, G. M. (1972) *Group Technology, A Foundation for Better Total Company Operation,* McGraw-Hill, Maidenhead, UK
14. BURBIDGE, J. L. (1979) *Group Technology in the Engineering Industry,* Mechanical Engineering Publications, London
15. FAZAKERLEY, G. M. (1974) 'Group Technology, Social Benefits and Social Problems', *The Production Engineer* (October)
16. EDWARDS, G. A. B. (1974) 'Group Technology, A Technical Answer to a Social Problem', *Personnel Management* (March)
17. INTERNATIONAL LABOUR OFFICE (1979) *New Forms of Work Organisation. Vols 1 and 2,* International Labour Office, Geneva
18. LEONARD, R. and RATHMILL, K. (1977) 'The Group Technology Myths', *Management Today* (January)
19. LEONARD, R. and RATHMILL, K. (1977) 'Group Technology – A Restricted Manufacturing Philosophy', *The Chartered Mechanical Engineer* (October)
20. BURBIDGE, J. L. (1978) 'Whatever Happened to GT?', *Management Today* (September)

Chapter 5

Designing flowline operations

5.1 The nature of flowlines and the problem of work allocation

The ideas behind flowline working are not new. The principle of moving the 'product' along a series of 'work stations' can be traced back to the 15th Century when ships being victualled and armed at the Venice arsenal were towed along a canal being progressively loaded from the windows of houses on either side[1]. This technique was later extended into true manufacturing when needles, coins. pulley blocks, etc. were produced by a series of machines or processes arranged to provide a more-or-less continuous flow of materials from beginning to end of the system.

Henry Ford's well-known flowline for assembling his 'Model T' was developed in 1913. It was probably the first large-scale line for producing a complex consumer product and was soon copied by those who recognized the benefits that could be achieved in terms of production cost.

The unfavourable features of flowline systems have been discussed in Chapter 3 but there remain advocates who consider that they are still outweighed by the benefits. The continuing popularity of flowline principles can now be witnessed by their growing use in the service sector. In catering, for instance, the 'cafeteria' approach is widely used for low-cost delivery of food, while banks use the technique for processing documents at their centralized offices[2]. A very recent development reported from the Soviet Union is the use of a flowline for routine eye surgery whereby patients are literally passed along a line from one surgeon to another, each of whom performs a small part of the total operation.

This widespread and continued use of flow production justifies a discussion on the design of flowlines and some of the problems associated with their operation. The purposes this will serve are twofold: firstly, it will provide an account of the design considerations and methods of allocating work to stations in order to fulfill certain criteria, and secondly, it will supply a more detailed explanation of the physical disadvantages of flowline working. This second part of the discussion will in turn provide much of the basis for Chapter 6 on Autonomous Working. To start with, however, it is appropriate to describe the basic types of flowline together with their characteristics and relevance to particular types of product.

Essentially lines may be of two types – assembly or analytical[3]. The assembly type produces a single finished product by using human and/or physical resources to bring together materials and components at a series of workstations (as shown in *Figure 5.1(a)*).

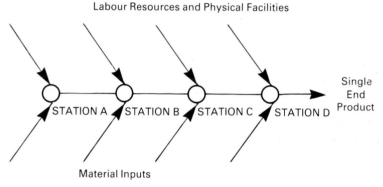

Figure 5.1(a) The assembly type of flowline

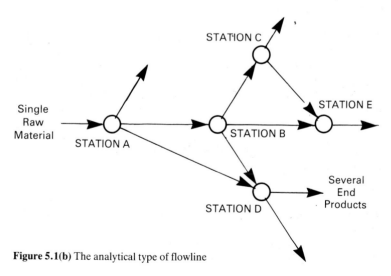

Figure 5.1(b) The analytical type of flowline

Alternatively, this type of line may not involve the addition of material but merely the performance of a series of operations on a single item as it proceeds from one station to another. An example of this would be a series of machines linked to form a transfer line, which diagrammatically would also appear as *Figure 5.1(a)*, although the only material input would be at the beginning of the line.

The analytical type of line is used where a number of finished outputs are produced from a single raw material (see *Figure 5.1(b)*). Although less common than assembly and transfer lines, they are still widely used, particularly in the chemical and petro-chemical processing industries.

An example of the analytical type of line, for instance, is the oil refinery where crude oil is refined and subsequently blended and combined to produce different grades of petroleum, diesel oil, paraffin, tar, etc. The analytical function usually presents fewer design options since the station sequence and work allocation is often pre-determined by the underlying chemical or physical process. For this reason the following discussion will be limited to the previously described assembly type of line.

5.1.1 Work allocation

When designing a line there are a number of basic decisions which need to be made relating to the allocation of work. These are:

(i) deciding on output rate or cycle time;
(ii) determining the required number of stations;
(iii) assigning tasks to each station;
(iv) deciding on the need for station replication or multiple resourcing.

The principal objective of flowline design is to produce the desired output while still maintaining a high degree of resource efficiency and a good balance of work between stations. This would be relatively simple if any task could be assigned to any station in any order, but in practice the line designer is limited by two types of constraint, namely:

(i) *Precedence constraints*. These are restrictions on the order in which tasks can be done, i.e. certain tasks will have *predecessors* which must be carried out before subsequent tasks can be performed (e.g. holes must be drilled before they are threaded, washers must be fitted before nuts, etc.).
(ii) *Zoning constraints*. These are restrictions on where certain tasks or combinations of tasks should, or should not, take place

(e.g. an immovable piece of equipment may already exist at a workstation or two tasks performed together may present a safety hazard).

To demonstrate the nature of the flowline design problem, consider the following simple example:

The tasks below represent the assembly requirements for a toy motorized double-decker bus which is to be produced on a flowline. Predecessors and task times are also given. There are no zoning constraints.

Task number	Description of task	Immediate predecessors	Time for task (seconds)
1	Install seats into top section	–	7
2	Install seats into bottom section	–	10
3	Fix steering wheel	–	5
4	Assemble top and bottom sections	1,6,3	10
5	Rivet top and bottom sections together	4	15
6	Install motor unit	2	12
7	Connect motor to rear wheels	6,10	7
8	Install switch	6	6
9	Fix front wheels	–	8
10	Fix rear wheels	2	8
11	Apply stickers	–	9
12	Put into packaging	5,7,8,9,11	13
		Total assembly time = (work content)	110 seconds

A useful first step is to draw a network illustrating task precedence. This is usually done using 'node' notation and the time for each task is shown against its respective node. Hence the precedence network for the example is as shown in *Figure 5.2*.

If the toy bus is to be produced continuously on an assembly line, the twelve tasks must be assigned to stations along the line. One solution would be to assign tasks to stations as soon as their predecessors had been completed, with all the initial tasks (those

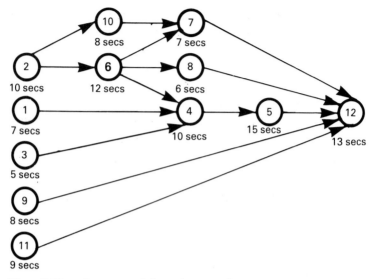

Figure 5.2 Precedence network for toy bus example

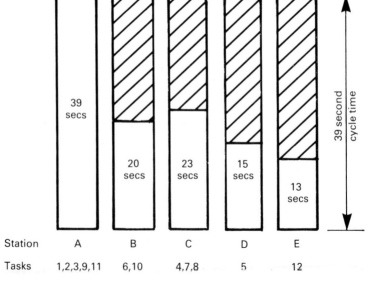

Figure 5.3 A feasible allocation of tasks to work stations yielding low efficiency and uneven balance

with no immediate predecessors) on the first station. This would yield the feasible allocation shown diagrammatically in *Figure 5.3*. The cycle time, which determines the output from the line, is 39 seconds, which with the five stations gives a total available work station time of $5 \times 39 = 195$ seconds. The total time required to assemble the toy bus (work content) is 110 seconds, so the line efficiency is $110/195 \times 100\% = 56.4\%$. This is rather low and the *balance* of the line (distribution of work between stations) is also uneven (note the difference in loading between stations A and E); a better solution is, therefore, desirable.

Furthermore, the assignment of tasks to stations was made without first considering the required output from the line. The resultant cycle time of 39 seconds could be greater than that required to satisfy the market demand. Considering this last point – say the line worked for 40 hours per week (without stoppages) then the output from the line with a cycle time of 40 seconds would be 40×60 (mins/hr) $\times 60$ (secs/min)$/39 = 3692$ buses per week. If market requirements were for 6000 buses per week then the required cycle time would be $40 \times 60 \times 60/6000 = 24$ seconds, and a different assignment would be required.

Clearly the range of possible assignments could be quite large in the case of a more realistic example (e.g. motor vehicles, domestic appliances, etc.) so to rely on 'trial and error' would not be practical. A number of procedures have, therefore, been developed to tackle the problem of assigning tasks to work stations. Although some of these give *exact* solutions based on mathematical treatments such as linear programming[4], they are only really of academic value since their procedure is so complex that realistic problems would require vast computations which would be an impractical proposition even with the assistance of a computer.

Of much greater value, therefore, are the 'heuristic' techniques which provide good but not necessarily optimum solutions. Some of these are fairly simple to operate, being designed for manual application, while others are slightly more elaborate requiring a computer to perform the necessary calculations.

5.1.2 Heuristic techniques for task assignment

Among the better known heuristic techniques for assigning tasks to work stations on flowlines are the 'Kilbridge and Wester' method[5] and 'ranked positional weights'. Using the second of these, each task is assigned a *positional weight* which is the sum of the time for that task and the times of *all subsequent* tasks.

For example, task 6 has a positional weight

p.w. = time for 6 + times for 7, 8, 4, 5 and 12
      = 12 + 7 + 6 + 10 + 15 + 13
      = 63

In *Table 5.1* the positional weights are given for each of the twelve assembly tasks. These are then ranked in *descending* order of positional weights (where there is a choice, the task with the longest time is ranked first).

Table 5.1

Task no.	Task time (secs)	Positional weight (p.w.)	Rank
1	7	45	3
2	10	81	1
3	5	43	4
4	10	38	5
5	15	28	6
6	12	63	2
7	7	20	10
8	6	19	11
9	8	21	9
10	8	28	7
11	9	22	8
12	13	13	12

Now tasks are assigned to work stations according to their ranking with each station being 'closed' when the cumulative time reaches the 24 second limit (the required cycle time). In the example the solution given in *Table 5.2* would be reached in this way:

Table 5.2

	Rank	Task no.	Time (secs)	Cumulative time ($\leqslant$24 secs)
Station A	1	2	10	10
	2	6	12	22
Station B	3	1	7	7
	4	3	5	12
	5	4	10	22
Station C	6	5	15	15
	7	10	8	23
Station D	8	11	9	9
	9	9	8	17
	10	7	7	24
Station E	11	8	6	6
	12	12	13	19

This solution is shown diagrammatically in *Figure 5.4*. Clearly this is a preferable allocation to the previous one since, first of all, the cycle time of 24 seconds will yield the desired output of 6000 buses per week. The total available work station time is, on this occasion, 5 × 24 = 120 seconds, so the line efficiency is now 110/120 × 100% = 91.7%. Furthermore, not only is the efficiency much better, but the balance is also greatly improved with only 5 seconds difference between the busiest and least busy work stations (D and E).

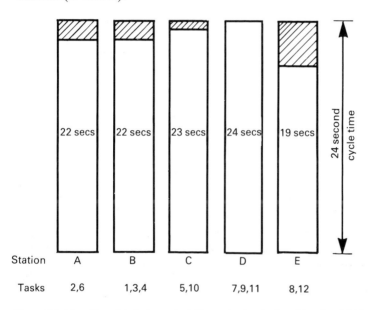

Figure 5.4 Allocation of tasks to work stations using 'ranked positional weights'

In most cases, heuristics like 'ranked positional weights' will provide solutions that meet the precedence conditions and provide acceptable levels of efficiency and station balance. However, they do not guarantee that precedence constraints will not be violated nor that the assignment cannot be improved upon. For this reason a running check on precedence should accompany the operation of the technique and the final result should be examined to determine whether further manipulation can yield any improvements.

The fairly simple heuristic procedure just described can be operated manually on even fairly complex problems, but in order to ensure strict adherence to the precedence constraints and to avoid the need for further manipulation, a computerized version is preferable. It is possible, of course, to program a computer to perform the relatively simple procedures of one of the manual heuristics; use of such a program will ensure that a large problem will be solved without error. Alternatively, methods are also available which have been specifically designed for computerized computations[7,8] and which can, therefore, be based on a more elaborate algorithm.

5.2 Dealing with product variety

Ideally, products which are processed on flowlines should be completely standardized in order that maximum benefit is derived from the economies of scale that can be achieved. This, of course, was the rationale behind Ford's statement 'You can have it any colour as long as it is black', the implication being that any variation whatsoever would create higher production costs.

Today, however, the situation is very different. Marketers wish to offer potential customers a wide degree of choice as well as a competitively priced product. This choice could be of a number of essentially different finished goods (i.e. refrigerators, freezers, fridge-freezers, etc.) or it could be of a range of options which may be selected to provide differentiation in an otherwise basic product (i.e. the practice nowadays with motor cars).

Another reason for variations needing to be produced is that goods are often now produced at single locations to supply world markets. For instance, electrical equipment needs to be made with different voltages and to different safety standards, and vehicles need to be equipped with different engines, heating equipment, emission control devices, etc.

Clearly the manufacture of a variety of products or options necessitates that, for each, a different set of tasks will be required and different times will be involved. The single-model flowline described previously would, therefore, need to be modified in order that these differences can be accommodated.

There are basically two methods of dealing with the problem of producing a variety of products on a flowline. The first is to re-organize the line periodically, when required, so that for each product or variant a different allocation of tasks to work stations is used – this is sometimes referred to as using a *multi-model* line. The second approach is to design a versatile flowline which will be capable of producing any one of the variations without any re-organization – this is a *mixed-model* line.

Both approaches have their advantages and disadvantages. Multi-model lines can provide good levels of efficiency and balance for each of the models produced, but the need to re-organize them periodically results in a loss of capacity. Mixed-model lines do not require re-organizing between models but their design must involve a compromise, with their versatility sometimes being paid for by relatively poor levels of efficiency and balance.

5.2.1 The use and design of multi-model lines

For the reasons stated above, multi-model lines are normally used where differences between models are significant and where a long run of each can be allowed. A manufacturer of power tools, for instance, may design a line to produce electric drills, change the task allocation to produce jigsaws, then change it again to produce sanders, and so on.

Mixed-model lines, on the other hand, are far more likely to be used where the variations are on what is basically a standard product. This is typically the case with motor cars where variety is derived from a choice of engine sizes, accessories, number of doors, etc. Here it would be impractical to re-organize the line specially to accommodate each variation so the mixed-model line is employed to allow uninterrupted production with a mix of products being manufactured on the line at any one time.

Looking respectively at the main design problems of multi and mixed model lines, it can be seen that the re-organization which takes place in the first case merely requires a repetition of the approach just described for the single model line. The extra dimension to the problem, however, is the need to minimize the total time taken to change the line, successively, from one model to another.

Assume, for instance, that as well as making toy buses, the line in the previous example is also required for the assembly of toy trucks, aeroplanes and tractors. *Figure 5.5* shows in matrix form the time taken to change from one to another. An operational research technique known as the assignment method of linear programming[9] can be used to arrive at the optimum sequence (i.e. the order in which products should be produced to minimize total changeover time).

The technique is not presented here in detail, neither is each step in the modification of the matrix shown. It is sufficient to note the iteration shown in *Figure 5.6* where there is a set of four 'unique' zeros (i.e. being in not more than one row or column).

Changing To:

	Buses	Trucks	Aeroplanes	Tractors
Buses	—	36	42	48
Trucks	38	—	44	36
Aeroplanes	52	34	—	38
Tractors	38	42	46	—

Changing from: (row labels above)

Figure 5.5 Multi-model line – times to change from one model to another (minutes)

To:

From:	Buses	Trucks	Aeroplanes	Tractors
Buses	64	0	0*	12
Trucks	2	64	2	0*
Aeroplanes	18	0*	60	4
Tractors	0*	4	2	62

Production Sequence
which minimises
changeover time:
Buses—Aeroplanes—
Trucks—Tractors

*Zeros in unique positions

Figure 5.6 Modified matrix using assignment method which gives unique zeros in rows and columns

These four zeros correspond to the optimal assignment which is to change from buses to aeroplanes to trucks to tractors to buses etc. with a total changeover time of 150 minutes required to complete the model production cycle.

5.2.2 Mixed-model line design

A quite different approach is required in the case of the mixed-model line. As was indicated earlier, this needs to be designed so that a composite solution is reached which *on average* provides good efficiency and balance.

Again taking the previous example of the toy bus: say, for instance, that a second type is to be produced which has no electric motor. If this were the case, then tasks, 6, 7 and 8 would not be required in its assembly.

A modification to the ranked positional weights method can be used to arrive at an allocation of tasks to stations. The times are firstly adjusted in recognition of the relative number of times each task must be performed. Assume, therefore, that the demand for buses with motors is now only 1000 per week, while for those without it is 5000 (i.e. the total demand is still 6000 per week). A new table (see *Table 5.3*) can be drawn up where each task time (t) is multiplied by the relative number of times it must be performed (n). The value ($n \times t$) is now used to calculate the positional weight for each task with the ranking as before being on the basis of descending p.w. order.

Table 5.3

Task no.	Relative no. of times task must be performed (n)	Task time (t)	(nxt)	Positional weight (p.w.)	Rank
1	6	7	42	270	2
2	6	10	60	361	1
3	6	5	30	258	3
4	6	10	60	228	5
5	6	15	90	168	6
6	1	12	12	253	4
7	1	7	7	85	10
8	1	6	6	84	11
9	6	8	48	126	9
10	6	8	48	133	7
11	6	9	54	132	8
12	6	13	78	78	12

Tasks are now allocated to work stations in a similar manner as before except that individual task times cannot be used since their frequency of occurrence varies. Instead the allocation is based on the time spent on each task to produce the desired output of 6000 buses per week with the maximum station loading being the available hours for their production (i.e. 40 hours in this example). The times for each task are, therefore, as follows:

Table 5.4

Task no.	Individual task Time (secs)	Time to produce 6000 buses (secs)	Time to produce 6000 buses (hours)
1	7	42000	11.7
2	10	60000	16.7
3	5	30000	8.3
4	10	60000	16.7
5	15	90000	25.0
6	12	12000*	3.3
7	7	7000*	1.9
8	6	6000*	1.7
9	8	48000	13.3
10	8	48000	13.3
11	9	54000	15.0
12	13	78000	21.7

* These tasks are only carried out 1000 times for every 6000 buses.

Assigning tasks to work stations in order of their ranking and limiting the loading on each station to 40 hours the following solution results:

Table 5.5

	Rank	Task no.	Task time for 6000 buses (hrs)	Cumulative time (≤ 40 hrs)
Station A	1	2	16.7	16.7
	2	1	11.7	28.4
	3	3	8.3	36.7
	4	6	3.3	40.0
Station B	5	4	16.7	16.7
	7	10	13.3	30.0
	10	7	1.9	31.9
	11	8	1.7	33.6
Station C	6*	5	25.0	25.0
	8*	11	15.0	40.0
Station D	9*	9	13.3	13.3
	12	12	21.7	35.0

* These tasks could not be assigned to earlier work stations without overloading them.

This resultant station loading is shown diagrammatically in *Figure 5.7*. The *average* cycle time can be seen to be 24 seconds so the total available work station time is $4 \times 24 = 96$ seconds. The *average* work content is 89.2 seconds so the line efficiency is $89.2/96 \times 100\% = 92.9\%$.

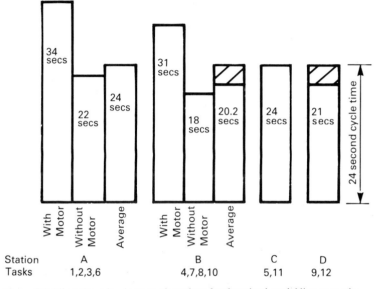

Figure 5.7 Allocation of tasks to work stations for the mixed model line example

In order to achieve this high level of efficiency the scheduling of models onto the line must be carefully controlled to ensure the maintenance of an average work station time on Station A of 24 seconds. If too many buses with electric motors were sequenced together then the loading on Station A would be excessive. If this happened then either the line would need to be stopped periodically in order to allow work at Station A to be completed, thereby creating delays further down the line, or buses would leave Station A without the necessary work having been completed. In the event of the latter situation arising, additional work would need to be done, off the end of the line, to complete the required assembly tasks.

Another point to note concerning the design of mixed-model lines is that the desired station allocation is based on the assumption that the relative number of each model to be produced is fixed. It can readily be seen that if the mix in the example were to change from the stated 5000 to 1000 ratio, then this would change all the calculations on which the allocation was based, and consequently render the solution 'invalid'.

5.3 System losses

Reference was made above to a situation where, because of excessive loading on a work station, tasks may not be completed, and unfinished products would result. The reason suggested for this was that too many variants involving extra work could be sequenced together onto a line designed for a more even distribution of models.

However, this is only one circumstance in which work is not completed at a particular station. Perhaps a more common reason is that operator speed tends to be variable, and that the time taken to complete the required tasks may simply be longer than planned for. The term 'system loss' is given to incomplete work which can result from such a situation.

There have been many studies into the variability of work times under paced and unpaced conditions[10]. By pacing is meant the degree to which the work rate is controlled or determined by the production process. Therefore, unpaced work occurs where operators are totally free to work at the rate of their choosing, whereas rigid pacing occurs where operators must work at precisely the same rate as a machine (which they cannot control). Rigid pacing occurs on flowlines when workers are allowed a fixed time to perform their set of tasks and the line then moves on, regardless of whether or not they are completed, allowing no opportunity to make up for lost time.

Figure 5.8 shows time distributions for paced and unpaced work. It can be seen that the unpaced work time distribution is positively skewed while for paced work the distribution is much more symmetrical. To avoid any system loss if rigid pacing were adopted on a flowline, the cycle time would need to be sufficiently long to embrace all the times in the distribution. However, since the longer times only have a low probability of occurrence the resulting efficiency would be adversely affected since the average time each station is occupied would be much less than the time allowed.

Fortunately there are other ways in which variability can be allowed for, and system losses reduced. One common approach is by using bufferstocks between work stations, a technique already described as being used in the Philips experiments which were

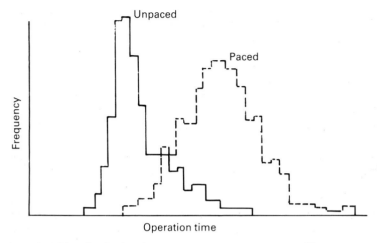

Figure 5.8 Time distributions for paced and unpaced work (Dudley[10])

introduced in Chapter 1. The idea is simply to allow operators the opportunity to vary their work rate by providing space for items to accumulate during periods when they work faster than average. Then as they work slower, the next work station would still have these stocks to draw on and output could be maintained.

Obviously the disadvantage of bufferstocks is that they represent an investment in materials and space, so accountants view them unfavourably. However, if a proper costing exercise is carried out this disadvantage can be weighed against the benefits derived from not needing to complete the manufacture of products in expensive rectification areas.

There are occasions where very large bufferstocks are deliberately built up between adjacent work stations apart from following for variability of work rates. First, they can permit machines and processes to be changed, reset or repaired without needing to stop the line. Secondly, they can be used in instances where the number of operators is less than the number of work stations. In this case an operator can build up a stock of items before moving on to another work station, so providing continuity of production with limited manning.

The use of bufferstocks is just one way in which pacing may be reduced on flowlines. The effect of introducing a buffer is to make it possible for some items to be available to the operator for extended periods of time. Another way of doing this is by slowing down the line speed.

Reducing the speed of a flowline may seem a strange way of increasing its efficiency. However, the reduction in speed would be coupled with a closing-up of the spaces between items, and in this way the cycle time can be maintained. It may be seen that with a slower speed and closer spacing, an operator will, for a given distance of reach, be able to work on a greater number of items. This makes it possible to vary the pace of work while providing the opportunity of finishing the set of tasks before the item passes to the next work station.

In some situations the same effect can be achieved by permitting the operator to 'ride on the line'. With this technique items can again be made available for quite long periods of time and in some cases work stations can even overlap allowing a quick operator temporarily to overtake a slower one further down the line. Naturally the ability to move too far would be prevented by the availability of equipment and materials. Precedence constraints would also restrict the amount of overtaking which could take place. Nonetheless, this type of approach is fairly common in, for example, the motor industry where line speeds are comparatively slow and where precedence constraints are often quite loose.

5.4 Summary

The use of flowlines remains widespread where products are required to be manufactured in large quantities. Traditionally a highly standardized design of product was an essential prerequisite for flowline working and the lines used were of the simple, single-model type. The need to produce a greater range of products or variants, however, has resulted in a modified approach using mixed and multi-model lines.

Whatever type of line is employed, tasks must be allocated to work stations within previously defined precedence and zoning constraints. This should be done with the objective of achieving the desired cycle time and also with the aim of maximizing efficiency and creating good station balance. However, as the number of variants increases the problem of line design becomes more complex and it is increasingly difficult to achieve an optimum solution.

A further problem associated with flowline working is the effect of pacing and the likely variability of operation times. The greater the degree of pacing, the more chance there is that tasks will be unfinished, making it necessary for work to be completed later. This unfinished production work is known as 'system loss'. System loss can be reduced by making items available to operators for longer periods of time and thereby making an allowance for the variation in operation times. On conventional flowlines this can be achieved in a number of ways including the introduction of bufferstocks between work stations and reducing line speeds while decreasing the spacing between items on the line.

However, it should be appreciated that all the measures described to solve the problems of task allocation, balance, variability, system loss, etc. are only solutions to some of the 'physical' problems described in Chapter 3. It was also pointed out then that several 'human' problems are also associated with flowline working which in turn could adversely affect quality, labour turnover, absenteeism, etc.

Many of these problems are a direct or indirect result of the monotony associated with working on a line rather than on a different production system where work is far less regulated. Although lines can be modified to reduce the degree of monotony and provide for some job enlargement, the extent to which it is possible to go is limited. As a further step towards tackling the human problems the idea of autonomous working was developed, based on an entirely different philosophy to the one from which the flowline idea emerged.

Autonomous working seeks to remove many of the regulatory aspects of flowline working so that operators can work more freely and flexibly. In this way, it is claimed, many of the human problems can be solved and the adverse effects can be reduced. What is more, autonomous working not only has benefits in terms of the human aspects – it also, in a different way, solves many of the physical problems which demanded modification of the conventional flowline.

References

1. WILD, R. (1973) 'The Origins and Development of Flow-line Production'. *Chartered Mechanical Engineer* (July)
2. REED, J. (1971) Sure It's A Bank But I Think Of It As A Factory, *Innovation,* No 23
3. BENNETT, D. J. (1981) 'Operations Planning and Control', in *Operations Management in Practice,* edited by C. D. Lewis. Philip Allan, London
4. BOWMAN, E. H. (1960) 'Assembly Line Balancing by Linear Programming', *Operations Research,* **8,** No 3
5. KILBRIDGE, M. and WESTER, L. (1961) 'A Heuristic Method of Assembly Line Balancing', *Journal of Industrial Engineering,* **12,** No 4

6. HELGESON, W. B. and BIRNIE, D. P. (1961) 'Assembly Line Balancing Using the Ranked Positional Weight Technique', *Journal of Industrial Engineering* (Nov/Dec)

7. ARCUS, A. L. (1966) COMSOAL – a Computer Method of Sequencing Operations for Assembly Lines, *International Journal of Production Research,* **4,** No 4

8. BUXEY, G. and BURKE, M. (1974) 'Assembly Line Balancing by Computer: A Case Study', *The Production Engineer* (September)

9. DAELLENBACH, H. G., GEORGE, J. A. and McNICKLE, D. C. (1983) *Introduction to Operations Research Techniques.* Allyn & Bacon, USA

10. DUDLEY, N. A. (1968) *Work Measurement: Some Research Studies.* Macmillan, London

Chapter 6

Autonomous working

6.1 The make-complete approach using individuals and work groups

Autonomy means, literally, freedom to act as one pleases. It is self-evident, therefore, that complete autonomy is impossible within the context of a production system. However, the degree of autonomy may vary and it is in situations where this is high that forms the subject of this chapter.

Autonomous working is a typical characteristic of job production systems. In Chapter 3 it was stated that

> 'From the worker's point of view, job production provides enlarged work elements requiring a range of skills and giving individuals greater responsibility for both quality and output'.

Job production, however, is associated with low volume or one-off manufacture. High volume production is by contrast usually achieved using flow systems and it is on flowlines that very little autonomy exists.

The main aim of this chapter, therefore, is not to look at autonomous working in all types of production but to examine ways in which changes can be made to provide autonomy in continuous, flow production situations. It is in this latter category of production where the 'human problems' have been most severe and where the increased job enrichment associated with autonomy can provide the greatest benefit. It is also the case that many of the physical disadvantages of flowlines can be overcome by adopting autonomous working, so this aspect will also merit some consideration.

In practice, the provision of autonomy is just one aspect of job design or redesign which is aimed at achieving greater complexity of work in a deliberate attempt to reverse the trend towards work simplification. As well as by providing autonomy, complexity can also be achieved by increasing variety and allowing for 'completeness of task' (carrying out a whole and identifiable piece of work)[1].

In many jobs these three aspects of job design may be exclusive, but in production they are usually inseparable so autonomous working, by implication, includes both increased variety and completeness of work. Furthermore, while in non-productive jobs redesign may be facilitated by changes in work content and organization, systems for the production of goods must undergo physical changes in order that variety, autonomy and completeness are achieved.

In the case of flow production using line layouts, this need to change the physical system implies a different kind of configuration to the one normally associated with this form of production.

Figure 6.1(a) shows the traditional division of tasks for flowline working. Each operator is given a limited number of the total tasks (here twelve) required to produce the complete product. They are all dependent on each other for continuous and uninterrupted production and, in the case of mechanical lines, the whole system is at risk in the event of a breakdown at any work station. The short work cycle at each station provides for minimum training of operators while work study techniques and financial incentives can be applied since production is highly regulated.

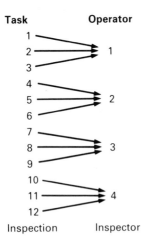

Figure 6.1(a) Traditional division of tasks for flowline working

6.1.1 Achieving autonomy

An alternative approach, providing greater autonomy, is for each operator to make a complete product; this is shown diagrammatically in *Figure 6.1(b)*.

Task	Operator	Task	Operator	Task	Operator	Task	Operator
1		1		1		1	
2		2		2		2	
3		3		3		3	
4		4		4		4	
5		5		5		5	
6	1	6	2	6	3	6	4
7		7		7		7	
8		8		8		8	
9		9		9		9	
10		10		10		10	
11		11		11		11	
12		12		12		12	

Figure 6.1(b) The make-complete approach using individual operators

Such a division of total work content, giving each operator more tasks and a longer work cycle, might be seen by some behaviourists as merely job enlargement rather than enriching the work and increasing autonomy. In response to this possible criticism, it is worth making a few extra comments.

Firstly, as well as creating extra work, the new task division has created completeness of work. In this case, operators are producing complete products for which they are fully responsible so they can identify with this product rather than just a limited set of tasks.

Secondly, rather than being dependent on their fellow operators, each operator is able to work independently. Reliability is, therefore, improved because there is no 'knock-on' effect in the event of breakdown and, since pacing can be completely removed, there is in theory no system loss.

Lastly, recognizing that autonomy and enrichment come with additional responsibility, a number of otherwise separate functions can be included in the set of tasks allocated to each operator. Among these can be included material control and ordering, routine maintenance, some of the more detailed planning activities, and responsibility for quality. On this last point it will be noted that in *Figure 6.1(a)* a separate inspection task is added after completion of the productive tasks. In *Figure 6.1(b)* this is omitted, the argument for this being that separate inspection ought not be necessary if operators are responsible for products rather than tasks.

There is still a great deal of controversy concerning the extent to which the quality control function can be devolved down to the operators. Some respected authorities on the subject will insist that independent quality control inspectors are essential in order that high quality levels are maintained. Others contend that inspection is an unnecessary overhead – provided that the job is done 'right first time' (Is there a need for policemen if there is no crime?).

Leaving this argument aside until later (in fact, a subsequent chapter deals entirely with quality control), the question remains how, in terms of the physical system, make-complete production can be facilitated in cases where flowline methods would otherwise be used. *Figure 6.2(a)* shows the typical layout of a flowline with operators positioned at work stations along the line. Items move continuously down the conveyor and production is progressive with completed goods leaving the line at the last station. In *Figure 6.2(b)* a layout is shown which will allow make-complete production.

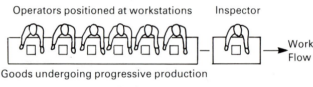

Figure 6.2(a) Typical flowline layout

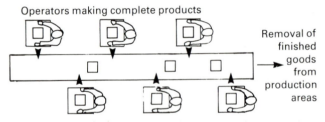

Figure 6.2(b) Layout to facilitate make-complete production

Work is located in a fixed-position where operators, at their own pace, can undertake all the tasks required for their completion. Each separate production area is provided with the materials, tools and equipment necessary to do the work required and finished goods are placed onto a conveyor which serves merely as a means of transportation away from the production areas.

Clearly one of the disadvantages of this arrangement is that it requires duplication of equipment and tools together with a larger stock of material than was required for flow production. Nevertheless, layouts of this type are quite common for the assembly of small electrical devices (e.g. circuit breakers, contactors, etc.) and clothing manufacture. In such examples, equipment costs are relatively low and the independence of the production areas makes it possible for each operator to be making a different variant (e.g. circuit breakers with different current ratings, different clothing styles etc.).

Where tooling and equipment costs are higher, it becomes desirable that they be shared by all the operators. *Figure 6.2(c)*, therefore, shows an alternative layout for make-complete production where this is possible. In this arrangement goods are produced progressively as they move along the line but, rather than being positioned at fixed work stations, operators stay with the product and move with it around the 'circuit'. Only one set of tools or one piece of equipment is needed for a particular task with the operator visiting the points where they are located.

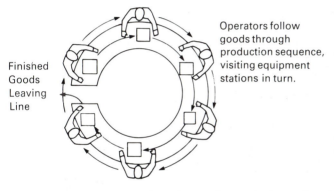

Operators follow goods through production sequence, visiting equipment stations in turn.

Finished Goods Leaving Line

Figure 6.2(c) Alternative layout for make-complete production to allow sharing of equipment

Once the operator has completed the product it leaves the line at a point close to the beginning so that production can immediately commence on another. Despite its attractions in terms of reduced investment, this alternative layout does itself have a number of disadvantages. Most importantly, it can be seen that operators are not as independent as is normally desirable under autonomous working since they must all work at more-or-less the same pace (though in some circumstances overtaking could be allowed). It is also more difficult (though not impossible) to produce a number of different variants using this arrangement since separate materials and unique tasks cannot easily be incorporated into the line.

An example of a product where this technique is used in assembly is a motor-car gearbox where the new layout has replaced the traditional flowlines which employed an operator at each fixed work station. The high equipment cost for gearbox assembly (which involves the use of hoists, jigs, torque wrenches, etc.) precluded the purchase of additional equipment but make-complete assembly was still thought beneficial. One of the new lines is for instance, designed so that operators can assemble two gearboxes at a time with the line accommodating up to ten operators. Average output for each operator is 2.7 per hour giving a line capacity of 20–30 gearboxes per hour using maximum manning and with reduced capacity being achieved by utilizing fewer operators.

One of the fundamental questions relating to make-complete production concerns the amount of work that can sensibly be assigned to one operator. In the case of the gearbox example the time required to assemble a complete product was $60/2.7 = 22$ minutes, but there are cases where much longer times are found to be possible. A useful indication of how long the time can practically be extended is provided by the case of a diesel engine manufacturer. Here the total time taken to assemble an engine was four hours.

The experience, however, was that this was too long a job for a single operator to undertake without involving excessive training. The solution was for an operator to follow an engine to the half-way point (i.e. taking two hours) where it was then taken over and completed by another person.

6.1.2 Autonomous work groups

The type of autonomous working described so far enables single operators to work independently on the manufacture of complete products. Since at most only a couple of hours work can sensibly be allocated to a single person, the approach cannot as it stands be extended to the manufacture of highly complex products. In such cases autonomy is often achieved by allowing operators to work in groups known usually as 'autonomous work groups' or sometimes 'parallel groups', where several such groups work in parallel to produce the desired output.

Although the use of autonomous work groups is often thought of as a recent phenomenon, a few exceptional examples have been reported which demonstrate their earlier existence. For instance, Hoover (the domestic appliance manufacturer) is cited as using a system known as 'new team working' at its plant in Perivale, UK, which originated in 1950[2]. Autonomous groups were also formed as a result of the Norwegian Industrial Democracy Project which started in the early 1960[3] and, of course, the 1950s coal mining studies, described briefly in Chapter 1, demonstrated the benefits of group working as opposed to the 'factory approach'.

A diagrammatic representation of group working is shown in *Figure 6.3* where it may be seen that all the twelve tasks previously assigned to individual operators in *Figure 6.1* are now undertaken by the group. The allocation of work within the group is generally left entirely up to its members, the only condition being that they organize their work within certain broad parameters relating to output, quality and cost.

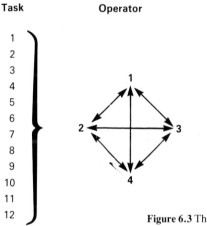

Figure 6.3 The structure of group working

Obviously groups cannot operate in isolation since their activities require co-ordination and certain supporting functions are necessary (which can themselves be provided by another specialized group). *Figure 6.4*, therefore, shows how a large 'product' group can comprise a number of linked 'producer'

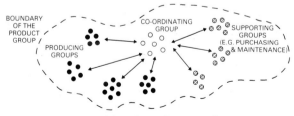

Figure 6.4 The composition of a product group (based on Bowey and Connolly[4])

groups (each responsible for a part of the product), together with groups of supporting functions and a group of facilitators (the foremen and supervisors in a traditional structure).

Needless to say such a widespread adoption of group working in an organization requires considerable application on the part of management and a high degree of participation of the workforce. This partly explains why their development has been most significant in Scandinavia and, to some extent, central European countries such as the Netherlands and West Germany. For it is in these counties that greater industrial democracy exists making easier the introduction of such novel forms of work organization. It is also often the case that industrial workers have been educated to a higher level in these countries which increases the demand for more meaningful jobs.

An example of a company which introduced the idea of autonomous working using the 'linked group' approach is Alfa-Laval in Lund, Sweden. The product group approach was introduced in 1970 for the manufacture of heat exchangers, and now the Thermal Engineering Division is arranged entirely into 'product workshops' and 'flow groups' (i.e. the production groups) with each workshop having its own planning, purchasing, production engineering, maintenance and quality functions[5].

As well as being justified on economic grounds, the product workshop and flow group approach has greatly simplified administration and created better and more interesting jobs. A particular point to note is that the groups are responsible for their own storekeeping and material re-ordering using computer terminals. The groups' autonomy ensures that this is done properly since any wrong transactions will have a direct affect on their own production.

6.2 Factory design to allow for group working

The point was made earlier of the need to change the physical system in order to allow for autonomous working. The scale of such changes to create the type of system described for make-complete manufacture can be relatively small, involving the creation of a number of fixed or moving work places instead of a flowline.

However, in the case of group working, particularly with linked groups producing altogether larger products, a quite different approach may be necessary. At the very least this will require completely new layouts within existing factories and often, to remove the constraints imposed by the previous methods, it could involve the provision of a wholly new system. There are a number of examples of organizations which have made substantial changes to the facilities and their layout in order to allow for group working to take place. Among these is Alfa-Laval which has just been mentioned, while others range across a number of industries of various types and sizes.

To illustrate the scope of these novel forms of production system, a set of cases will be described which embrace a variety of production situations. Several of these relate to some aspect or other of motor vehicle manufacture, but this is not by coincidence. The motor industry has tended to be the pacemaker in experimenting with various forms of group working and many of the most innovative developments in the field have emerged from this sector.

CASE 1: The manufacture of automobile bodies

Saab Cars is a major part of Saab Scania, Sweden's sixth largest company. Its principal manufacturing plant, at Trollhättan, is where bodies are produced and final assembly takes place.

In the early 1970s Saab, along with many other Swedish companies, experienced labour turnover and absenteeism problems where flow lines were being used. This included the body shop at Trollhättan where labour turnover averaged about 50% per annum in the four years from 1971 to 1975. In the same period, absenteeism also rose steadily from 15% to 23%, causing such severe manning difficulties that on some days it was virtually impossible to build a complete car.

Saab had experimented with the use of autonomous groups at Trollhättan since 1970, and in 1971 a group was established on a trial basis to produce doors for the two-door '99' model. This proved to be a success so, when production of the Combi Coupe model started in 1973, it was decided not to use conventional, driven flowlines. Instead the work would be carried out by autonomous groups.

A new workshop building was, therefore, completed in 1974 in which various sub-assemblies for the '99' and Combi Coupe were produced by the groups. At the same time work was started on the most ambitious application of group working to date: the replacement of three driven lines for welding, grinding and adjustment of bodies by a number of parallel workplaces known as the 'line-out' system[6]. Before the changes the driven line transferred car bodies between work stations where the various

Lanchester Library

operations were carried out, *Figure 6.5*. The line was mechanically controlled with a cycle time of 3 minutes. Workers were directly supervised, and there was an extensive inspection system so no responsibility for quality or other parts of the work was placed on the operators themselves.

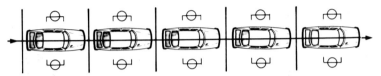

Figure 6.5 Driven line at Saab cars for body welding, grinding and adjustment (Karlsson[6])

Under the line-out system, work is carried out at eighteen parallel stations divided up into six groups of three workplaces in every group (*Figure 6.6*). Each group comprises eight members – six operators working in pairs on the car bodies, one the 'liaison man' and one a stand-in (in the event of illness). The liaison man's duties include inspection, maintenance of the equipment and liaison with other functions within the Company. New group members are predominantly trained within the group following

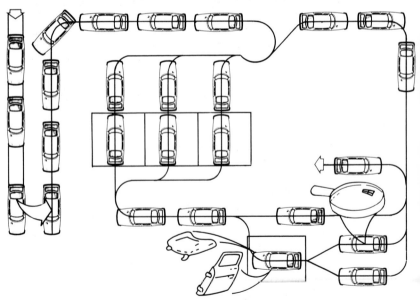

Figure 6.6 Line-out system at Saab cars (Karlsson[6])

basic training in welding and grinding. A new member starts by being assigned simpler duties and, under the leadership of experienced group members, is instructed in an increasing number of working operations. All members of the group are trained to instructor level whereas with the conventional line there was a strict hierarchy of instructors, adjusters, stand-ins, operators, transporters and cleaners.

In the line-out system bodies are transported on an overhead conveyor by means of independent electrically-driven 'tractors'. After going through a buffer store, each is automatically manoeuvred into an empty workplace where the groups carry out the welding, grinding, adjustment and inspection operations. A working group decides itself when a new body is to be taken into the workplace.

The two operators at each workplace can divide up the work to suit their knowledge and personal requirements. It is even possible for the workplace to be manned by only one person. Job rotation is employed within the group so every member takes their turn at being the liaison man and stand-in.

The cycle time at each workplace is approximately 45 minutes and, with buffer storage both before and after, there is wide scope to vary the pace and each group inspects its own work. On completion of the work, the group dispatches the body through the buffer store to further assembly stations where doors, engine bonnet and the luggage compartment lid are fitted. After a final quality check, the body is transported out of the system and on to painting or, if further work is needed, it can be taken via a return loop back to the groups.

As well as enlarging the direct work and allowing responsibility for quality, the further responsibilities that can be assigned to a group are:

- that the production programme is followed;
- checking of incoming materials;
- adjustments to defects on incoming materials;
- return of defective materials;
- return of materials damaged in transit;
- transport, including the ordering of transport;
- maintenance of hand machines and daily inspection of mechanical equipment;
- cleaning;
- training of new members;
- the right to take time off without pay;
- materials requisitions;

- contact with maintenance services in the event of disturbances in production;
- consumables;
- rationalization of work within the department through the Suggestions Scheme;
- feedback of defects on random sampling inspection of finished products;
- adjustments to their own production;
- budget, comprising indirect hours for stand-ins and extra personnel.

Remuneration is on a group basis with a fixed payment being made for the production of one-hundred-and-fifty bodies per week. A group responsibility allowance is also payable on an increase in responsibility. The responsibility which can be delegated to a production group is divided into five main sections:

- production responsibility;
- quality responsibility;
- economic responsibility;
- administrative responsibility;
- social responsibility (no rejection of members).

The acceptance of responsibility in each section can take place in several stages which gradually give an increased allowance up to a prescribed maximum.

It is always difficult to make an accurate assessment of the effect of changes such as the move to the line-out system. However, thorough research at Saab proved that using autonomous groups in parallel stations provides greater job satisfaction and is an economically viable alternative to driven lines.

In particular, the introduction of the line-out system had a beneficial effect on labour turnover while quality costs were also reduced. The line-out system also had technical advantages. Balancing loss, for instance, was 16% on the old driven line but using parallel groups it was only 2%, and similarly system losses were reduced by two-thirds. The overall labour costs were also less, due mainly to the reduction in number of instructors and adjusters.

In summary, therefore, the move to parallel autonomous groups in the body shop at Saab Cars can be regarded as successful. However, it should be noted that, despite this, extending the system to final assembly could be seen as presenting difficulties. The various reasons for this were the relatively higher cost of equipment and of the buffers needed to provide autonomy, together with the problems of material handling when dealing with complex assembly work.

Nevertheless, the final assembly of automobiles is an area where autonomy is desirable so alternatives to conventional driven lines are still required. This issue will, therefore, be taken up in a later case.

CASE 2: The assembly of small complex items

(a) Typewriters

The IBM plant at Amsterdam in the Netherlands employs approximately 2000 people in the production of electric type-writers and related products. When it was built in the early 1970s, final assembly was undertaken on two long mechanized lines with cycles times of about 3 minutes.

IBM chose to examine the possibility of changing this system for a number of reasons:

- the labour turnover rate of 30% per annum and absenteeism of 12% was considered too high;
- there was an inordinately large number of inspectors and rectification workers needed to maintain quality;
- excessive overtime was needed to maintain output.

The use of long assembly lines also presented technical difficulties. Since the Amsterdam plant supplied typewriters throughout the world, a large number of variations needed to be produced with different colours, voltages, keyboards and other special features. This required complex material planning and control where traditional lines were concerned as well as causing reductions in line efficiency. The increasing educational level of the plant's workers was also a consideration since it raised the expectation for participation and creation of larger jobs, a factor borne out in attitude surveys carried out by the Company.

The conclusion reached was that assembly work needed to be carried out by smaller groups with wider responsibilities. Therefore, the concept of 'mini-lines' was devised which were short E-shaped lines manned by approximately twenty-one operators (*Figure 6.7*). The reason for the mini-line shape was simply to allow easy communication between all members of the group while still providing the length of line required for completion of all the assembly operations.

Many of the components previously assembled on the long line were put together as sub-assemblies elsewhere in the plant and, in some cases, were bought complete from outside suppliers. In this

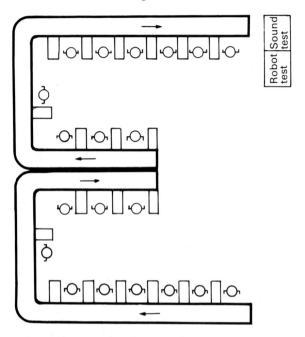

Figure 6.7 Mini-line for typewriter assembly at IBM Amsterdam

way the group size working on the mini-lines could be reduced. Cycle times were approximately 10 minutes. Transfer of typewriters between work stations was via roller conveyors which could also be used to create a buffer, thereby reducing the pacing effect.

Responsibility for quality was assigned to operators with two inspection stations being staffed by members of the group rather than by separate quality control inspectors.

As well as being used solely for inspection, these group members could also do all the assembly tasks on the line, making them the most versatile and highly paid operators. Less experienced operators might be capable of working on two or more stations (i.e. they could act as relief operators), while relative newcomers could probably only work on one station. No incentive pay was available, a standard daywork rate being payable provided the group produced fifty typewriters per day. The line was managed by a foreman who held overall responsibility for production and had to explain variations from the daywork target. The foreman could also recruit labour directly into the group, using the Personnel Department as a service function for advertising posts and for payment purposes.

The use of mini-lines was an immediate success and by 1980 about twenty-three such lines were in operation at Amsterdam, each being capable of producing a different model or variation. Furthermore, when IBM built their new typewriter plant in Berlin-Merienfelde the mini-line idea was incorporated in the original design[7], demonstrating the Company's confidence in the group assembly idea.

(b) Televisions
Bang and Olufsen (B & O) produce consumer electronic goods at Struer in Denmark. The Company relies heavily on its image for aesthetically pleasing and high quality products which carry a commensurately high price ticket. In the early 1970s B & O's colour television manufacture ran into similar difficulties to those just described at the IBM typewriter plant, i.e. 15% absenteeism, 30% labour turnover rate and, most seriously, deteriorating quality[8].

The orthodox assembly line which was used to produce the sets was also rigid and inflexible. Designed for the manufacture of two-hundred-and-thirty sets per day it could not make more and, without working short-time, could not make less.

The introduction of a new model of TV set in 1973 provided B & O with the opportunity of switching to an alternative type of production[9]. The workforce was split into thirty-four groups ranging in size from individuals working alone to teams of ten or twelve. By a fortunate coincidence the design of the new set lent itself to the group working principle; modular approach having been used to ease customer service and maintenance. Separate, easily replaceable modules contained colour controls, sound controls, etc., and could be regarded as products in themselves with manufacture being assigned to different groups who worked on short lines. Within each group job rotation was encouraged and a group incentive scheme was put into effect.

Cycle times were typically increased from 8–12 minutes to 40 minutes and fault correction was carried out by the groups rather than as a separate operation. The most radical part of the new production methods, however, was in the final assembly stage. Here the work was done entirely by individuals who fitted the various modules and components into the set, then checked and adjusted it, at a production rate of twenty sets per day.

The changes to the production system at B & O improved matters considerably. Labour turnover was cut to almost zero and output per labour hour was doubled. Throughput time for products was reduced from an average of twenty days to five, and the decline in quality was reversed. The system also proved far more flexible, allowing production to fluctuate by simply reducing or increasing the size of groups as appropriate.

CASE 3: Automobile assembly

One of the major pioneers in the use of group working is Volvo – Sweden's largest corporation. Since the late 1960s Volvo has been committed to changing the organization of work so as to create small, product-oriented units. These changes within the Corporation have taken place not just on the factory floor but also at plant and divisional level. They have been largely due to the efforts of Pehr Gyllenhammar, Volvo's President, who has masterminded this fundamental change in Company philosophy.

The automobile assembly plant at Kalmar is probably the best-known example of this new philosophy. Despite being just one of many plants within Volvo employing group working, Kalmar has achieved some notoriety, due probably to the fact that it challenged a view towards automobile assembly which had persisted since Henry Ford's day.

The plant commenced production in 1974 but the decision to build at Kalmar, a small coastal town in south east Sweden, was made in 1971. Volvo interviewed one thousand of its 15 000 workers at the parent factory in Gothenburg to determine their likes and dislikes before deciding, in the autumn of 1972, to build a plant with a totally novel technical system which created the atmosphere of small 'workshops' in which operators could work in groups.

The plant itself, built on reclaimed land outside the town, has a total floor area of about $40\,000\,m^2$ with three-quarters of the structure having two levels. The plant's shape is described by fitting four hexagons together[10]. It is, therefore, quite unlike any other car assembly plant, providing every worker with a nearby wall giving views through large picture windows. As well as providing a clean, quiet working environment the plant's designers provided a changing room for each of the twenty-nine groups – every one having toilets, showers and a sauna. Separate coffee corners were also provided for each group, adjacent to their working area.

Volvo Kalmar's most important feature, however, is its technical system. Rather than using the conventional driven line, each body is mounted on an 'autocarrier' guided by a wire embedded in the floor (*Figure 6.8*). These battery powered wagons, having two speeds (3 and 30 m/min), can be stopped and

Figure 6.8 Volvo, Kalmar Autocarriers

started at will by the operators. As well as being capable of responding to manual control, the autocarriers can receive instructions from a central computer which also checks their progress and can quickly detect interruptions to production. The autocarriers are of two types, high and low, and on the low type the bodies can be tilted through 90 degrees allowing easy access to the underside.

Each of the teams, which average fourteen operators, works on a specific and clearly identifiable part of the car – suspension, electrical system, doors, etc., providing the 'completeness of task' feature required of autonomous working. Pacing is reduced by allowing a buffer of cars between each group. Normal rate of production is eighteen cars per hour and each car stays in a group's work area for approximately 20 minutes.

Group members are free to arrange the necessary work among themselves so, by rotating between the left- and right-hand side of the cars, a maximum 40-minute work cycle is possible for each operator. A break of about 8 minutes can be gained by speeding up production and filling up the buffers, a common practice just before lunch and the official coffee break.

When the Kalmar plant was first commissioned, the work flow within the groups was organized in two ways. The first of these, line assembly, allowed the carriers to move through the work area with the operators following the cars and completing the necessary assembly work (*Figure 6.9(a)*). Under the second arrangement, dock assembly, the carriers remained stationary at parallel workplaces (in a similar fashion to Saab's line-out system) until the work was completed and the body sent on to the next group.

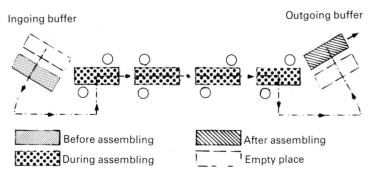

Figure 6.9(a) Line assembly at the Volvo factory at Kalmar (Aguren, Hansson & Karlsson[11])

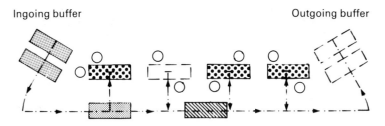

Figure 6.9(b) Dock assembly at the Volvo factory at Kalmar (Aguren, Hansson & Karlsson[11])

Four groups were organized using dock assembly. This did not prove successful, so they were changed to the line system. The problems were found to be with the extra space required for materials and the necessary duplication of tools; the dock system was also not popular with the operators.

Notwithstanding the abandonment of the dock system, the Kalmar project has on most counts been a success. A joint evaluation was carried out at Kalmar in December 1983 and January 1984 by the employers' organization and trades unions which followed a similar survey conducted in 1976[11]. The main findings were as follows:

- between 1977 and 1983 the assembly time of a vehicle had been reduced by 40%;
- faults had been reduced by 39%;
- utilization had increased from 96% to 99%;
- inventory turnover rate increased from nine to twenty-one times per annum.

Added to which, almost without exception, employees had given a favourable assessment of their work. On top of this the plant changed from assembling the Model 240 to Model 740 in February 1984, and production was only lost for 1½ working days due to the technical changes which could be made to the assembly carriers while they were previously taken out for routine maintenance.

Finally, these independent assessments of the plant's success were confirmed by Volvo's own efficiency measures which, in 1984, judged Kalmar as number one in its productivity league table which compares all its plants worldwide.

CASE 4: Truck assembly

Compared with motor cars, trucks are produced in much lower volumes. This might suggest that, even using conventional production systems, the consequently longer cycle times offer the opportunity for enlarged jobs with greater autonomy.

The Volvo Truck Corporation, has a different view. It is the second largest manufacturer of heavy trucks in the world with a total annual production of 35 000 units. Of these 18 000 are built near Gothenburg in Sweden.

In the mid-1970s a decision was made to increase the truck capacity which at that time was concentrated in their plant at Lundby. This factory used traditional flowline techniques but an alternative system was sought which could adopt the principles of group working. From 1977, therefore, a series of experiments was carried out aimed at testing a whole range of possible methods whereby group working could be accommodated.

Despite its use being discontinued for car assembly at Kalmar, the dock system proved to be a feasible proposition (*Figure 6.10*) and, in fact, an assembly system using three docks had been established at the new bus plant opened in 1977 at Borås.

The final choice for truck assembly, however, was a system using two short parallel 'flows' and a new plant was built at Tuve to incorporate this principle (*Figure 6.11*). Completed in 1981 the Tuve plant has a capacity of 6000 trucks per annum, single shift. Each flow, therefore, produces on average thirteen trucks per day with a cycle time of 40–45 minutes. A special feature of the new assembly system is the extent to which sub-assemblies are prepared by separate groups.

In particular, engines and cabs are brought to a state of near-completion so their installation at the appropriate point on the flow is relatively quick and simple. Each 'flow' comprises just four assembly groups (for frame and axle assembly, engine installation, cab installation, tyre and final assembly), each comprising about seven operators. Assembly is followed by inspection and adjustment, then painting. Groups are responsible for their own quality inspection and one member is also designated an 'inspector'. The final inspection personnel constantly feed back information so the performance of the assembly groups can be monitored and improved.

In some ways the arrangement at Tuve is similar to the line assembly system at the Kalmar car plant. Each group is separated by a buffer of two trucks and group members follow the vehicle through the sequence of work required. Transportation of frames is via wheeled assembly carriers which are controlled manually by the operators. Similar devices are used for moving engines except that they employ an air cushion principle.

Figure 6.10 Dock system evaluated for assembly of heavy trucks (Almgren[12])

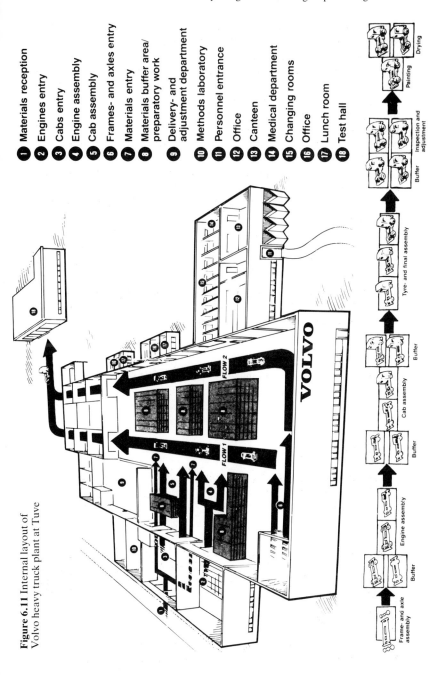

Figure 6.11 Internal layout of Volvo heavy truck plant at Tuve

1. Materials reception
2. Engines entry
3. Cabs entry
4. Engine assembly
5. Cab assembly
6. Frames- and axles entry
7. Materials entry
8. Materials buffer area/preparatory work
9. Delivery- and adjustment department
10. Methods laboratory
11. Personnel entrance
12. Office
13. Canteen
14. Medical department
15. Changing rooms
16. Office
17. Lunch room
18. Test hall

Although the Tuve plant was primarily designed to provide good working conditions and better jobs, a special point needs to be made about its efficiency. Trucks, more so even than motor cars, are subject to wide variations on their basic design. This means that when single line assembly is used there are significant losses in efficiency since the line must be designed for the most complex model, and production of simpler variants results in under-utilization of resources.

By putting in two 'lines' rather than one, Volvo immediately achieved 12% higher productivity for this technical reason alone. Overall the Tuve plant achieves 90–95% efficiency, which is extremely high for a facility manufacturing products in such a wide variety of types.

6.3 Special features of group systems

The development of autonomous group working in manufacturing industries has necessitated a completely new approach to the design of production systems. The cases just described have demonstrated the extent to which this can be achieved within existing factories and how new plants can be built specially to provide for group work.

From these general descriptions a number of specific aspects emerge which deserve further discussion. In particular, product design, material handling, production control, and group responsibility and payment merit examination, since in group working they all need to be given special consideration.

6.3.1 Product design

One of the most important requirements for successful implementation of group working is that the design of the product lends itself to the 'completeness of task' principle previously described. In all the cases presented the product in some way suited the system which was developed for its manufacture. In the case of Saab Cars, the relative simplicity of a car body was the key to their being suitable for the line-out system, whereas the complex nature of the total product prevented the easy translation of the system to final assembly.

Where group working has been successfully adopted for complex products, its success tends to depend on the availability of modules within the product's design. B & O by coincidence (to provide ease of servicing) had already modularized the design of its TV sets so the group working system could be arranged around these pre-existing sub-assembly modules.

However, in the case of some other products a conscious decision has been needed to design goods which can use 'product-focused' systems in their manufacture. To some extent this is true in the case of Volvo's trucks and motor cars. For instance, the Tuve factory is just one 'product-focused' workshop for which the end-product is a finished truck made up of a number of 'building-blocks'.

Similar product workshops within Volvo are themselves producing the blocks or modules which are still regarded by the workers as *their* end-product (i.e. cabs at the plant in Umeå, engines at Skövde, gearboxes at Köping). In this way the most complex of finished products can comprise identifiable elements to

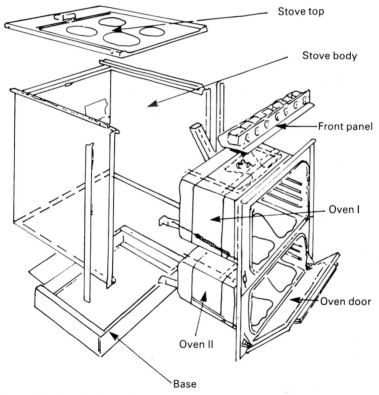

Figure 6.12 Modular design of stove to allow for assembly using autonomous working (Agurén and Edgren[13])

which the producing groups can relate and which make product-focused systems feasible.

Ideally, therefore, new products which are intended for manufacture by groups should be designed from the start on a modular basis. An example of such an approach is provided by the 'prefabricated stove' designed by Husqvarna (*Figure 6.12*). The design work for this product was carried out in very close co-operation between designers and the industrial engineers who were responsible for its manufacture. The resulting product consists of a number of modules – the stove body, top, front panel, oven doors, and the base. These are pre-assembled by separate production groups before going via a buffer store to final assembly. Final assembly takes place at parallel stations where every operator does the entire remaining assembly work required to produce the finished stove.

6.3.2 Material handling

In order to make group production systems workable, new forms of material handling need to be devised. Their main feature must be flexibility, since materials can sometimes follow a number of alternative routings between groups or workplaces and buffers need to be provided to allow for variations in pace.

In the case of smaller products, materials can be moved on simple devices such as roller conveyors or can be mounted on small wheeled trolleys which are manoeuvred manually from place to place.

It is where larger items are to be moved that more novel and sophisticated material handling systems are evident. Common among the devices used are those relying on the air cushion principle. These are used in the assembly of heavy diesel engines and for carrying large heat exchangers (at Alfa-Laval). They can allow an item weighing several tonnes to be moved with just a gentle push from an operator and do not require any motive power.

The alternative to the air cushion carrier is a wheeled vehicle but to move heavy loads these must be powered, typically by electric motors. Such carriers are often used in conjunction with an automatic guidance system comprising wires buried in the factory floor. The signals fed through these wires can instruct a carrier to follow different routes, so products being made with several variations or options can be guided to an appropriate workstation automatically and often under computer control.

An interesting point to note is that Volvo, being pioneers in group working, have generated sufficient in-house knowledge of such material handling equipment that they are now a major manufacturer of such devices. ACS (Auto Carrier Systems) produces and sells a range of automatically guided vehicles which are sold worldwide and used in a variety of applications including flexible manufacturing cells of the type which will be described in Chapter 7.

6.3.3 Production control

Group working requires a different type of system for production control than would be suitable for conventional flowline production. The control system needs both to monitor products and sub-assemblies as well as guide them to correct workplaces at the correct time. At Volvo Kalmar the system uses five small computers, fifty display screens, thirty-seven print-out terminals and a number of direct connections to the work group areas, fixed mechanical equipment and the carrier control 'loop' system.

One of the computers is for direct control of production and plant processing equipment while another computer functions as a link. It is through this computer that all bulletins are passed between the production computer and the display screens or printer terminals in the plant. Computer number three is a spare and can replace the unit controlling the carriers or the terminal computer. It can also be used for further development of the programme.

The remaining two computers are used for material control, assembly planning, computer registration, balancing, communications with Volvo-Data (the group's central data processing service) and a number of other administrative jobs.

When the assembly process starts a body is placed on a carrier, the designation of which is registered in the computer. The system can then follow the carrier through the entire assembly process with a visual representation of the plant and the position of each of the carriers provided on VDU screens. Special sensors report the position of the carrier to the production system which produces assembly instructions from its register for the body that is at that time mounted on the carrier.

The assembly instructions are printed out in good time to the pre-assembly stations which depend on variants, and information is provided about the parts that are to be fitted. When the carrier reaches the assembly point, the team there has already had time to build up subsidiary components that are to be installed in the body.

Since the position of each carrier is reported to the computer through a sensor and the assembly instructions are not printed out until a certain position is known, the carriers can be given an irregular sequence through the assembly process. Thus if a carrier or product presents problems it can be withdrawn from the system, the problem dealt with, and then put back without the need to reschedule production completely.

The versatility of the control system at Kalmar is in stark contrast to a typical system for controlling flow production. Normal practice here would be for a computer simply to dictate to production the number and type of item to be produced and the order of production to ensure that the correct parts are fitted together. Monitoring and feedback of progress is usually not necessary since once the ordering is determined it is unchanged with products remaining on the line regardless of any problems.

6.3.4 Group responsibility and payment

The extent to which added responsibility is given to workers under autonomous working depends on more than just the physical arrangement. Ancillary, non-productive tasks that are normally carried out by functional specialists must be deliberately re-assigned if job enrichment is to be provided using the principles of vertical job loading. In most cases of group working additional responsibility is provided for quality and planning but there are some examples where greater steps have been taken to give groups a much wider range of duties and responsibilities than is usually common.

The Volvo factory at Vara, which manufactures marine diesel engines, has allowed sufficient responsibility to be devolved to the production groups that it operates without foremen. Three supervisors control the one hundred or so workers who are divided into groups for machining, assembly, testing, painting, etc. A group member is then assigned responsibility for each of the following: personnel management, production planning and control, quality, 'economy' (i.e. budgets) and production technology. The roles are re-assigned each year. Thus the foreman's normal duties are shared among the group, even including the selection of new members. Guidance is provided by a standard reference manual describing the expectations for each of the assigned roles.

Autonomous working also demands systems of payment that are based on a variety of factors other than just output. At the Kalmar plant a payment plan has been devised which applies to every worker in the plant, including office staff and excluding only the factory manager.

There is a fixed part based on job evaluation and a further part which is result-related and based on seven factors

1. Cost of factory workers.
2. Cost of staff.
3. Rejection and adjustment.
4. Operational supplies and tools.
5. Added material.
6. Store value.
7. Quality index.

The scheme has increased the interest of employees to contribute to improvements in all areas such as ensuring quality is right first time, maintaining uninterrupted production, keeping down stock levels, etc. An element in the pay of each individual worker is also based on their length of service and absenteeism record.

At Tuve and Vara a similar scheme is operated except that job evaluation is applied to the group rather than the individual. The evaluation is based on the group's performance in the five areas mentioned previously (i.e. personnel management, maintenance, etc.). A 'merit rated' element is also provided for individual group members based, among other things, on the number of tasks they can perform.

Very rarely is payment linked directly to output under group working. The most common arrangement is for some form of measured daywork whereby groups are paid at a standard rate for a predetermined level of production. Once daily or weekly targets have been achieved no further production need take place and workers can normally spend the rest of their attendance time doing ancillary tasks such as cleaning, maintenance etc. It is not usual for workers to be allowed to leave early since this might encourage jobs to be completed in haste, having a detrimental effect on quality.

6.4 Summary

Both the physical and human problems associated with flow line production can be alleviated by adopting autonomous working. The physical problems are reduced because under autonomous working tasks are performed at a number of independent workplaces rather than at a series of stations which depend on each other for continued production. Reliability is, therefore, increased since if production stops at one workplace the others can continue uninterrupted.

Balancing and system losses are reduced since a larger set of tasks is allocated to each workplace and the amount of pacing is far less than on a short-cycle line. High labour turnover and absenteeism are both indicators that human problems exist within a production system. Most documented cases suggest that both these measures improve with the introduction of autonomous working. Also, where quality has deteriorated, this trend is usually arrested and reversed with quality levels eventually becoming higher than those previously achieved.

There are many alternative arrangements to facilitate autonomous working. Operators may perform a set of tasks as individuals or in groups. Tasks may be carried out in parallel or using short lines separated by buffers, with operators following the products in order to lengthen the cycle time.

The choice of actual system used is often determined by the product to be manufactured. Small items and those of simple construction are suitable for production by individuals or using parallel groups. Complex items are often more suited for manufacture on short lines, unless their design is simplified using a modular approach.

A further physical consideration is the handling of materials in autonomous working systems. Flexible and versatile equipment is needed to allow movement between different workplaces at intermittent intervals. In some cases this requires the use of sophisticated, automatically guided vehicles, monitored and controlled by a central computer which organizes the total production process.

Autonomous groups also accept many of the responsibilities normally carried by functional specialists and foremen. This allows them greater discretion and provides for enriched jobs. Such job changes are usually reflected in the method of payment which can have a significant 'merit rating' element in recognition of the increased responsibility for such matters as maintenance and quality. The dependency of pay on output is in most cases very small.

Lastly, it must be noted that, on occasions, autonomous working systems do encounter problems and need to be changed. At Kalmar, Volvo abandoned the dock system in favour of short lines, and more recently the Saab-Scania engine plant altered production from a group system to a new method based on individuals working in parallel and supported by assembly automation.

In all cases, however, problems have been solved by changing from one type of autonomous working to another. Rarely has the solution been to revert back to the conventional flowline.

References

1. WALL, T. D. (1982) 'Perspectives on Job Redesign', in *Autonomy and Control at the Workplace*, edited by J. E. Kelly and C. W. Clegg, Croom Helm
2. DYSON, B. (1973) 'Hoover's Group Therapy', *Management Today*. May
3. SANDBERG, T. (1982) *Work Organisation and Autonomous Groups*, Liber Förlag, Lund, Sweden
4. BOWEY, A. and CONNOLLY, R. (1975) 'Application of the Concept of Working in Groups', *Management Decisions*, **13**, No 3
5. BENNETT, D. J. (1984) *Activity Report on ESRC/HSFR Research Exchange Visit to Sweden to Study Developments in the Design of Production Systems*, University of Aston (April)
6. KARLSSON, U. (1979) *Evaluation of Alternatives to the Traditional Assembly Line at the Body Shop of Saab-Scania in Trollhättan, Sweden*, Chalmers University of Technology, Gothenburg
7. PHYTHIAN, D. (1974) 'Tightly Knit Teams Beat Assembly Blues', *Metalworking Production* (August)
8. DUNDELACH, P. and MORTENSEN, N. (1979) *New Forms of Work Organisation – Denmark, Norway and Sweden*, International Labour Office, Geneva
9. TIEFENTHAL, R., ed. (1975) *Production*, McGraw-Hill, Maidenhead, UK
10. LINDHOLM, R. and NORSTEDT, J-P. (1975) *The Volvo Report*, Swedish Employers' Confederation, Stockholm
11. AGURÉN, S., HANSSON, R. and KARLSSON, K. G. (1976) *The Volvo Kalmar Plant; The Impact of New Design on Work Organisation*, The Rationalization Council, SAF-LO
12. ALMGREN, B. *et al.* (1980) *UARDA Elva Olika Produktionssystem för Lastvagnsmontering*, Chalmers University of Technology, Gothenburg
13. AGURÉN, S. and EDGREN, J. (1980) *New Factories*, Swedish Employers' Confederation, Stockholm

Chapter 7

New technology and production

7.1 The automation of production processes and their control

Many of the more important developments in the design of production systems have related to the machines and processes used for converting materials. The Industrial Revolution saw a change from processes which were largely dependent on natural sources of power to those which, using steam and then electricity, enabled output to be raised to seemingly impossible levels. At the same time the increasing costs of labour caused machine and process designers to reduce the need for skilled operators, and so the concept of automation was developed.

Automation is not new. The machines made by Maudsley for producing pulley blocks, described in Chapter 1, are an early example. However, these earliest forms of automation, along with those which emerged during the first half of the 20th Century, can be described as 'rigid' or 'hard'. When the word 'automation' is used today, the reference is usually to a more flexible type of system which can also be regarded as having some form of intelligence. This type of automation became available as a direct result of the invention of the electronic computer and heralded what some consider to be a second industrial revolution[1]. Under the new revolution, however, automation is not just confined to the machines and processes for manufacture, it can also be applied to all aspects of the production function including design, engineering, planning, monitoring and control.

More recently still the term 'new technology' has become generally used in connection with the latest generation of automated systems. This term refers to a wide range of equipment utilizing micro-circuitry and associated software. The newness of new technology lies not so much in the application of electronics to data processing, since this has been commercially available and used in automated systems since the 1950s, but rather in the radically changed nature of the equipment now being produced.

This has enormously increased the range of its practical applications.

Micro-electronic technology is distinguished by its compactness, cheapness, speed of operation, reliability, accuracy, and low energy consumption. When combined with suitable data inputting and communication facilities, new technology permits information to be collected, collated, stored and accessed with a speed not previously available[2].

7.1.1 Numerical control

Machines and processes which have been automated using some form of electronic system are said to use 'numerical control' or NC (i.e. literally, control by numbers). The first generation of NC system, introduced commercially about 1954, used thermionic valves and hard-wired circuitry, and proved extremely unreliable. NC systems were often added-on to existing machines providing linear point-to-point movement of tools or machine elements. The second and third generations of NC system using, respectively, transistors and integrated circuits, provided greater speed of operation, reliability, and more complex processing capabilities.

A feature of early numerical control was the lengthy and often rather skilled job of producing the control medium, usually a punched or magnetic tape. Computers would often be used to assist the 'part programmer' in this job but they would be large mainframe machines located separately from the production facilities[3]. Thus the fourth generation of NC, introduced in the mid-1960s, is known as Computer Numerical Control or CNC. This system incorporates a mini-computer which carries out many of the functions previously accomplished using a separate computer.

Some of the possible functions of the computer in a CNC system include diagnosis of faults in the control system, modifying the control program in the event of design changes, machine errors, etc., and adaptive control (making alterations to suit changing conditions). CNC systems can also store relatively simple programs so the control tape need not be read for every item manufactured. This is an advantage since tapes and tape readers tend to be the least reliable components of an NC machine.

The next logical step, therefore, is for the necessity for tapes as a control medium to be removed completely. This is the idea behind Direct Numerical Control or DNC where programs for a number of NC machine tools are stored in a single computer of larger capacity than the type used in CNC. The central control feature of

DNC also facilitates the integration of a number of machines and processes into a complete manufacturing system, with parts scheduling and process monitoring, which is a real step towards a completely automated factory.

Automation by numerical control was originally limited to metal machining processes such as drilling, milling, turning, etc. Over the years, however, the number of NC applications has increased until few production processes are left which have not been automated in some way. Nowadays automation has been applied to spot-welding, arc-welding, tube bending, sheet-metal pressing and forming, plastic moulding, adhesive application, painting, chemical processing etc., while, most important of all, considerable progress is now being made towards automating the most labour intensive aspect of manufacturing-assembly work.

Although the trend is now more towards flexible automation by numerical control, any discussion on the general theme of automation cannot ignore the more traditional 'rigid' or 'hard' type. This form of automation has served high volume manufacturers well throughout most of this century and systems such as the 'transfer machine line' are still available as a cheap, reliable option in some circumstances.

Their disadvantage, however, lies in the fact that they cannot be quickly and inexpensively changed from the manufacture of one item to another. They are appropriate, therefore, in situations where demand is high and variety low, but when demand falls and the number of variants increases, 'flexible' or 'soft' automation becomes more favourable.

7.1.2 Justification

Leaving aside for a moment the description of automated systems, it is relevant at this point to re-address the question of their justification. It was stated earlier that higher labour costs originally encouraged designers of machines to remove the need for an operator. The subsequent reduction in direct labour cost, therefore, became the main factor when originally choosing an automated process rather than its conventional, manually operated, counterpart. Indeed, this particular factor remained the most important single reason for justifying an investment into automation while the hard type was the only form available.

Justification of numerically controlled systems, on the other hand, can be made on a number of other grounds. Firstly, there are factors to consider, apart from direct labour cost, which can be assessed directly in monetary terms. These will include, in some cases, material cost reductions and a reduction in overheads attributable to the process, the most important of which is likely to be setting cost. Secondly, there are a number of less tangible factors which may affect costs. The savings made in these areas should always be taken into consideration, and the value of NC production cannot be fully appreciated until the impact in all areas has been evaluated. They are (adapted from [4]):

(a) *Inspection costs.* NC reduces the need for full inspection, hence the costs of inspection and transport to inspection sections are lowered; time is saved and delay in waiting for transport and inspection is avoided.

(b) *Cost of scrap.* Certain errors, e.g. incorrect hole locations, are almost entirely eliminated. Other errors, such as oversize holes, may not be so drastically reduced but in general NC cuts the cost of scrap, often by more than 50%.

(c) *Machining accuracy.* A consistent and high degree of accuracy in machining is achieved. Consistent products lead to easier assembly and reduced fitting costs.

(d) *Cost of modifications.* Production is not stopped while a modification is introduced, a new program can be quickly prepared and few fixtures need to be modified.

(e) *Tool storage costs.* Cutting tools are readily located in the machine's tool storage system and the need for fixture storage facilities is reduced.

(f) *Transportation costs.* The use of versatile NC machines reduces the number of times components have to be moved from machine to machine; the time spent awaiting the availability of secondary machines is eliminated, thus speeding the turnover of work.

(g) *Cost of floor space.* The output from just one NC machine is often equivalent to that from several conventional machines; rental or building costs, as well as those for lighting and heating, are reduced.

(h) *Work-in-progress costs.* The reduced number of operations per component, and the limited need for inspection and re-setting, ensure that components are processed with minimum delay. The reductions in waiting time help to lessen the number of part-finished jobs and so reduce the amount of money tied up as work-in-progress.

An additional point which must be made relating to the justification of numerically controlled-automated systems concerns the strategic advantages derived from their use. In recent years manufacturers of goods have seen factors such as quality, reliability, delivery and design emerging as competitive weapons in winning customer orders. Rarely is price alone taken into account when choosing between rival products. Numerical control increases the opportunities for manufacturers to compete in all these areas, thus ensuring their continued survival and growth.

Before leaving this general discussion on automation, some mention needs to be made about its application to production control. It was argued in Chapter 1 that many of the production control problems can be 'designed out' by paying careful attention to the production system itself (e.g. by reducing setting times, etc.). Indeed the underlying philosophy of numerical control endorses this argument.

However, the production control function can never be entirely eliminated so improvements in its efficiency are as desirable as those which have been achieved in the production processes themselves. The use of computers in the production control area is an example, therefore, of how the philosophy of automation can be applied in a wider sense than to just the immediate hardware for converting materials.

Capacity planning, order processing, purchasing, material requirements planning (MRP), scheduling, progressing, and stock control are all examples of production control subsystems which have been automated to a greater or lesser degree. Although there is some debate as to whether automation has provided *better* control, there can be no disputing the fact that the labour requirement is lower while more complex calculations can be performed.

Other functions outside the confines of the material conversion process which can be automated include product design, process planning and other engineering aspects of production. These developments, together with the powerful breakthrough into robotics, will be discussed in the next section which extends the theme of automation into the wider concept of a computer integrated manufacturing system.

7.2 CADCAM and robotics

CADCAM stands for Computer Aided Design and Manufacturing[5]. In its widest sense, CADCAM implies the automation, using computer control, of all activities necessary to take a product from concept through to its completed manufacture. These activities include not just product design and parts manufacture but also process planning, costing, tool design, production planning, material ordering, assembly, testing, etc. The rate of development of CADCAM is extremely rapid, and accelerating, so today there is no design and manufacturing subsystem that has not benefited from some form of computerization.

The computer integrated, fully automatic factory has still to emerge but its individual elements already exist. All that is required are the linkages, and it is expected that these will be available and complete systems running by the end of the 20th Century[6].

When examining the elements of CADCAM it is logical to start by looking at the design function. Not only is this where the whole production cycle starts, it is also one of the most important elements since it can ensure the ultimate success of a completely automated system. The term 'designing for production' has been used for many years. It simply means that designers must give consideration to how their designs will be produced rather than handing over a set of drawings which present the manufacturing engineers with an impossible challenge.

In fact, the same basic principles apply to designing for computer integrated manufacturing that were previously outlined in connection with 'group technology' and 'autonomous working'. These are, firstly, to ensure components are designed as members of families rather than making each one unique and, secondly, to adopt the modularized, 'building block' principle which simplifies the manufacture of even the most complex of products. The reasons for these two principles being adopted are that component family formation facilitates production using 'flexible manufacturing systems' (which will be described later) while modular design enables assembly work to be more easily automated.

7.2.1 Design

Computer Aided Design (CAD) is not a new technique. In fact, designers have used computers since they first became commercially available in the early 1950s[7]. Originally the computer was used to assist in the mathematics of design work, and this is still an important part of CAD. However, this aspect has been augmented by two other common uses to aid the designer, so the three main areas of CAD today are:

(i)   Using the computer to perform design calculations;
(ii) Design storage and retrieval;
(iii) 'Graphics'.

The use of computers to perform design calculations is an important aspect of design work where structures are subject to loads and stresses. Their use is, therefore, widespread in the construction and aerospace industries[8]. The complex nature of such calculations made them ideal applications for scientific programming languages such as FORTRAN (FORmula TRANslator), and other higher level languages which have been specifically developed for manipulating mathematical data.

Storage and retrieval of designs and design information can often be justified as a labour saving application alone. 'Standard' parts such as screws, bearings, gears, etc. can be recorded on computer file and called-up when required, avoiding the need to 'redesign' such items every time a product or assembly is generated or modified. More important still, a storage and retrieval system is an essential prerequisite for designing parts which are standardized or form part of a component family. The unique parameters for a required part can be specified and the computer selects existing designs which are used as they stand or modified, so preventing any unnecessary proliferation of parts requiring new production methods and processes.

Computer graphics enable the VDU screen to be used, literally, as a drawing board. Drawings can be generated using a light-pen, tablet, joystick, etc. and then stored. Standard parts or shapes can be called-up from storage and displayed on the screen, then moved, enlarged or reduced as required. Hard copies of designs are produced using high speed pen and ink plotters which can generate a drawing on paper in a matter of minutes rather than days. More sophisticated graphics programs can even generate designs in three dimensions, enabling a part to be viewed from any chosen angle, for mechanical performance to be assessed, and allowing complex shapes, such as aerofoils and turbine blades, to be 'described' in a form which can be recognized by NC machines.

Computer Aided Design systems require such extensive development work that they are rarely developed in-house by their end-users. Today the industry is dominated by a relatively small number of 'turnkey' suppliers (suppliers of both hardware and software), most of whom are American in origin. Among these firms are 'Computervision', which was established in 1969, and IBM, which started developing CAD in 1974[9].

7.2.2 Process planning

The term 'process planning' embraces a set of activities which are necessary to take detailed product designs through to the point when production at the required level can commence. These activities will include deciding the logic for manufacture (i.e. determining the product 'structure'), taking 'make or buy' decisions, method and process selection, and issuing manufacturing instructions[10].

A number of ancillary activities will also accompany those which are central to process planning. These will include tool design, specifying purchase requirements, and designing layouts. Process planning can be regarded, therefore, as deciding *how* a product is to be manufactured. The input to the process planning system is: *what* is to be produced? (design data), *when* is it to be produced? (the introduction date), and *how many* are to be produced? (the forecast demand or firm orders).

Process planning is traditionally laborious and time-consuming, which explains why manufacturers often need to plan several years ahead when intending to introduce a new product into the market-place. Another important feature of process planning is that, when being carried out manually, it requires an intimate knowledge of manufacturing techniques, equipment and level of plant skills. Computer-Aided Process Planning (CAPP) uses existing company manufacturing data – for example, synthetic time standards and process data for machining, welding and assembly – to create a manufacturing engineering database[11].

Ideally, the system should also perform all calculations, generate descriptive user-defined documentation and data files, be applicable to all types of manufacture, be capable of extension or update by manufacturing engineers to reflect changing manufacturing processes and equipment, and evolve towards automatic links with CAD. The requirements of a CAPP system, and the fact that they do the work of experienced and knowledgeable personnel, mean that it must be 'rule-driven' so in essence it is an *expert system* which interacts with the manufacturing base data.

The number of available CAPP systems has increased considerably over the last few years with universities, consultancies, research institutes and hardware manufacturers offering a wide range of packages which vary in terms of their complexity and usefulness. Among these is MIPLAN offered by Computervision which can be integrated with their CAD system[12].

Activities which are ancillary to process planning can equally be computerized en route to the final objective of creating a fully integrated manufacturing system. For example, tool design work can be done on computer by recalling component designs and then, using graphics, constructing the required design of tooling using standard clamps, bushes, etc. taken from the computer's file.

Sometimes parts and tools may even be designed together, an approach which can offer greater efficiency since problems relating to clamping, clearances etc. can be seen and solved at the outset.

Purchase requirements are generated as a result of make or buy decisions. Parts which will not be manufactured in-house can have their designs automatically sent for tender to a selection of approved vendors who will be retained on file. Individual purchase orders can then be produced by the computerized material requirements planning (MRP) system and transmitted, together with due date and delivery requirements to the chosen vendor.

Layouts of tooling and machinery can be designed using a number of proprietary computer programs, some of which have been available since the early 1960s. More recent programs enable the layout designer to use interactive graphics in much the same way as the product designer using a CAD system[13]. Alternatively a system simulation packaging can be used where the interaction between machines and processes is important. The subject of simulation will be dealt with later when the manufacturing system is discussed in more detail.

7.2.3 Robotics

One of the biggest obstacles standing in the way of developing a completely automated factory has until recently been the problem of moving, transferring and manipulating materials. Transporting materials from the stores, and then between machines, continued to be a manually-operated job long after the machines and processes themselves had been automated. Likewise, operations requiring dexterity or complex movements (such as assembly work or paint spraying) remained as manual jobs unless volumes could justify the heavy investment needed to automate using specially-built equipment. Today, however, this particular area is one where the move towards automation is most rapid; the reason being the development of 'robotics'.

There are many definitions of a robot but the Robot Institute of America offers the following useful interpretation of the term:

> A robot is a reprogrammable multi-functional manipulator designed to move material, parts, tools, or specialized devices through variable programmed motions for the performance of a variety of tasks.

If the RIA definition is interpreted liberally, then robots could include a range of devices including AGVs (automatically guided vehicles), computer controlled warehouse cranes, and simple component handling devices fixed to machines for the purpose of loading and unloading. More strictly though an industrial robot is usually regarded as a stand-alone device having three principal components[14]:

(i) One or more arms, usually situated on a fixed base, that can move in several directions;
(ii) A manipulator, the business end of the robot, being the 'hand' that holds the tool or the part to be worked;
(iii) A controller that gives detailed movement instructions.

Most industrial robots in use today are employed in engineering manufacture, although they are also being developed for use in hazardous environments (e.g. bomb disposal and mining) and for non-engineering applications (e.g. food preparation).

A particular country or industry's robot population is often used as a barometer to measure the extent of its development towards fully automated manufacturing. It is arguably a useful, if crude, measure but can often be misleading since, as was previously suggested, the count could include simple 'pick and place' devices of the type commonly used in hard automation. For this reason the Japanese robot population has (in 1983) been estimated at anywhere from 3000 to 47 000. However, by any definition the Japanese population is today the highest in the world, followed by that of the USA and USSR, then the major European industrial nations including West Germany, Sweden and the UK[15].

Adjusting robot population figures to take account of the number of people employed in manufacturing shows that Sweden has the highest density (30 robots in 1981 per 10 000 employed), Japan (13 per 10 000), West Germany (5 per 10 000) and USA (4 per 10 000)[16]. The major robot manufacturers in the West are Cincinnati Milacron and Unimation (both of the USA) and ASEA (Sweden), while in Japan they are produced by FANUC, Hitachi, Kawasaki, Nachi, Seiko and Yaskawa. IBM's determination to break into the field of automated manufacturing is again demonstrated by the fact that it is working hard to gain a major market share, particularly of robotic assembly applications (the main activity in IBM's own factories).

When looking in detail at industrial robots it is helpful to classify them according to one or more of a number of factors. They can be grouped according to characteristics such as: their drive system, number of degrees of freedom, load capacity, sensory perception, price, motion control, application etc. For the purpose of this discussion the most appropriate characteristic is probably application.

Looked at in terms of their operational mode, therefore, robots can be grouped as follows:

(i) Handling robots (those which grip or carry workpieces or material);
(ii) Process robots (those which handle tools or equipment)
   – welding, glueing and other jointing applications
   – spray painting
   – deburring, polishing, cutting and other metal working
   – other process applications (mainly inspection)
(iii) Assembly robots.

When examining the number of robots within each of these groups an interesting fact emerges. This is that, in only a few years, the emphasis on using robots for handling has greatly reduced. Process applications have replaced handling in terms of popularity while assembly uses are growing rapidly and look like dominating within the next few years.

In terms of robot design this trend has a great deal of significance. Handling robots can be, on the whole, of the simple 'programmable' type while process and assembly robots need to be more sophisticated. Important among the features of a process robot is its 'sensory perception', which is its ability to display a degree of intelligence and act in different ways depending on certain conditions.

The types of sensor used in robotic applications include proximity sensors (e.g. optical or electro-magnetic devices), range sensors (e.g. acoustic or laser devices), and tactile sensors (e.g. simple micro-switches or devices measuring stress, torque, etc.).

A more recent breakthrough in terms of robot technology has been the development of vision sensors. Giving a robot eyes (a vision system) can reduce the need for component fixturing and ease tolerances on parts. It also makes the robot capable of performing all kinds of assembly and inspection tasks.

7.3 Flexible manufacturing

Reference has been made in this and previous chapters to 'flexibility' as an attribute of modern production systems. It could be argued, because of their ability to produce a range of components and products, that traditional job and batch production systems are, and always have been, flexible. However, current usage of the term 'flexible manufacturing' implies something more specific. Firstly, it relates on the whole to automated manufacture, an area where flexibility has not traditionally been evident. Secondly, the term 'flexible' relates not just to the range of components the system is capable of producing but also to a number of other factors not normally regarded as open to a high degree of variation. It is, therefore, more appropriate to refer to flexible *automation* rather than manufacturing, with flexibility being not only in terms of component design but also operation sequence, batch sizes, and overall production capacity.

In many ways the logic behind flexible manufacturing is similar to that which led to Group Technology (GT) manufacture. The objective of GT in the first instance was to reduce setting times by identifying families of components and, later, to reduce lead times, material movement and work-in-progress levels by grouping machines into cells or lines. In fact, if the GT argument is taken to its logical conclusion it becomes evident that both the machines and material handling system between them should be automated to produce an unmanned GT cell.

These were the very thoughts of Dr Theo Williamson when he joined the Molins Company in the UK during the 1960s. Williamson came from Ferranti, a company renowned for its GT applications, and he led Molins (a cigarette machinery manufacturer) into not just using GT but into developing and producing an automated system based on GT principles[17]. Called the Molins System 24, the development was an automatic process consisting of a bank of NC machine tools separated from a row of work-setting operators by a pigeon-holed rack.

Work was transferred automatically to and from this storage rack by units known as 'Molacs' (Molins on-line automatic conveyors). The only manual operation required was that of fixing unmachined billets to pallets and removing the finished work. Other operations such as taking jobs to and from the machine tools, supplying the machines with control tapes, checking the provision of the correct tools for a particular job and supplying the raw material were all catered for automatically under computer control.

System 24 was designed to operate twenty-four hours a day with labour only needed for eight hours and was in many ways the forerunner of the type of automatic system subsequently developed in Japan and the USA. Indeed, it was generally recognized that System 24 was ten years ahead of its time but, as often happens in such cases, the venture ultimately failed[18].

Among the reasons cited for the lack of success of System 24 is the fact that it was capable of machining only relatively small components and, more important, its very high speed of operation confined it to non-ferrous metals (of the type used in cigarette machinery). Thus, outside the aerospace and instrument industries few applications could be found, despite Williamson's argument that the superior economics of manufacture would convert companies to using light alloys. Molin's Machine Tool Division was, therefore, closed in the early 1970s and today many engineers quote System 24 as another of Britain's missed opportunities.

Molin's concept of an automated cell of machine tools, linked by conveyors and with automatic transfer of materials to and from a store, is essentially that of a modern Flexible Manufacturing System (FMS). An FMS can be defined as

> '...a system dealing with high level distributed data processing and automated material flow using computer controlled machines, assembly cells, industrial robots, inspection machines and so on, together with computer integrated materials handling and storage system'[19].

Flexible Manufacturing Systems can be used in a wide variety of industrial processes including sheet-metal work, cutting, welding, pressing, painting and assembly work. Most progress, however, has been made in metal machining, an area where NC was already well-established.

Figure 7.1 shows the elements of an FMS cell. Its basic functions are: to perform the conversion process, to allow buffer storage and/or holding of a workpiece or workpieces, to provide the physical links to the materials handling systems in the 'outside world', and to provide the data communication links to the control system. Its physical links allow the transport of parts, tools, pallets etc. FMS systems are justified using a set of factors which are essentially a combination of those already specified for group technology and numerical control.

The physical appearance of an FMS will vary not only with the type of production process being used but also with the type of hardware adopted for the transportation, transfer and storage of materials, parts and tools. For transportation purposes the following may be used: conveyors, rail guided vehicles, automatically guided vehicles (fixed height and high lifting), and stacker cranes.

Tool and component transfer will normally be effected by some kind of robotic device. Simple pick and place robots, for instance, can be used for loading and unloading small components and similar devices have been used for many years as tool changers on numerically controlled machining centres. Where larger items are to be transferred, pallet changing robots are available which can

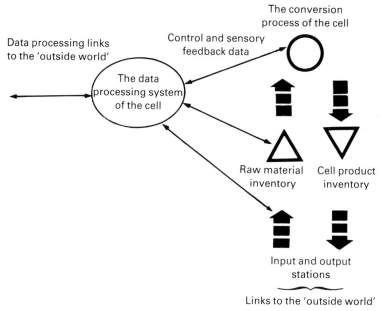

Figure 7.1 The elements of an FMS cell (Ranky[19])

move heavy loads on and off the table of a large machine tool. In some cases the transfer of tools and parts requires quite complex movements (e.g. in assembly work), calling for a more sophisticated industrial robot with manipulative capabilities and some form of sensory perception.

The type of system used for tool and parts storage will depend on the required capacity and desired speed of access. Tools can, for instance, be stored in limited numbers on drums, carousels and chain-type magazines, all of which provide quick change-overs but limited capacity. Similar devices can be used for parts storage and small buffers of parts can even be maintained on conveyors. However, such systems can only enable the facility to run unmanned for limited periods so remote storage of materials, parts and tools becomes necessary if long-duration automated manufacture is to be achieved. In this case the transportation devices mentioned earlier would be used not just for conveying material between machines but also for moving material and tools into and out of store.

The transmission and processing of information to and within a flexible manufacturing system is an important aspect of its design which can be approached in a number of slightly different ways.

Essentially though it is achieved by some form of distributed data processing, i.e. a system where computers 'talk' to each other.

The most common approach is to use a network whereby a central computer (or computers) is linked to the CNC controllers on the processing machines and, where applicable, the industrial robots, AGVs, etc. Thus, the central computer will deal with the overall production control activities such as programming, work scheduling and monitoring. Then, on instruction from the main computer, the controllers will direct their machine or device to go through the necessary sequence of activities, reporting back their completion at the appropriate time.

An alternative to linking together all the computers in the system is to use some form of 'labelling' method. Here, part details or instructions are carried, literally, with the material and are read by the machines before they select the necessary CNC program. The label, which is usually fixed to a pallet, can be mechanical, in which case a simple trip-switch mechanism will read its coded information. Mechanical labels, however, can only carry limited amounts of information (sufficient to distinguish between about thirty or forty different pallets) so other devices employing microwaves, for example, are used enabling hundreds of different sets of instructions to be carried.

Bar code labels of the type commonly used nowadays in connection with stock control can carry information in FMS systems, but only in a clean environment since any contamination immediately creates reading problems. They are suitable, therefore, for assembly work rather than for machining, where they are rapidly gaining acceptance as a means of transmitting information on the required variations to complex products.

To illustrate the scope of FMS and the wide variety of sizes and system elements a number of examples will now be described. Each represents a different configuration of machines and handling equipment. They also demonstrate the range of complexity and versatility which is embraced by the general heading of flexible manufacturing.

Example 1: Machines and machine cells served by industrial robots

The simplest and most elementary form of FMS is a single machine or a cell of two or more machines served by a robot. Such an arrangement often represents an organization's first step towards a full system capable of producing a complete range of parts or products.

Figure 7.2, for instance, shows a CNC machining centre around which there are a number of pallet stations. A simple robot transfers pallets, as required, from station to machine, removing completed work and returning it to an empty pallet station. A wide range of components can be produced since it is possible for every pallet to contain a different set of parts.

Figure 7.2 A CNC machining centre with pallet stations and a pallet robot (AB Sajo Maskin)

The main constraint on the system's versatility would normally be the number of tools which can be stored in the machine's magazine. 'Yasda' of Japan, however, produce machining centres which are equipped with capacity for three hundred tools and 'Sandvik' of Sweden has developed a magazine for turning machines which can carry more than one hundred tool blocks. This number of tools will usually enable systems of this type to run unmanned for at least a complete shift on a range of different components, each having widely differing machining requirements.

A somewhat different arrangement, built around the same idea, is a cell of machines served by a more versatile manipulative robot. Here individual components, rather than loaded pallets, are picked up by the robot's grippers and then transferred from machine to machine (*Figure 7.3*). The robot's agility and range of possible movements makes the cell capable of producing a number of components requiring different positioning and different

Figure 7.3 Machine cell served by a manipulative industrial robot (ASEA Robotics)

machine sequences. Robots used in this type of application are also much faster in operation than pallet robots since they are used in conjunction with simpler, short-cycle operations such as pressing and drilling.

Example 2: Machine cells served by linear material transporters

The type of arrangement just described is obviously restricted to a very small number of machines, which in practice is determined by the limit of the robot's reach. If the idea is to be extended to include a complete workshop of machines then some further means of automatically moving materials will be required.

The simplest method of achieving this is by providing some form of mechanism for transporting pallets or components between stations from where a robot can then load them on or off the machines. The system used could be a linear powered roller conveyor of the type employed in early FMS such as System 24 and Cincinnati's 'Variable Mission I'[20].

This is still a popular approach where smaller parts are involved, and was chosen by the 600 Group for their SCAMP (Six hundred

Computer Aided Manufacturing Project). This is a system developed for automatically producing a range of turned parts[21].

The load carrying capacity of a roller conveyor is rather limited, however, so an alternative type of transporter for linear movement of heavier parts is a rail guided vehicle[22]. Proprietary transporters of this type are available which enable cells to be extended at reasonably low cost (*Figure 7.4*). A large workshop using a rail-guided parts transportation system is in operation at the Yamazaki machine tool plant in Japan. Here eighteen machining centres are arranged in two lines, with each line being served by a rail-guided pallet transporter incorporating a machine loading robot. One transporter can carry 3 tons and travel at 60 metres/min, the other has 8 tons capacity and a speed of 40 metres/min. Twelve operators are required in this workshop compared with the two-hundred-and-fifteen needed using conventionally equipped machines.

Figure 7.4 Rail guided vehicle providing linear movement of heavier material (Kearney & Trecker Marwin)

Example 3: Machine cells served by stacker crane

A novel alternative to roller conveyors or rail-guided transporters is the use of a computer-controlled stacker crane. This was the approach adopted by BT Handling Systems in Sweden in preference to the alternative arrangements offered by current suppliers. As a manufacturer and experienced user of sophisticated material handling equipment, BT could see the merits of using their own products within an FMS. A conventional GT cell had been used for some years in which racks and a fork lift truck provided work-in-progress storage and parts handling.

Extending the idea using computer-controlled material handling and CNC machines became a relatively simple step achieved at a cost, in 1980, of £120 000 for the crane, racking and minicomputer system (*Figure 7.5*). Initially the system was set-up with one fully automatic station, a Yasda YBM 90N machine centre, and fifteen other machine tools also served by the crane but using operators. As the cell has been developed, further Yasda machines and fully automatic CNC lathes have been added, enabling more of the system to run completely unmanned during nightshift periods.

Figure 7.5 Machine cell served by a computer controlled stacker crane at BT Handling Systems

BT's approach to FMS is interesting in that it represents a view that progressive development using limited manning can be a more sensible alternative than the immediate introduction of a highly sophisticated, fully automated system. The view has been reinforced by the introduction of a second cell, also using a stacker crane, for welding. Again the system was set up using largely manual welding stations, but capable of being enhanced later by progressively replacing them with automatic processes.

Example 4: Machine cells served by AGVs

The use of AGVs (automatically guided vehicles) has already been described in Chapter 6 in connection with material handling for autonomous working. These highly versatile devices, whose use is well-established for assembly work and in automated warehouses, are now becoming an essential feature of manufacturing systems which are *truly* flexible. AGVs require nothing other than a reasonably flat floor and follow a buried wire, so installation costs are minimal. The development of radio-controlled and laser-guided AGVs could even remove the need for the second requirement in the future.

AGVs are, therefore, not as limited in their application as roller conveyors, rail-guided transporters and cranes. They can literally 'go anywhere' provided there is an adequate roadway, so they can visit a number of machines together with inspection stations, parts washing facilities, etc. A small FMS cell developed by Cincinnati Milacron, employing one AGV, is shown in *Figure 7.6*.

As well as providing a highly versatile FMS, the use of AGVs easily enables a system to be expanded or contracted. Extra AGVs can simply be added to increase the frequency with which

Figure 7.6 FMS cell using an AGV at Cincinnati Milacron

materials are moved and machines can be added or removed without disruption to the rest of the system.

An interesting variation on the conventional type of AGV, which increases its versatility still further is the high-lifting type. Developed from a fork lift truck, this AGV was first introduced by BT Handling Systems. It has the ability to lift work from floor level up to 3 m so can load and unload machines having different working heights as well as moving items in and out of a high-bay store. An FMS using high lifting AGVs with three machining centres has been installed at Sundsvalls Verkstäder in Sweden (*Figure 7.7*).

Figure 7.7 High lifting AGV developed by BT Handling Systems

Example 5: Full FMS with tool and parts storage

In order for an automated manufacturing system to be fully flexible there must be sufficient material, tool and program storage to allow uninterrupted running for long periods on the widest range of parts. There must also be a sufficiently sophisticated set of automated 'service' functions to prevent the system from periodically stopping due to relatively minor and correctable deviations from normal running conditions. A large material storage capacity can be incorporated into an FMS system by utilizing the sort of automated warehousing technology that is well developed in the wholesale and retailing sectors.

The automated warehouse is interfaced with the manufacturing system by a transfer device which moves parts between the AGVs (which serve the FMS cells) and the stacker crane (which puts the parts into store and picks them out again when required). FMS systems which are linked in this way to an automated warehouse have been installed by Murata Machinery and Mori Seiko in Japan[23].

Additional tool storage can be provided in a similar way. Drums or magazines from machines are made interchangeable and are transported to and from a tool store by some form of handling device. Cincinnati Milacron, for instance, has developed a technique using an AGV to change complete magazines, while Yamazaki uses a 'drum loader robot' which functions in a manner similar to an overhead crane. Yet another system involves the use of an industrial robot mounted on an AGV which is also equipped with a tool rack. The robot can thereby change individual tools, when necessary, rather than complete magazines.

Program storage is less of a problem than the physical storage of parts and tools. Although the mini- and micro-computers attached to machines and cells have limited capacity, they are invariably linked via a network to a larger computer. Moreover, the program storage capacity can be increased further still using a hierarchy of computers which can download the programs to the system and machine computers when required.

The monitoring of quality and process performance is an important requirement of any manufacturing system capable of running uninterrupted for long periods of time. Quality inspection is generally achieved using some form of in-process gauging device which will check dimensional accuracy, either while a component is being produced or immediately afterwards. The machine will automatically compensate for any error trend which is occurring by making adjustments to the appropriate settings. More complex parts will be inspected on separate, numerically controlled, co-ordinate measuring machines which check a wide variety of different dimensions without delaying the production processes.

The other important type of monitoring, i.e. fault-detection and diagnosis, is still in its infancy but when fully developed it will be the key which will unlock the door to fully unmanned production. Detection and replacement of broken tools is becoming a common feature of automated production systems. The idea will doubtless be extended to include other machine components and systems, thereby automating the traditionally labour intensive maintenance function.

Example 6: FMS for sheet metal fabrication and welding

Most of the earlier development work into flexible manufacturing involved metal-cutting machine tools. In practice, however, the range of production processes goes much wider and the need for automated systems extends to a number of other areas where numerical control is less well-established. The last two examples are, therefore, different in that they relate to some of the more important of these areas which, if fully automated, will open up the benefits of flexible manufacturing to a much larger population of producers.

Recent years have shown a trend towards sheet metal fabrication and welding as low cost substitutes for more conventional casting, forging and machining work. Their use is justified on the basis of reduced capital and material costs, together with the shorter production cycles associated with pressing and welding operations. Automation, on the other hand, has proved difficult due to the problem of handling large sheets of raw material and work-in-progress. Welding has also tended to be a manual process since it is usually conducted 'by eye' and requires a certain degree of operator skill.

The creation of an FMS system for producing sheet metal fabrications follows essentially the same steps as for the more conventional systems already outlined. The first step is the application of numerical control to the individual processes. For shearing, punching and folding, proprietary machines equipped with NC and CNC are becoming more readily available. For welding, industrial robot welders are being produced with probes and vision systems removing the need for operator control.

The next step is the introduction of automatic loading and unloading systems to allow uninterrupted running of the individual processes. This would involve the use of an 'add on' device capable of handling large metal sheets with electro-magnetic grippers or suction cups. The final step is to link together the various processes with material transport and transfer devices. For this purpose the limitless versatility of the 'peripatetic' AGV can again be utilized to advantage. Suitably modified, a proprietary AGV is capable of transporting sheets, either singly or in batches, from one process to another where they can be linked-in with the automatic loading and unloading system.

Example 7: Flexible assembly systems

Assembly work is a major area of application for FMS technology. As was the case with component production, automated assembling was limited to high volumes when using conventional technology. New technologies and, in particular, robotics have now changed this and flexible assembly systems are one of the most rapidly growing areas of production.

Compared with other manufacturing processes, assembly is unique in that it requires a far higher degree of manipulative and corrective skill. For this reason conventional automation and even early generation robots were incapable of performing the sophisticated movements that could only be carried out by dexterous human operators. The availability of robots with sensory perception, however, has meant that many of these tasks need no longer be carried out manually since the requirement to feel or see can be fulfilled by the robot itself.

A further important aspect of assembly work is that the amount of 'pacing' is (relatively) quite high, especially where lines are being used. This enables both automated and manual assembly operations to be carried out on the same product, provided they are separated by a suitable buffer. Full automation can, therefore, be introduced gradually by progressively replacing manual operations with individual robot stations.

An example of this approach can be seen at Saab-Scania's plant for the production of petrol engines[24,25]. An increased range of engine options was being offered by Saab Cars, but conventional 'hard' automation was not appropriate for their assembly because of the relatively low volumes and resulting high frequency of changeovers. Scania, therefore, opted for a flexible assembly system which initially consisted of six ASEA robots installed in a line of otherwise manual operations.

The robots, which assembled sundry items such as valve springs, collets, timing covers and flywheels, could be changed to produce a different engine variant in about 15 minutes. Once this initial installation had been proved, Scania then added another three robots to automate more of the manual operations and move one further step towards the ultimate goal of a completely automated system.

A contrasting approach to Saab-Scania's is that of Perkins Engines (a subsidiary of Massey Ferguson) in the UK[26]. Perkins, a large diesel engine manufacturer, opted for a complete flexible assembly system costing £1m for the production of its full range of cylinder heads, together with an automated component handling system costing a further £2.5m. The system provided immediate capacity to produce 1000 cylinder heads per day, automatically, in a random mix of sizes and types (three, four or six cylinder). The inclusion of automated inspection equipment also ensured that defective components were detected before rather than after being built into a complete engine.

The system at Perkins, and even that at Saab-Scania, represents a fairly large scale and specialized case of flexible automated assembly. However, a number of relatively inexpensive robots is becoming readily available which are designed specifically for assembly work (see *Figure 7.8*).

Figure 7.8 An industrial robot designed for assembly work (ASEA Robotics)

To conclude this section on Flexible Manufacturing, some final words are appropriate on justification and introduction. In order to understand the criteria on which FMS is justified, it must first of all be stressed that Flexible Manufacturing represents a wholly new philosophy towards the design of production systems. It is not merely the next generation of automation, nor must it be regarded as an automated process or cell within a traditional batch production environment.

Flexible manufacturing is a response to changes in both the demands of the marketplace and in the demands which are today placed on productive resources. A number of strategic issues may be identified which affect competitiveness[27]. These are:

Price reduction;
Lead time reduction;
Improve response to customer orders;
Update products;
Increase variety;
Reduce non-conformance;
Reduce warranty claims and failures.

To be fully competitive, therefore, manufacturers need to address all of these issues since they are a reflection of the demands placed by consumers and the modern environment. Furthermore, any improvement must be made without an adverse effect on cost. Given the mix of issues described the only answer would seem to be the FMS type of solution since it carries the cost advantages of conventional automation with the strategic advantages attached to batch production using the group technology approach.

Thus any justification procedure must not be based simply on a calculation of unit production cost. Full account must also be taken of all the strategic issues, even if they cannot be directly quantified. Conventional methods of financial appraisal would often not favour investment in FMS but most such methods ignore the more intangible strategic advantages. Procedures must be adopted which account for all the factors involved, giving favourable weighting to the important criteria which would otherwise have been disregarded using these more conventional approaches.

On the question of the introduction of FMS, a particular note should be made of the usefulness of *simulation*. With more conventional systems of production the demand pattern is often sufficiently predictable to enable the system to be designed for efficient running with minimum interference. In cases where demand is less predictable, sufficient stocks of material and work-in-progress can usually be held to allow the effect of any interference to be absorbed elsewhere in the system.

FMS systems, on the other hand, are intended to handle unpredictable demand patterns while at the same time requiring the minimum of material and work-in-progress stocks. Unless they are properly designed, therefore, they run the risk of operating at below optimum efficiency due to an over-dependence of one part of the system on another.

Simulation is a means of operating a production system before it is actually installed. A system is usually simulated using a computer-based model which has been designed to represent all the important facilities. Different inputs of demand can be tried out, their effect ascertained and parameters changed until the desired configuration is reached. The 'real' system can then be installed in the knowledge that its performance has been anticipated in advance. There are several simulation packages on the market which can be used to predict the behaviour of complete manufacturing plants[28] or of a robot working in a production cell[29].

7.4 Summary

A whole new set of opportunities is open to designers of production systems as a result of developments involving new technology. In particular, Computer Numerical Control (CNC) and robotics have enabled the introduction of flexible automated systems rather than the more conventional rigid automation, the application of which was restricted to high volume production.

The use of computers in connection with other activities such as design, process planning and production control has also brought the reality of a fully automated factory much closer. There are already numerous examples of sub-systems and even complete manufacturing systems which operate with limited manpower. Complete integration can be achieved by linking together the automated elements, placing the whole under computer control.

To many organizations the idea of a completely unmanned factory would probably be regarded as only a distant vision. This being so the case for total automation should never be over-sold. However, there are few situations which would not benefit from at least some selected applications. Even if they cannot be seen as financially viable, their justification might still be confirmed on grounds of quality, delivery lead time, humanization of the workplace etc. It, therefore, remains an inescapable fact that the future design of production systems will be greatly influenced by the emerging technologies and their practical use in product design, planning, manufacture and control.

References

1. GRABBE, E. M. (ed) (1957) *Automation in Business and Industry,* Wiley, New York
2. CHILD, J. (1983) Managerial Strategies, New Technology and the Labour Process, in *Job Redesign*, edited by D. Knights, H. Willmott and C. Collinson. Gower, Aldershot

3. OLESTEN, N. O. (1970) *Numerical Control,* Wiley, New York
4. MARTIN, S. J. (1970) *Numerical Control of Machine Tools,* The English Universities Press, London
5. SMITH, W. A. (ed) (1983) *A Guide to CADCAM,* The Institution of Production Engineers
6. GROOVER, M. P. (1980) *Automation, Production Systems, and Computer-Aided Manufacturing,* Prentice-Hall, New Jersey, USA
7. ALLAN, J. J. (1973) 'Foundations of the Many Manifestations of Computer Augmented Design, in *Computer-Aided Design,* edited by J. Vlietstra and R. F. Wielinga. North Holland
8. WALTER, H. (1973) 'Computer-Aided Design in the Aircraft Industry', in *Computer-Aided Design,* edited by J. Vlietstra and R. F. Wielinga. North Holland
9. KAPLINSKY, R. (1982) *Computer-Aided Design: UNIDO Study,* Frances Pinter
10. BENNETT, D. J. (1981) 'Facility Decisions', in *Operations Management in Practice,* edited by C. D. Lewis. Philip Allan, London
11. LOGAN, F. (1984) 'Automated Process Planning – The Route to CIM', *The Production Engineer* (September)
12. BROOME, G. J. (1984) 'The Introduction of Computer Assisted Process Planning Within Austin Rover Group', *MBA Thesis. University of Aston Management Centre.*
13. CARRIE, A. S. (1979) *Computer Aided Layout Planning – The Way Ahead,* Vth International Conference on Production Research. Amsterdam (August)
14. HUNT, V. D. (1983) *Industrial Robotics Handbook,* Industrial Press, USA
15. AYRES, R. V. and MILLER, S. M. (1983) *Robotics: Applications and Social Implications,* Ballinger
16. CARLSSON, J. (1983) *Production and Use of Industrial Robots in Sweden in 1982,* Computers and Electronics Commission, Ministry of Industry, Stockholm
17. BLEE, M. (1968) 'Batch Production Via Numerical Control', *Data Systems* (June)
18. FOSTER, G. (1976) 'The Makings of Molins', *Management Today* (March)
19. RANKY, P. G. (1983) *The Design and Operation of FMS.* IFS Publications/North Holland Publishing
20. – (1968) 'The Cincinnati Automatic Manufacturing System', *Factory Management* (February)
21. – (1983) 'SCAMP is Revealed', *The Production Engineer* (January)
22. – (1983) 'Pallet Transporter for the Small Machine Tool User', *The Production Engineer* (May)
23. HARTLEY, J. (1984) *FMS At Work.* IFS Publications/North Holland Publishing
24. – (1983) 'Robots Mark Major Change in Engine Assembly at Scania', *The Production Engineer* (December)
25. CHARLISH, G. (1984) 'Robots Which Can Put It All Together', *Financial Times* (10 July)
26. RODGER, I. (1984) 'Perkins Spends £3.5m on Automated Engine Plant', *Financial Times* (27 November)
27. MORTIMER, J. (1982) *The FMS Report.* IFS Publications
28. CAPES, P. (1983) 'BL Systems Puts The Future In a Software Package', *Metalworking Production* (December)
29. BONNEY, M. C. *et al.* (1984) 'The Simulation of Industrial Robot Systems', *OMEGA,* **12,** No 3

Chapter 8

Liability and safety aspects

Most of the developments in the design of production systems which have so far been described are the result of some change in organization or technology. These changes have all enabled steps to be taken towards improving output, efficiency and flexibility. Some developments, however, are the result not of *enabling* factors but of *constraining* ones. It is the purpose of this chapter, therefore, to examine the major factors relating to product liability and environmental safety which are the concern of engineers and managers when designing products, services and production systems.

8.1 The background to product liability

Manufacturers have naturally always regarded quality and reliability as important competitive factors, along with price and design. This has been reflected in the increased use of 'product warranties' which, it is recognized, can contribute to the consumer's assessment of overall product value[1]. Warranties are, in effect, an 'added value' component by which the manufacturer commits himself to a given level of responsibility (usually over a specific time period) for the performance of the product he sells. They can have a significant effect on demand levels for a particular make or brand and, as such, their purpose is often 'promotional' rather than 'protective'.

In terms of cost, the implications of offering warranties are limited to the replacement or repair of individual items which prove defective during the warranty period. Unless there is a serious generic fault, therefore, firms can usually offer product warranties without incurring a high financial risk. The incentive to strive for high levels of quality and reliability is also small if warranty costs are the only penalty to be incurred.

In recent years, however, there have been many changes to the level of protection available to consumers which, in turn, has increased the potential cost to manufacturers when items prove defective in use. In the first place, media coverage of events and greater consumer awareness ('consumerism') has meant that the cost of a defect extends much further than simply replacing or repairing individual items. Secondly, the amount of legislation covering producers' liability for damage or injury resulting from goods which prove defective has greatly increased. This has meant that legal costs, compensation and damages can all be considerable when serious loss or injury is involved.

The various costs which can be incurred as a result of producing defective products are summarized in *Figure 8.1*. They are firstly sub-divided into 'consequential costs' and 'legal costs' before being further broken down into the individual headings which merit specific attention. As well as warranty costs, the consequential costs include the cost of a reduction in sales and that of trying to restore goodwill with customers. The legal costs include those relating to professional representation, together with those incurred as a result of awards being made against the manufacturer.

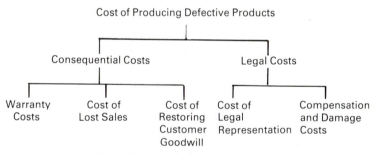

Figure 8.1 The costs incurred as a result of producing defective products (Bennett[14])

The extent to which losses in sales can result from widely publicized defects is witnessed by cases such as the Chevrolet Corvair and the McDonnell Douglas DC10, both of which are clear examples of products killed-off by public concern. As far as attempted restoration of goodwill is concerned, this is obviously difficult to measure. An indication of how expensive it might be though can be demonstrated by the DC10 case where, to restore confidence in its thirty DC10 aircraft, American Airlines demanded modifications costing £230 000 to each[2].

If the consequential costs alone are not enough to convince manufacturers of the need to maintain high standards of quality and reliability, the possible legal costs are bound to demand an examination of their capabilities. The law is complex and there are many parts, both civil and criminal, which relate to liability for defective products. Likewise there are variations in the detail and severity between countries in which it is administered.

The common factor, however, is that in general there has been a move away from the old concept of 'caveat emptor' (let the buyer beware) towards one of 'caveat vendori' (let the seller beware). This move is leading to greater adoption of the principle of *strict liability*, i.e. attribution of liability in all circumstances, even when the manufacturer could not be proved negligent[3]. In the USA, for instance, the California Supreme Court ruled in favour of strict liability in 1963 and within fifteen years the doctrine had been adopted in more than forty states.

In the UK the situation has not moved so far in this direction. Consumers have rights under the 'Sale of Goods Act' 1893 (and its subsequent additions and modifications) which states that goods must be reasonably fit for the purpose and of merchantable quality. However, the Act only applies in cases where a contract has been made, so third parties are not covered and claims can be complicated by the chain of wholesalers and retailers separating the manufacturer from the purchaser.

Where the 'Sale of Goods Act' does not apply, a consumer has recourse to the law of tort and may try to prove negligence on the part of the manufacturer. The difficulty here is that, to succeed, the claimant must prove the defect was attributable to lack of reasonable care on the part of the producer, an almost impossible task in the case of complex products or chemicals made by large corporations.

In fact, the only legislation in the UK which approaches the imposition of strict liability for defective products is Section 6 of the *Health and Safety at Work Act 1974*, in which it states:

'It shall be the duty of any person who designs, manufactures, imports or supplies an article for use *at work*:
(a) To ensure, so far as is reasonably practicable, that the article is so designed and constructed as to be safe and without risks to health when properly used;
(b) To carry out or arrange for the carrying out of such testing and examination as may be necessary for the performance of the duty imposed on him by the preceding paragraph;
(c) To take such steps as are necessary to secure that there will be available in connection with the use of the article at work adequate information about the use for which it is designed and tested, and about any conditions necessary to ensure that, when put to that use, it will be safe and without risks to health'.

The words '. . . when properly used' in paragraph (a) limit the liability to occasions when a genuine fault occurs or there is misleading (or a lack of) operating information. This offers the manufacturer a defence of contributory negligence where the user had stupidly tampered with the product or used it for a purpose for which it was not intended.

From the above, it may be seen that, in the UK, there is a range of different remedies for product liability situations under criminal law, contract, or in tort, depending on the precise circumstances of the case. Likewise within the rest of Europe there is a diversity of laws which has been identified by the EEC as being not only unfair to consumers in the Community, but also distorts fair competition in the Common Market[4]. For this reason the European Commission proposed, in 1976, that the laws be harmonized via a Directive from the Council of Ministers[5].

The proposed EEC Directive contains fifteen articles which, broadly speaking, seek to define terms ('producer', 'defective', etc.), assign responsibility, and specify the limits of operation of any proposed legislation. In essence the Directive is one which proposes greater protection for consumers than currently exists in most countries by saying (Article 1)

> 'The producer of an article shall be liable for damage caused by a defect in the article, whether or not he knew or could have known of the defect. The producer shall be liable even if the article could not have been regarded as defective in the light of the scientific and technological development at the time when he put the article into circulation

It also says (Article 4)

> 'A product is defective when it does not provide for persons or property the safety which a person is entitled to expect'.

There are few defences open to the producer under the Directive so in essence it is advocating the application of the strict liability concept. The Council of Europe, on the other hand, in its Convention published in 1977, did advocate further defences – adding, in particular, the provision for contributory negligence.

In the UK the response to the perceived need to make legislative changes took the form of a Law Commission Report published in 1977[7], and the much more wide-ranging report of a Royal Commission on Civil Liability and Compensation for Personal Injury presented in 1978[8]. The second of these represents, if anything does, the 'official' view and states in the case of products that 'Producers should be strictly liable in tort for death or personal injury caused by defective products'.

The Royal Commission does, however, recommend that the defence of contributory negligence should be available to a producer. So, in practice, the type of legislation envisaged differs from that which operates in the USA and some other countries where contributory negligence is not widely accepted.

This last distinction is an important one since much of the criticism levelled at product liability laws cites unusual but nonetheless disturbing cases from the USA, such as that of the lady who cooked her poodle when trying to dry it in a microwave oven – and successfully sued the oven's manufacturer[9]. The logic of allowing contributory negligence to be a defence was, therefore, accepted by the EEC when amending the Council Directive in 1979 to read

> 'If a victim or any person for whom he is liable has by his fault contributed to the damage, the compensation may be reduced or no compensation may be awarded'[10].

So, in summary, it may be seen that most industrialized countries have moved, or are moving, towards a position which provides much greater protection to the users of manufactured products. There are differences in the permitted defences and the level of damages and compensation which would be awarded but, despite these variations, there is still a pressing need for producers not only to express concern but also to take positive action. Product liability must be given serious consideration when designing goods, systems for their manufacture, and when marketing and providing customer services. There are various ways in which the problem can be dealt with and these will now be examined and discussed.

8.2 The effect of product liability on the design of goods, production and marketing systems

The preceding section has outlined the likely implications, both at present and in the future, of circulating defective or potentially dangerous products in the marketplace. Whatever shape any forthcoming legislation takes, a greater burden of responsibility is bound to fall on manufacturers of goods. What is more, not only will the law provide greater protection for the consumer, but media coverage and pressure from consumer groups will further increase the pressure on manufacturers to devise the ways and means of ensuring that they are protected from the financial consequences of a product liability 'incident'.

Clearly, no manufacturer can be totally immune to the situation which is developing. There is always a risk, however small, of running into trouble – sometimes with very serious consequences. The aim, therefore, should be to manage that risk and keep it within control. To do this there are four broad options available[11]:

retention,
transfer,
reduction, or
avoidance.

Any one or more of these may be selected depending on the particular circumstances which surround the manufacturer, the product and the market.

Retention, i.e. keeping the risk entirely within the business, would normally only be an option open to the largest businesses since, unlike smaller concerns, they could meet possible defect costs from their own finances. It must be stressed that confidence in the product should not itself be a reason for retaining the risk since defects can materialize long after the product has left the manufacturer, despite rigorous final inspection procedures.

In most cases where risk is not retained it is transferred to another party. This would commonly be an insurance company which, of course, would charge an appropriate premium depending on the level of risk assumed. Since product liability is a relatively new area of the insurance business the level of risk is often linked to crude measures such as the total value of sales. Using historical data is often of little value because of the rapid development of totally new products and new materials for which there is no past experience.

The modern underwriter must base his judgements more on information about current trends, new circumstances, perils and exposures, and the probability of previously unexperienced losses in terms both of type and size. Risk evaluation for product liability requires much greater use of scientific information and is a process which involves constantly looking ahead rather than looking back. It is a complex task requiring liaison between an insurer's engineering, claims and underwriting staff with full co-operation from the insured[12].

The other way in which risk, or more correctly responsibility for compensation, might be transferred is via a *no-fault* scheme. Under such an arrangement compensating payments are made from a fund rather than by the person responsible for the injury or his insurer. Such schemes are common all over the world for work accidents and in North America the system is widely used to compensate road accident victims. In 1974, New Zealand introduced the first comprehensive no-fault compensation scheme in the world for personal injury by accident.

Many countries, including the UK, do not favour the widespread use of no-fault compensation, but this tends to be because some provision for the whole population already exists. In fact, medical and hospital cover under the British National Health Scheme is open-ended, whereas most USA no-fault schemes for road accidents provide only limited cover. The other argument against comprehensive no-fault schemes is the possible adverse effect they might have on accident prevention and the possible weakening of incentive on the part of manufacturers to guard against the production of defective goods.

Reducing the risk is a self-evident means of reducing the likely costs associated with product liability. Reduction can be achieved in a variety of ways but essentially it will involve a process of identification, quantification and control. Some detailed procedures will be described later in this section. Even if the risk is being retained or transferred, reduction is still a desirable option since it minimizes the cost of failure and insurers will look more favourably on manufacturers who can demonstrate competence in risk reduction. It will also lessen the chance of being the subject of adverse publicity in the event of injury being caused by defective products.

Avoidance is probably the simplest approach to risk management, involving the business in *not* manufacturing a new product or discontinuing an existing one. It is, of course, an easy option to pursue but has implications for economic survival and growth. In fact, the potential risk of bringing new drugs onto the market has discouraged many pharmaceutical manufacturers from developing new products – a paradox considering such drugs might possibly save more lives than they endanger.

Of the four options described, it can readily be seen that risk *reduction* is likely to be favoured in the majority of cases. It is not an alternative to retention or transfer since it is likely to supplement these options if they have been chosen. Even manufacturers who avoid the risk by discontinuing products or curtailing new developments will still benefit from a risk reduction programme covering its remaining product range.

In planning such a programme it is first of all necessary to recognize that risk is incurred at all stages of the product's life cycle. Chronologically these stages are as follows, together with the potential areas of risk involved:

1. *Conception and design*
A formula or fundamental design idea may be misconceived.

2. Development
Potentially sound designs may not be adequately developed before being translated into marketable products.

3. Production
Errors may be made when following drawings or instructions;
Faulty components and/or faulty or contaminated materials may be used;
Errors may occur in material processing or assembly.

4. Packaging
Products may be damaged or contaminated by the packaging itself;
Ruptured or faulty containers can expose the product to external hazards;
Containers or packaging may cause injury rather than the contents themselves.

5. Marketing and distribution
Over-optimistic claims can be made of a product's assets;
Warnings or instructions may be absent or incorrect;
Damage may be incurred during transport or warehousing.

6. After-sales service
Defective spares might be supplied;
Wrong advice could be given;
Servicing work could be faulty.

From the above areas where risk is incurred, it can readily be seen that manufacturers must regularly negotiate a minefield of potential product liability problems. The only sensible way forward is a systematic examination and evaluation of each area to ascertain the degree of risk involved with, where necessary, action being taken to reduce this risk where it is considered too high.

The design stage is clearly one of the most important in terms of potential widespread problems being incurred. A defect in design or misconceived formula will affect not just a single item but every derivative of the original design. For mass producers of consumer durables, chemicals, etc., the implications are so great that massive efforts are made to test prototypes and pre-production items in large numbers, under representative conditions, over prolonged periods of time. This is obviously an expensive and time-consuming procedure which may nevertheless be considered unavoidable in the highest risk cases.

There could be occasions, however, when the expense and time can be reduced by a variety of approaches without incurring commensurate reductions in safety. One of these is to avoid making radical departures from established practice. Novel end-products can still be designed by combining and adapting existing designs whose performance is established and well-known. Similarly, the idea can be extended to ensuring that designs are based on the use of materials, processes, treatments etc. for which there are recognized standards and audits[13].

A further approach is to use simulation rather than 'real world' testing. This could involve using a scale model or mock-up product in real conditions. Alternatively, the actual product might be tested in simulated conditions. There may be some cases where testing can take place using merely a computer simulation which models the key parameters and variables; the lives of astronauts regularly depend on products which have been tested in just such a manner.

In product liability terms, the difference between design and development is often a fine one, with development being an extension to the design stage which ensures that designs are ready to be produced in quantity. A key part of the development stage is confirming that designs which have been proved to perform satisfactorily do so over the likely lifetime of the product. Since performance may change with time, this raises for discussion the concept of *reliability* and, in particular, the idea of failure rates.

Reliability data can be gathered from two sources. The first of these is from products in the field whose occurrences of failures are noted, together with the time at which they took place. Products can be of two types – those which fail completely and must be replaced (e.g. light bulbs, drive belts, etc.), and those which can be repaired and put back into service.

In analysing the data from the two types, it will be seen that in the first the original population of products decreases as they fail, while in the second the population remains constant (unless products are deliberately taken out of service). Using field data obviously means that a long wait is incurred until there are sufficient failures to provide a failure pattern for the product's useful lifetime. For this reason the second source of data is often used, from testing which takes place under accelerated laboratory conditions (e.g. by applying high frequency cyclical load to generate data relating to fatigue failures). However, there is a danger attached to accelerated life testing in that the conditions simulated in the laboratory may not be a good representation of reality.

Once the data relating to failure has been generated, standard techniques of statistical analysis may be used to determine the distribution of failures over time[14]. The most informative function which can be produced from the analyses is probably the failure rate, which is essentially the number of failures in a period expressed as a proportion of the number still surviving (i.e. the original population of products if failed products are always repaired). There are basically three 'shapes' the failure rate curve can take.

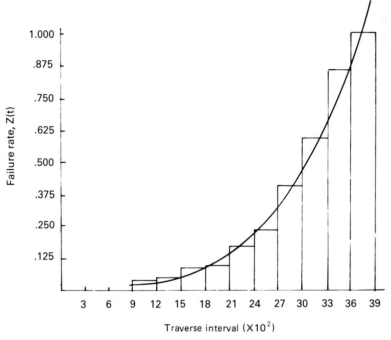

Figure 8.2 Failure rate function for a drilling machine component (Bennett[14])

Figure 8.2 shows the actual failure rate for a particular part on a machine tool which clearly has a tendency to become less reliable with time. *Figure 8.3* illustrates what would be the second case, constant failure rate, indicating randomness and, therefore, no change in reliability. *Figure 8.4* shows the third possibility, decreasing failure rate, indicating an improvement in reliability as time proceeds. This third example is often demonstrated in the case of electronic equipment which has a tendency to exhibit a large number of early-life or 'burn-in' failures which become fewer as repairs are made.

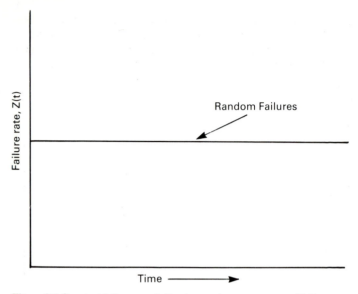

Figure 8.3 Constant failure rate indicating random occurrence of failure

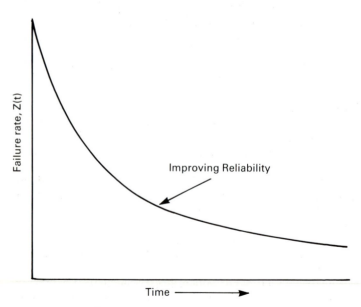

Figure 8.4 Decreasing failure rate indicating reliability improvement

Some products often exhibit more than one of the failure rate 'types' and *Figure 8.5* illustrates the failure rate function for a product which exhibits all three. In this particular case, the product is 'homo sapiens' since the data is taken from the human mortality statistics of the UK Office of Population Censuses and Surveys.

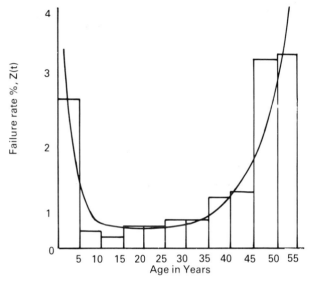

Figure 8.5 Failure rate function for human mortality (data source: Office of Population Censuses and Surveys, UK)

Failure analyses can provide management with an indication not just of the immediate risk but of the potential risk throughout the lifetime of the product. If it is considered too high then further development work can be carried out to reduce it to acceptable levels. Alternatively, the predicted pattern of failure can be used to devise the most effective schedules for maintenance, overhaul and replacement. It may even result in advice being given not to tamper with the product when the failure rate is naturally decreasing since what is thought to be *preventive* maintenance could actually be *destructive* maintenance.

During production there is a range of activities available to reduce the risk of producing faulty components and end-products. They would usually all come under the generic heading of *quality control* and, in fact, the next chapter will be devoted to this particular topic. At the production stage, quality control activities are aimed basically at ensuring that individual components and products conform to the specifications and standards set down by the design department. This will involve checking the acceptability of incoming materials and parts, monitoring and controlling production processes and audit testing finished products to validate the preceding controls.

It must be stressed that quality control does not just mean inspection, it involves feeding information both backwards and forwards in order that appropriate corrective action is taken when necessary.

The procedures for reducing liability risks connected with packaging are essentially similar to those which are appropriate for the product itself. Careful attention needs to be paid to package design and testing, which ideally should be done in conjunction with the product it is to contain. In the same fashion, the quality control techniques which are applied in accepting incoming materials should also be extended to cover packaging received from outside suppliers, while finished goods audits should embrace packaged products in the form in which they are delivered to customers.

As with design, marketing is an important stage in the product life cycle since risks can be incurred across a complete type or even the entire product range. The risk here is one of selling products with a 'presentational defect', that is a lack of adequate instructions for use and warnings of hazard together with inaccurate data about the product's performance. In practical terms a manufacturer can become liable on four counts[15]:

(i) Failure to warn or instruct;
(ii) Incorrect warnings and instructions;
(iii) Inadequate warnings and instructions;
(iv) Untimely warnings or instructions.

Liability applies to any form of presentation, be it via the packaging, manuals, leaflets, media advertising and salesmen. Care must be taken to ensure consistency across all of these and to ensure that any ambiguity does not arise. If close attention has been paid to ensuring that instructions on the package are carefully worded, then all the good may be undone by conflicting or misleading press advertisements. It is helpful, therefore, to take guidance from the basic structure of presentation of warnings and instructions which is:

1. Attract the user's attention to the instructions and warnings.
2. Inform the user about correct usage and incorrect usage, and describe the directions for correct usage that should be followed.

3. Warn the user against improper use and the circumstances that can lead to misuse.

4. Warn the user of any inherent hazards that may not be obvious to the user.

5. Warn the user about the nature and extent of injury if the hazard materializes.

6. Instruct the user on corrective action that must be taken if injury or misuse occurs.

7. If no corrective action is available, then warn the user of this fact.

Three additional rules supplement this basic structure to ensure maximum effectiveness. First, the information should be separated into three distinct groups – warnings, instructions, and sales information. Second, the information should be presented in a clear, concise and non-technical way, using diagrams if appropriate. It should also be durable and attached or positioned adjacent to the product. Third, the emphasis must be right with the greatest hazards being given the greatest prominence rather than everything receiving equal emphasis.

The importance of adequate warnings and instructions cannot be overstated. If contributory negligence is to be a defence against strict liability, then this is an area where much of the manufacturer's attention should be directed. The law will only see a product's use as being improper if instructions or warnings have clearly been ignored. Absence of any instructions will undoubtedly place the burden firmly on the shoulders of the manufacturer.

The last area to be considered – after-sales service – presents additional complications to the manufacturer since it is an activity over which there is often little control. There are the added problems of service sometimes being provided by an independent contractor who may use spares supplied by the original equipment manufacturer or which might be purchased from an alternative source.

Therefore, all the previous discussion relating to instructions in the use of products applies just as much to persons who might service them as to the product's users. More desirable still is that service personnel, even those not directly employed by the manufacturer, should be fully trained in all aspects of servicing before being authorized to carry out any work.

A final, but critical, aspect connected with products which are operational in the field relates to recalls. Product recall is becoming more commonplace, not because products are necessarily becoming less safe but rather because they are one way of reducing risk of further liability once a defect has been detected. Examples of products which are often subject to recalls include motor vehicles, foodstuffs, and electrical appliances. A recall becomes necessary because of design or manufacturing defects which may affect every unit produced, a specific batch, or a limited production run.

Failure to warn may be another reason, although this could be rectified via a special notice in the press or sent to all users. A further reason to recall products, which has been the subject of much publicity recently, is *sabotage*, particularly to pharmaceuticals and foodstuffs.

A product recall is essentially a process of putting the distribution system into reverse[16] and to be conducted successfully requires a great deal of advanced thinking and forward planning. The ability to recall a selected batch demands that close and accurate records are kept of individual products, components and materials, production processes and times.

It is also important to have a means of identifying individual products and components using serial numbers, markings, colour differentiation etc. This is a costly exercise, but the only alternative may be widespread notification via the mass media which would attract the attention of a much wider audience than is absolutely necessary and thereby create adverse publicity for the company as a whole.

To summarize what has been said about risk reduction, it involves a company-wide programme which will often need to be placed under the direction of a single individual or group with sufficient status in the organization to influence the process of change. The position of 'Product Safety and Liability Controller' has been proposed[17] in one case, being a direct appointment by the company's Chief Executive. Another company, an American-based multinational manufacturer of power tools, has a 'Product Safety Policy Committee' chaired by the Divisional President and with representation from General Management, Technical Management and Legal Counsel[18].

The programme, which will be under the general direction of the responsible individual or group, will extend across the product life cycle risk areas previously identified. It will be based on information gathered and analysed by the company about its products and processes. It will also use standard reference data relating to product safety and reliability which will provide recommended working principles, methodologies and practices[19,20]. To some extent the programme will be an extension and intensification of the company's existing design, development, production and marketing activities. These will be supplemented by the additional tasks necessary to meet the special demands made by impending legislation and greater consumer awareness.

8.3 Safety and health at the workplace

This chapter has so far dealt with the background to product safety, the legislative situation relating to product liability and procedures for dealing with the associated risks. Much of the discussion, however, can equally be applied to the workplace where safety and health are also important considerations when designing the production system.

As before, the attention which has been directed towards the subject is a result of both 'public' pressure and legislation. However, pressure on this occasion has come not from the consumer lobby, but rather from the workforce and, in particular, the trades unions and other employee organizations. The demand for an improvement in safety and health was originally prompted by the poor conditions which arose as a result of rapid industrialization during the 18th Century. These conditions were such that lighting, ventilation and sanitation were minimal and machine guarding was virtually unknown. Occupational deaths and maimings were frequent and workers suffered poor health as a result of environmental pollution, dust and noise.

Protection for workers was initially only provided by the more benevolent organizations so the need for government intervention is common to most industrialized countries. In England, for instance, factory inspections were introduced as early as 1833 and the Factory and Workshop Act was passed in 1878. Massachusetts was the first State in the USA to legislate for the appointment of factory inspectors in 1867, and France passed a similar law in 1874[21]. Standards of safety and health have naturally improved dramatically in the subsequent hundred years and legislation has been changed and updated to reflect this trend. So today a rigorous set of laws exists with equally severe penalties attached to their contravention.

In the USA the legislation is embodied in the Occupational Health and Safety Act of 1970, while in the UK the equivalent mechanism is the Health and Safety at Work Act of 1974. The main purpose of the UK Health and Safety at Work Act was to provide for one, comprehensive, integrated system of law dealing with the health, safety and welfare of work-people and the health and safety of the public as affected by work activities. It deliberately avoided setting down detail but was rather intended as an 'enabling' Act having six main objects[22]:

(i) To overhaul and modernize the existing law dealing with safety, health and welfare at work;
(ii) To put new *general duties* on employers, ranging from providing and maintaining a safe place of work to consulting with their workers;
(iii) To create a new Health and Safety Commission;
(iv) To re-organize and unify the various Government Inspectorates;
(v) To provide new powers and penalties for the enforcement of safety laws;
(vi) To establish new methods of accident prevention, and new ways of operating future safety regulations.

The UK Health and Safety at Work Act, and the emerging legislation in other industrialized countries, thus takes a new approach to industrial safety. Prior to the Act, over a hundred years of piecemeal introduction of highly specific laws led to a plethora of separate documents rendering the whole lot largely unenforceable. The onus has now been placed on manufacturers to examine carefully their workplaces, equipment and working practices to ensure that they fulfil a general duty to provide acceptable levels of safety as outlined in the various sections of the Act.

In dealing with the issue of health and safety a number of broad options are available, similar to those described in connection with product liability, whereby the associated risks can be managed. Of the options previously described, however, retention is not in this case viable, the reason being that the Inspectorate has the power to issue prohibition notices if persistent disregard is made of the general duty. Thus, even the largest of organizations cannot just retain the financial risk since the ultimate sanction of a production stoppage is a levelling mechanism which equally affects firms of any size.

Transfer is an option which does exist and indeed in the UK it has been compulsory since 1972 for employers to insure against their liability to pay damages for bodily injury or disease sustained by their employees arising out of and in the course of their employment[23]. In addition, public liability insurance is available providing cover against liability for injury to or illness of third parties (other than employees). Such insurance usually operates on the same basis as that covering employer's liability, covering costs and expenses as well as damage to property.

Risk avoidance is again a self-evident option. The probability of accident or danger to health is reduced to zero if machines or processes are eliminated and working practices ceased. However, avoidance can inhibit process innovation as well as product innovation so, as with products, the most sensible option is reduction – not necessarily exclusively but more likely accompanied by one or more of the other options available.

The approach taken to safety and health risk reduction is essentially similar again to that applied to products. Areas of risk need firstly to be identified and the level of risk quantified using a system of records and reports. A variety of published material is available to assist in the process of identifying the main sources of hazard[24]. A list of the potential areas might include – plant, machinery, material, transport, tools, electricity supply, gas, guards, floors and stairs, clothing, chemicals, gases, radiation, atmosphere and combustion. Physical danger is associated with all these areas and, in addition, there are psychological and behavioural implications associated with some other areas of risk such as lighting frequencies, space and colour.

The prevention of accidents and maintenance of health at work is such a complex and specialized discipline that it justifies a professional approach. The American Society of Safety Engineers exists in the United States to provide recognition for the expertise, and in the UK the equivalent professional body exists in the form of the Institution of Occupational Safety and Health.

Ultimate responsibility for safety and health still rests, however, with Production Management[25]. Decisions must be made based on advice given and managers must provide the required level of training and instruction. For their part, workers must act responsibly and according to the instructions given. Safety is provided by the organization but the organization comprises individuals. Managers are vested with the authority to ensure that adequate control is exercised over those individuals for which they are responsible.

8.4 Summary

Both product and workplace safety represent areas of concern in connection with the design of production systems. Pressure comes from both consumers and employees, while mass media coverage of events means that incidents are widely publicized, often with a detrimental effect on sales and the reputation of the organization as a whole.

The emerging legislation relating to product liability places greater responsibility on manufacturers for injury and damage caused by goods and services, regardless of negligence. This can impose a heavy financial burden on the firm, comprising legal costs and damages, which in some cases could put its future operations in jeopardy. The risk of incurring such costs can be managed by retention, transfer, reduction and avoidance. Reduction will, in the long term, provide the greatest benefit to the organization and the community since it will ultimately lead to improved design, quality and reliability.

Safety and health at the workplace is likewise an important aspect relating to the general issue of organizational liability. As with product liability, there have been developments in legislation which require that firms become more active in seeking to make improvements. The cost of improving the safety of products and workplaces is often criticized on the basis that it must be reflected in the price of goods and thereby reduces competitiveness. This possibly may be true in the short term. However, safer products and places of work must lead to lower costs in other areas and, directly or indirectly, will help enhance the organization's ability to compete.

References

1. MASON, R. S. (1973) The Economics of Product Warranties, *Management Decision,* **11**
2. JACKSON, H. (1979) 'Extensive Changes Demanded for DC10', *The Guardian* (17 October)
3. DEWIS, M., HUTCHINS, D. C. and MADGE, P. (1980) *Product Liability,* Heinemann, London
4. EEC (1979) *Liability for Defective Products,* European Communities Commission Background Report ISEC/B48/79 (30 November)
5. – (1976) *Proposals for a Council Directive Relating to the Approximation of the Laws, Regulations and Administrative Provisions of the Member States Concerning Liability for Defective Products,* Bulletin of the European Communities, Supplement 11/76
6. – (1977) *Convention on Product Liability in regard to Personal Injury and Death,* The Council of Europe, Strasbourg (January)
7. – (1977) *Liability for Defective Products,* Report of the Law Commission and the Scottish Law Commission, Cmnd. 6831, HMSO
8. PEARSON (Chairman) (1978) *Royal Commission on Civil Liability and Compensation for Personal Injury,* Cmnd. 7054, HMSO
9. CARVEL, J. (1978) 'The Sad Case of the Poodle and Product Liability', *The Guardian* (23 June)
10. – (1979) *Amendment of the Proposal for a Council Directive relating to the Approximation of the Laws, Regulations and Provisions of the Member States Concerning Liability for Defective Products,* Official Journal of the European Communities, No C271/3

11. BRETT, C. (1978) 'The Product Liability Problem', *Management Today* (May)
12. HUGHES, J. O. (1978) *Product Liability Insurance,* Commercial Union Risk Management Ltd (April)
13. ABBOTT, H. (1980) *Safe Enough To Sell? Design and Product Liability.* The Design Council, London
14. BENNETT, D. J. (1981) 'Quality and Reliability', in *Operations Management in Practice,* edited by C. D. Lewis. Philip Allan, London
15. NOON, J. (1981) 'Marketing Management and Products Liability', *European Journal of Marketing,* **15,** No 2
16. ABBOTT, H. (1983) 'How To Manage Liability', *Management Today* (July)
17. McROBB, M. (1983) 'A Product Safety and Liability Policy', *Product Liability International* (August)
18. STRAUGHAN, G. F. (1978) *Black & Decker Ltd – Product Liability Policy and Company Defences.* West Midlands Productivity Association Conference, UK (18 April)
19. KOLB, J. R. and ROSS, S. (1980) *Product Safety and Liability – A Desk Reference.* McGraw-Hill, New York
20. HAMMER, W. (1980) *Product Safety Management and Engineering.* Prentice-Hall, New Jersey, USA
21. HEINRICH, H. W., PETERSEN, O. and ROOS, N. (1980) *Industrial Accident Prevention.* McGraw-Hill, New York
22. – (1975) *Health and Safety at Work,* Trades Union Congress, London
23. WEST, A. (1983) 'Insurance Cover and Compensation', in *Safety at Work,* edited by J. Ridley, Butterworths, London
24. BLAKE, R. P. (1963) *Industrial Safety,* Prentice-Hall, New York
25. MOORE, D. (1984) 'How To Keep Safe', *Management Today* (February)

Chapter 9
Quality

9.1 The nature and importance of quality

The quality of a product or service is an important factor to be taken into account when designing the system for its production. Both quality and reliability (the latter applying to the performance of products over time) have been the subject of discussion in material covered within several previous chapters.

Despite this, quality still merits separate and specific coverage so this chapter aims to look at what is understood by 'quality', together with how it can be monitored, controlled and improved. Most importantly though, the necessity will be stressed of taking quality into account as part of the production system design process rather than simply regarding quality as a secondary factor requiring a reaction from management in response to some measure of output performance.

The distinction between organizations which are proactive and those which react to the question of quality is a significant one. Proactive organizations see quality as a powerful weapon with which to compete in the marketplace, while reactive ones see quality solely in terms of costs which they then seek to minimize. There is no reason to suggest that one strategy is generally better than the other since naturally it depends upon particular circumstances. Research does show, however, that many organizations can owe their success to making quality a top priority concern and then capitalizing on this emphasis[1].

Quality should be thought of as an asset which may be offered to the potential customer of a product or service. It can derive from the original design and specification, or it can result from the production process. This difference is important and gives rise to the concepts of *quality of design* and *quality of conformance*.

Quality of design is a function of the materials, sizes and tolerances specified, and the safety factors allowed. It also depends on the skill, knowledge and experience of the designers. Good quality of design is the fundamental prerequisite for ensuring that the customer or user is offered a good quality end-product or service. It does not, however, provide a guarantee of its achievement during production.

Quality of conformance is necessary to ensure that the individual goods and services being produced conform to the standards laid down at the design stage. Conformance activities are ongoing and involve regular checks of materials, parts, assemblies, processes, procedures and finished products. They are usually the responsibility of the quality control function or department, although all organizational functions may contribute to the overall effort. Indeed, the concept of *total quality control*, being a company-wide approach rather than one of simply assigning limited responsibilities, has rapidly grown in popularity. The concept will be explored later in this chapter after the main elements of a quality system have been described.

It is useful to think of the quality system as comprising three main elements[2]. These are:

1. Inspection;
2. Quality control;
3. Quality audit.

Inspection procedures are the numerous activities which take place throughout the production system where components, materials, etc. are measured and assessed in order to determine whether they conform to the design specifications. The items inspected are simply accepted or rejected so such procedures are only of partial use in ensuring good quality finished products or services. Items which are rejected will be prevented from being included in the finished product but, apart from that, inspection is of limited value and cannot alone be regarded as a satisfactory means of maintaining a high standard of quality.

The term **quality control** has already been used in the wider context of conformance. Quality control goes further than inspection by using the information gained to monitor, maintain and, where necessary, correct or change processes, methods and procedures. Control can be achieved in two basic ways. Firstly, information can be *fed-back* so preceding processes might be corrected, or it can be *fed-forward* for the purpose of adapting succeeding processes. Secondly, if a number of items taken from a large batch are inspected the results can be used to assess the likely quality of the entire batch which can then be accepted, rejected or reworked.

Quality audit refers to activities which are designed to test the effectiveness of the inspection and quality control procedures. It is in essence the quality control system for the quality system! A number of procedures will be employed in conjunction with a quality audit. For example, finished products or services will be selected and tested at random, regardless of any checks which have been carried out previously. Each defect found will be awarded a number of points (demerit points) depending on the nature and severity of the fault. If the points total reaches a pre-defined level then it indicates a 'defect' somewhere in the inspection or quality control system which would subsequently need to be rectified.

The effectiveness of inspection and quality control is also highly dependent on the accuracy of measurement, whether done by machine or using human judgement. A further aspect of quality audit must, therefore, be the regular checking of gauges and other measuring equipment, together with an assessment of inspectors' abilities to discriminate accurately between acceptable and unacceptable quality. All quality audit procedures must naturally be unbiased and independent of the rest of the quality system.

Partly for this reason, some activities, particularly gauge checking, are often done by outside contractors. A footnote to the discussion on quality audit is a mention of its use as a means of assessing plant performance. Organizations with multi-plant operations, for instance automobile manufacturers who assemble finished products worldwide, can use a standardized demerit point system to compare quality across a number of locations. In this way customers can be assured that they are being offered consistent quality, regardless of where a product is made or purchased.

Turning now to the application of quality control, it will be seen from the literature that a number of distinct techniques is available in connection with monitoring and process correction. In order to appreciate the relevance of any technique to the situation at hand it is necessary to first understand two basic concepts which underlie the theory. The first of these relates to measurement, which can be done using either variables or attributes, and the second concerns that of the producer/consumer relationship.

Measurement using variables is effected where a particular quality parameter can be located on a continuous scale. For example, weight, length, diameter, surface finish, etc. can all be measured in this way (in grammes, millimetres or microns). Acceptable quality for variables is usually defined by tolerances (higher, lower or both) beyond which items are regarded as defective.

Where quality is measured using attributes, a 'yes or no' decision is made based on some appropriate feature of the item or items in question. Examples of attribute measurement include the inspection of metal castings for porosity, bottles for cleanliness, labels for smoothness and straightness, etc. An extension to the idea of an attribute measure, which needs to be understood, is that of the attribute *decision*.

The latter is a 'yes' or 'no' decision which could in practice be reached after measurement has been made using variables. For example, an entire batch of components may either be accepted or rejected on the basis of information derived from a small sample which has been weighed. It should also be appreciated that there are sometimes occasions when a variable is converted to an attribute, or vice versa. For instance, a diameter could be measured using a 'go/no go' gauge or the quality of carpets could be evaluated in terms of the number of defects occurring in a given area.

The difference between producers and consumers is important since their position determines the availability to them of certain types of technique. Producers have in their possession all the machines and processes used in production so they can control quality by controlling (i.e. monitoring and correcting) these processes. Consumers, on the other hand, do not have the benefit of being able to control the production processes. The strategy they would adopt, therefore, would be to assess batches of items being received from suppliers in order to judge whether, overall, their expectations are being met.

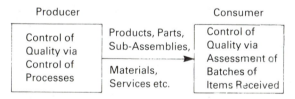

Producer   Consumer

| Control of Quality via Control of Processes | Products, Parts, Sub-Assemblies, | Control of Quality via Assessment of Batches of Items Received |
| Materials, Services etc. |

Figure 9.1(a) The producer consumer quality relationship (Bennett[2])

The immediate sanction would be the rejection or return of unacceptable batches while, in the longer term, a system of vendor rating can be used to decide whether supply should be continued. The producer/consumer relationship is shown in *Figure 9.1(a)*. It should be noted that an organization is rarely in the position of exclusively being either a producer or consumer. In most cases the organization is part of a long chain between the basic raw material supplier and the product's end-user. Thus, every consumer of material is also the supplier to the next link in the chain (see *Figure 9.1(b)*).

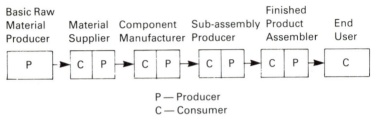

P — Producer
C — Consumer

Figure 9.1(b) A chain of producers and consumers

The ideas described can be reproduced diagrammatically in the form of a 2 by 2 matrix, as shown in *Figure 9.2*. The individual quality control techniques will be located in one of the four cells of the matrix, with the most common being those which control production processes using variables and those which assess batches of items using attributes (or attribute decisions).

	Using Variables	Using Attributes
Control of Production Processes	Most Common Techniques	Less Common Techniques
Assessment of Batches of Items	Least Common Techniques	Most Common Techniques

Figure 9.2 A matrix representation of quality control techniques

9.2 The techniques of quality control

The literature relating to quality control techniques is extensive and can supply the detail necessary to install the range of different schemes available to suit particular circumstances. Despite the widespread publication of these techniques, and the fact that some have been available for over fifty years, it is perhaps surprising how little used they are in some sectors of industry[3].

Even in the USA, where the techniques were originally developed by Shewhart[4] and by Dodge and Romig[5], their use diminished during the 1950s due to a huge domestic demand which placed less emphasis on quality. But perhaps the greatest irony is the fact that one of the early American advocates of quality control, W.E. Deming, when rebuffed by US industry, took his ideas to Japan instead[6]. The result is well-known; Japan has been transformed from a country that produced some of the poorest-quality products in the world to one that is now renowned for its high quality.

With these facts in mind, some of the more common quality control techniques will be described. No attempt is made to cover the statistical preliminaries; such a coverage is not warranted since the main purvose here is to provide an appreciation of their scope and usefulness. A brief account will be given of how a particular scheme operates, using practical examples to illustrate the mai features. The techniques described will firstly be those which would be used by producers to control processes. There will then follow a description of the type of technique used by consumers to assess the quality of batches of incoming goods.

9.2.1 Producer process control – control charts

The control of production processes is usually effected using some form of statistical control chart. The idea of using such a technique for controlling quality derives from work done by W.A. Shewhart in the 1920s at Bell Telephone Laboratories. The control chart is a device on which a process is monitored to confirm whether or not it is regularly meeting design expectations. By this means the output from the process should be maintained within the specified tolerances and an adequate warning provided in the event of the process going out of control.

In this particular context the term 'control' relates to the ability to detect 'assignable' causes of variation (i.e. those causes which can be assigned to some identifiable disturbance). Every process, however accurate, is subject to natural variability (due to 'unassignable' causes of variation). Therefore, the control chart must be designed so that any corrective action is taken when there is only a small chance of the change being due to natural variability. Statisticians use the word **confidence** to describe the probability of a correct decision being made. Two levels of confidence are normally used in designing control charts. 95% confidence is commonly used to set the **warning limits** while 99.8% is used for the **action limits.**

It must be stressed that, since the control chart is only a monitoring device, it can do no more than detect whether a process is going out of control. Having detected such an occurrence there must still be some mechanism for taking the necessary action to rectify the situation. This is generally achieved using some form of feed-back system, as shown in *Figure 9.3.* Here the output from a process is being monitored using a control chart and *significant* changes (i.e. those due to assignable causes) are reported to a 'control function'. The necessary corrective action is then taken to bring the process back under control. Such corrective action may be taken manually, by a machine setter.

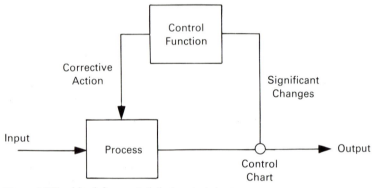

Figure 9.3 Feed-back from a statistical control chart

Alternatively the whole monitoring, detection and correction system may be automatic as is often the case with chemical plant and food processing. As indicated earlier, a feed-forward system could also be used so that the corrective action is taken at a subsequent processing stage.

There are basically three types of chart which can be used in connection with process control. The first two use variables and monitor *averages* ($\bar{x}$ charts) or *ranges* (R charts). The need for either or both is shown in *Figures 9.4(a) and (b).* It can be seen here that there are two ways in which a process may produce items which fall outside the specified tolerance. First, the average could shift while the range remains constant – for example, a cutting device may wear or slip. Second, the range could increase without a change in the average, as often happens if machine wear occurs or part of the processing equipment becomes loose.

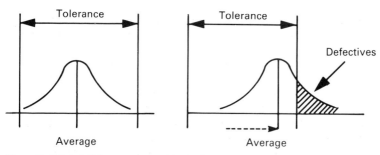

Figure 9.4(a) A shift in average resulting in defective items

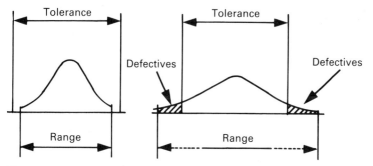

Figure 9.4(b) An increase in range resulting in defective items

The third type of chart is the number (or fraction) defective control chart. This uses attributes and operates on the basis of counting the number of defective items rather than using a measurement.

Average and range charts are normally based on the sampling distribution rather than the distribution of individual measurements. That is to say a small sample of approximately 5 to 10 items would be taken and the sample average plotted on the chart. The reason this is done is to make use of the 'central limit theorem' which allows the sampling distribution to be approximated by the *normal distribution*. Tables describing the normal distribution are readily available from which the control limits can be obtained for various levels of confidence. To illustrate the design and use of a control chart for variables, consider the following example:

A product is being packed using an automatic machine. The nominal weight is 450 grammes. A control chart is to be devised for monitoring the average and range of package weights using 95% confidence for the warning limits and 99.8% confidence for the action limits.

Method: A number of small samples are selected at intervals, while the machine is known to be 'in control'. The average and range of each small sample is calculated, from which the process average and range can be derived. Standard tables[7] can be used to set the control chart limits using, as a basis, either the standard deviation of the sample averages (σ) or the average range ($\bar{w}$).

Figure 9.5 shows the appearance of the control charts with process averages, warning and action limits drawn in accordance with the result of the previous calculations. Note that in the average chart both upper and lower limits are drawn to detect packets which are either too heavy or too light. In the case of the range chart, only the 'upper' limits are drawn since, clearly, 'lower' limits would detect a decreasing range and such a situation would not lead to defects being produced.

On both the charts some hypothetical data have been plotted relating to subsequent samples taken at intervals in order to monitor the process. The average chart has detected a shift and the process has been corrected. However, range has been maintained well within the warning limits, indicating that this has been kept under control.

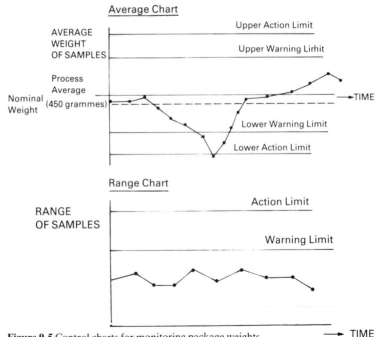

Figure 9.5 Control charts for monitoring package weights

Number defective control charts also use warning and action limits based on prescribed levels of confidence. They are based on the normal approximation to either the binomial or Poisson distribution, depending on the relative proportion of defects the process is producing. Again, the chart would be derived from data obtained while the process was in control with limits being set using the resulting standard deviation (2σ and 3σ limits are usually set). The following example illustrates the procedure:

A control chart is to be set up for monitoring a moulding machine producing plastic bottles. Bottles can be regarded as either good or defective.

Method: Samples of bottles are selected at regular intervals during a period when there are no unusual occurrences and the process is considered to be operating satisfactorily. (The sample size must be large enough to allow sufficient defects to be detected for calculation purposes – say, in this example, eight samples are taken, each comprising 200 bottles). The number of defectives found in each sample is recorded.

e.g.

Sample no.	Sample size, n	Number of defectives, c
1	200	7
2	200	11
3	200	3
4	200	18
5	200	16
6	200	6
7	200	15
8	200	12
$\Sigma n =$	1600	$\Sigma c = 88$

Process average proportion defective $\bar{p} = \dfrac{\Sigma c}{\Sigma n} = 0.055$

The Binomial distribution can be assumed since $\bar{p} > 0.05$

$$\text{Standard deviation (Binomial)} = \sqrt{\frac{\bar{p}(1 - \bar{p})}{n}}$$

$$= \sqrt{\frac{0.055 \times 0.945}{200}} = 0.016$$

Warning limit is $0.055 + (2 \times 0.016) = 0.087$
Action limit is $0.055 + (3 \times 0.016) = 0.103$
In samples of two hundred, this is:
  $200 \times 0.087 = 17.4$ (Warning)
  $200 \times 0.103 = 20.6$ (Action)

The chart is illustrated in *Figure 9.6* with subsequent hypothetical data plotted. This shows that the warning limit was crossed for a short time but the process soon came back under control so no action needed to be taken.

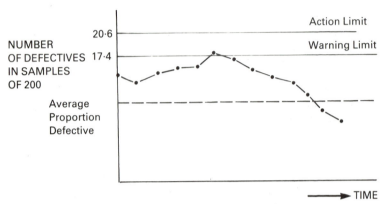

Figure 9.6 Control chart for number of defective plastic bottles

Note that if $\bar{p}$ had been less than 0.05 the Poisson distribution should have been assumed, in which case the limits are $\bar{c} + 2$ or $3\sqrt{\bar{c}}$ (where $\bar{c}$ is the average number of defectives found in each sample). The Poisson distribution could also be used where the sample is obviously large but does not constitute a number of discrete items, i.e. an area of carpet or a length of wire.

9.2.2 Batch quality assessment – acceptance sampling

It may seem logical for consumers to assess items being received by inspecting them all. However, for a number of reasons this is often impractical or undesirable, i.e.

(i) Inspection may be an expensive procedure compared with the value and importance of the item;
(ii) Inspection may require destruction of the item;
(iii) The inspection task could be tiring and may result, after a time, in defective items being accepted;
(iv) Handling the item may cause deterioration.

In all these cases the most appropriate procedure for maintaining quality standards is *acceptance sampling*. This is a method whereby a decision can be made regarding the quality of a large batch using information derived from a (relatively) small sample or samples.

The simplest form of acceptance sampling is where a *single* sample (size *n*) is taken *at random* from the batch and the number of defective items found is compared with an *acceptance number* (*c*). If this acceptance number is exceeded, the entire batch from which the sample derives is rejected (i.e. it may be returned or the batch completely inspected and the defectives rectified).

The procedure, of course, is simple but the size of the sample taken and the associated acceptance number must be chosen with care. They will depend on how well the scheme is required to discriminate between 'good' and 'bad' batches, the probability of the scheme rejecting 'good' batches and the probability of it accepting 'bad' batches. Normally the scheme will, therefore, be designed around four parameters, i.e.:

The Acceptable Quality Level (AQL). The percentage of defectives found in the batch below which it would be acceptable.

The Lot Tolerance Percent Defective (LTPD). The percentage of defectives in the batch above which it would be unacceptable.

The Producer's Risk (α). The risk, expressed as a percentage, of rejecting batches better than the AQL.

The Consumer's Risk (β). The risk, expressed as a percentage, of accepting batches worse than the LTPD.

The four parameters are shown, together with their relationship, in *Figure 9.7*. The *curve* is known as the 'operating characteristic' (OC). The steeper this curve the better the scheme's ability to discriminate between good and bad batches. Specifying the four parameters will define the shape of the OC curve and particular values of sample size (*n*) and acceptance number (*c*) will produce the desired operating characteristic. The following example serves to illustrate the technique:

A soft drinks manufacturer buys batches of plastic bottles from an outside supplier. If 1% or less are defective the batch is acceptable. However, if 3% or more are defective the batch is unacceptable since too many problems will be created on the bottling line. The bottle supplier will accept a 5% risk of 'good' batches being rejected, while the drinks manufacturer will tolerate a 1% risk of accepting 'unacceptable' batches. What should be the sample size and acceptance number if the soft drinks manufacturer uses a single acceptance sampling plan?

Method: The basic sampling theory which underlies the single acceptance sampling procedure is consolidated within specially prepared tables. These have been designed for ease of use and are suitable for a wide range of applications[7,8,9]. The example here

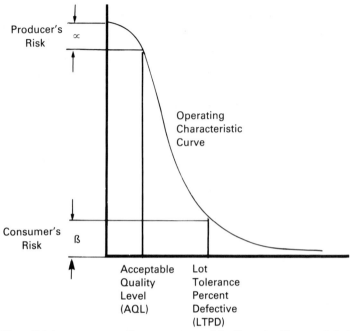

Figure 9.7 Acceptance sampling parameters and the Operating Characteristic (OC) curve

provides all the information necessary to devise the sampling plan using such a table (in this case, again, using [7]). It reveals that a sample size (n) is required of 692 while the acceptance number (c) should be 11.

The user of a sampling plan such as the one just designed is naturally concerned about its ability to detect batches of unacceptable quality. However, of equal importance to the *incoming* quality is that of the *outgoing* items. These will be of a quality determined by the effectiveness of the plan. The Average Outgoing Quality (AOQ) is thus derived from the formula:

$$AOQ(\%) = \frac{(N - n) \times PD \times PA}{100N}$$

where N = Size of the original batch;
n = Sample size;
PA = Probability of acceptance (%) for a particular *incoming* percentage defective, PD (%)

Say, in the previous example, the original batch size was 5000. PA values at various levels of PD could be found from the OC curve which in turn can be derived from an appropriate statistical table.

The Average Outgoing Quality may be presented graphically as shown in *Figure 9.8*. It may be seen that, initially, the AOQ(%) increases together with PD, but reaches a maximum before then decreasing. This maximum is known as the Average Outgoing Quality Limit (AOQL). It is a useful concept since knowing the value of this limit can be helpful for planning purposes. It is also valuable for product liability risk assessment.

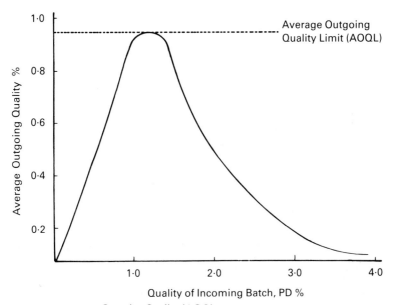

Figure 9.8 Average Outgoing Quality (AOQ)

The *single* sampling technique just described is obviously a simple and effective method of assessing batch quality. However, a sample of nearly seven hundred items, as required in the example, may still result in high inspection costs.

The reason for the sample size being so large is because the plan is designed to suit the complete range of possible quality levels, though in the case of extremely good or extremely poor batches a decision might have been made on the basis of a much smaller sample. *Double* sampling has, therefore, been developed in an attempt to reduce the *average* amount of inspection that needs to be done. This is a two stage sampling technique whereby very good or very poor batches are identified at the first stage while batches in the 'middle ground' will require the operation of the

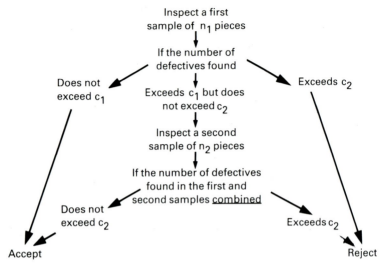

Figure 9.9 The structure of double sampling

second stage. The plan is illustrated in *Figure 9.9*, and the steps taken are as follows:

Stage 1. An initial sample is taken (n_1) and the number of defectives found is compared with *two* acceptance numbers c_1 and c_2. If the number of defectives does not exceed c_1 the batch is accepted. If it exceeds c_2 it is rejected. If it falls between c_1 and c_2 proceed to Stage 2.
Stage 2. A second sample is taken (n_2). If the *total* number of defectives in the combined sample $(n_1 + n_2)$ does not exceed c_2 the batch is accepted. If it exceeds c_2 it is rejected.

It follows that the procedure for double sampling could be extended to triple and multiple sampling where several samples are drawn from a batch with the possibility of acceptance or rejection at each stage. In practice, however, their operation would become laborious and complicated. Eventually it becomes more logical to use an item-by-item or sequential plan based on an individual sample size of one. To perform a sequential test the inspector uses a chart similar to *Figure 9.10*.

On the chart there are two sloping parallel lines, being the boundary of the acceptance and rejection regions. As the inspector draws and inspects each item (taken at random) the cumulative number of defectives is plotted against the number inspected so far. If the plot crosses the upper line the batch is

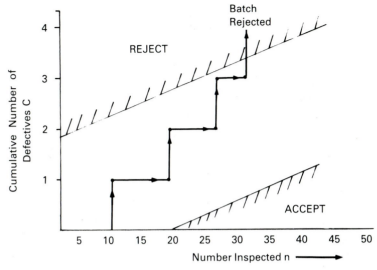

Figure 9.10 Item by item or sequential sampling

rejected, and if it crosses the lower line it is accepted. If it remains between the two lines sampling is continued, although a truncated plan may be used to avoid sampling ad infinitum.

The discussion on acceptance sampling is concluded with a brief mention of variables sampling plans. These are essentially similar to attribute plans except that a *measurement* is used to decide on acceptance or rejection rather than the *number* of defectives found. The OC curve is, therefore, plotted using a scale of values (e.g. weight, tensile strength etc.) as the X-axis. Variable plans are far less commonly used than their attribute equivalents.

9.3 Organization and motivation

It was pointed out earlier that the issue of quality has occurred on several occasions prior to its being given specific treatment in this chapter. The reason for this, of course, is that, conceptually, quality cannot be considered in isolation. It is a function of the output from the production system by which its performance is measured. Management will, therefore, use quality as one of the reference points when the effect of any change is assessed.

The idea that quality pervades all parts of the production system would seem to be at variance with the idea of it receiving specialized attention. Yet quality is often seen as exclusively the ·

province of a quality control *department* which has as its terms of reference the sole responsibility for monitoring and maintaining quality standards.

There are two main reasons why quality control is sometimes treated in this way. The first of these relates back to F.W. Taylor and his advocacy of functional specialization. The quality function, as with all other functions in the organization, is assumed to be most efficient when staffed by specialists who can focus on a limited range of quality-related tasks. The second reason why quality is separated out is that customers often regard its independence as an important factor. Without an independent quality function, it is argued, quality might be compromised in order to meet a production objective.

The extent to which this view has been held by major industrial customers, such as the automotive industry, forced suppliers into setting up separate quality control departments to ensure being placed on their approved list of vendors, making this arrangement very much the norm. For many years these two reasons for creating and maintaining a separate quality function were not questioned until examples emerged which demonstrated that a more participative approach could yield significantly better results.

9.3.1 Zero defects

The idea that everyone in the organization can make a contribution to quality is embodied in the 'Zero Defects' philosophy. Zero Defects resulted from a desire within the American defence industry to reduce the number of defects, almost literally, to zero. The Martin Company, contractors for the Pershing missile system, developed the concept at its Orlando, Florida plant[10]. The need for such an approach arose due to the complex nature of the Pershing system. Experience showed that with 25 000 parts, the system was likely to suffer from a high number of flight failures unless a concerted effort was made to detect and rectify each and every quality defect. The Company's solution was to devise a programme which encouraged a contribution from every employee towards the total quality effort.

Success of a Zero Defects programme depends on planning, organization and co-ordination. It would normally be run under the direction of a Zero Defects Administrator who has an open channel of communication with all the functions likely to be in a position to influence quality in any way. Participation in a Zero

Defects programme is voluntary, although full commitment is expected from all those who do participate, to the extent that a 'pledge' is often signed.

The other special feature of a Zero Defects programme is the launch or 'kick-off'. This is designed to create the greatest impact with a variety of devices being used to serve this purpose. A common feature of 'kick-off' day is a rally attended by all plant employees at which a senior executive makes a keynote address, introducing the ZD Administrator, explaining the programme and urging full participation. The kick-off is carefully preceded by a product and quality awareness campaign aimed at explaining, in advance, the purpose and benefits of the programme.

Also associated with the launch of the programme is the use of badges, stickers, posters etc., bearing slogans which are designed to motivate and maintain enthusiasm. One company, Garrett Manufacturing in Canada, even devised a cartoon character, 'Mr Q', who was given a Hollywood-style introduction and became the central theme of the campaign[11].

Of course, the promotional and motivational aspects of a Zero Defects programme cannot alone ensure success, although they are an essential ingredient. Equally important is the underlying organization which ensures that each individual contribution produces maximum yield. In this regard it should be noted that Zero Defects can only be achieved by preventing the occurrence of defects rather than relying on detecting them. An important feature is, therefore, Error Cause Identification (ECI) and Error Cause Removal (ECR) whereby an employee can formally make suggestions regarding elimination of the reasons for the generation of defective items.

Financial rewards are not normally given to employees in return for their contribution to quality improvement, but badges, certificates, prizes etc. are commonly used in recognition of any special achievement.

Although the Zero Defects programme, as described, is a uniquely American phenomenon, the concept can quite well be transferred to other countries. In Japan, for instance, the President of Nippon Electric Company introduced a programme in 1964 after witnessing its success at the Hughes Aircraft Co. Within a year one hundred Japanese companies had started some form of Zero Defects programme, and ten years later the number had grown to 7000[12].

Despite being based on the same philosophy, Japanese Zero Defects programmes differ in many areas of detail. Firstly, the kick-off is treated as far less of a carnival-like event but is rather more of a ceremonial meeting held after the programme is already underway. The idea of giving the individual a special recognition is also not in the Japanese nature. Instead, a nominal cash sum is given to the group.

The success of a Zero Defects programme of the type described depends on a high degree of planning, centralized control and commitment from a large proportion of employees across the organization. The requirement of workers is also to do nothing more than provide a personal contribution within the normal scope of their job or skill. In this way individual specialization still exists with extra attention to quality and the removal of defects being added.

An approach which stems from the same broad objective, but is based on a different philosophy, is the use of Quality Circles. Compared with Zero Defects programmes these have gained more widespread acceptance, having been adopted with success in numerous organizations throughout the world.

Quality Circles go under various other names such as Quality Control Circles and Quality Control Groups. They were established in Japan in 1962 so in fact preceded the introduction there of Zero Defects programmes. The idea was initiated through the Union of Japanese Scientists and Engineers (JUSE) following publication of a magazine, *Quality Control for Foremen*. As their name suggests, Quality Circles[13] are based on groups rather than relying on the contribution of individuals. Circles are usually led by a departmental foreman, supervisor, or other qualified person, and consist of between five and ten employees. Membership is always voluntary.

Apart from their focus on groups rather than individuals, the other distinctive feature of Quality Circles is the training aspect. Training of group leaders is fundamental to the success of the programme. A leadership course is usually provided aimed at teaching basic problem-solving techniques which the leader will then pass on to group members. This training, passed on via the group leader, is usually supplemented by additional courses in quality control methods.

Ideally every employee in the group should be equipped to use the so-called seven tools (i.e. Pareto analysis, cause and effect diagrams, stratification, check sheets, histograms, scatter diagrams, and control charts). The majority of these are established techniques for analysis and problem-solving, while cause and effect diagrams were specially devised for use by Quality Circles. They were originally developed by Professor Kaoru Ishikawa of Tokyo University as an aid to 'brainstorming'. Their structure is

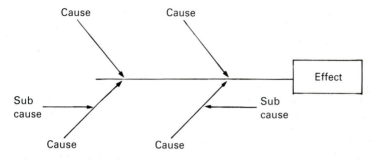

Figure 9.11 'Fishbone' (or cause and effect) diagram

shown in *Figure 9.11* from which it will be seen how they earn their other name – 'fishbone' diagrams.

The success of Quality Circles in Japan is evidenced by the fact that in 1980 it was estimated that some one million circles were operating in Japanese factories[14]. Furthermore, the spread of Quality Circles outside Japan has been rapid and extensive, their being employed in countries as far apart as Brazil, Korea, Sweden, Malaysia, the USA, and the UK.

It is often said that Quality Circles are suited to the Japanese industrial environment but will not succeed when translated into Western cultures. However, practice demonstrates otherwise. In the USA, for instance, Circles are found in some of the largest corporations such as Westinghouse, TRW, Northrop, General Electric, Honeywell, and General Motors[15]. In the UK they are operating in Ford and Rolls Royce, while their use in Marks & Spencer demonstrates their applicability in the service sector. In a period of thirty months Rolls Royce Aero Division at Derby claimed financial benefits amounting to £525 000 as a result of their using Quality Circles. Among the items contributing to this total were a reduction in defective welds on turbine blades from 24% to 1.8% by amending the weld parameters, and a reduction in machining scrap from 4% to 0.5% by re-organizing the workplace[16].

Of course, the methodology used by Quality Circles need not be limited only to solving quality problems. The approach can equally be applied to many other areas of work improvement as the Rolls Royce scrap example shows. As a more general problem-solving technique, however, the Quality Circle is just one of many programmes which are widely used throughout industry, although a comparison of the more popular of these programmes shows that Quality Circles, together with other 'worker involvement' techniques, are still not a substitute for good management and engineering[17].

The overall conclusion which can be derived from examining the various quality-related systems and programmes is that a broad approach is most appropriate, based on a mixture of methodologies. Thus, the concept of *Total Quality Control*, emerges which embraces all aspects of quality control and improvement including design, industrial engineering, organization, statistical control techniques, employee participation and motivation.

The dependence on human involvement will be recognized and full use made of ergonomic aspects which relate to inspection, detection and response[18]. A complementary but equally important effort will be directed to improving process reliability and automating process monitoring and control.

As a postscript, the following quotation captures this complete philosophy which is well understood by all organizations where success has been dependent on quality:

'Quality is free. It's not a gift, but it is free. What costs money are the unquality things – all the actions that involve not doing jobs right the first time"[19].

9.4 Summary

The design of a quality system should be regarded as a central activity in the whole production system design process. In this way quality can be viewed as an asset on which the enterprise can capitalize rather than being a complicating factor which places extra demands upon the system.

Quality of design is the essential prerequisite for ensuring that all derivatives of the original design are of the desired standard. It is a function of materials, sizes, tolerances, and safety factors, together with the skill, knowledge and experience of the designer. Quality of conformance describes all the activities which then seek to ensure that each individual item made conforms to the original specification. These activities can be grouped into inspection, quality control and quality audit. Inspection concerns measurement and assessment while auditing tests the effectiveness of the total quality system.

Quality control, as the term suggests, uses the information derived from inspection to provide control over the system. This is done by feed-back or feed-forward techniques and often uses statistical methods for process monitoring and batch quality assessment.

The extent to which each organizational function makes a contribution to quality may vary widely. It depends on the degree of specialization which exists and how desirable it is to maintain an independent quality control function. If a more widespread contribution to the quality effort is sought then a Zero Defects or Quality Circles programme may provide an appropriate mechanism. These are both worker involvement techniques aimed at directing and co-ordinating the thoughts and ideas of individuals and groups. They have been successful in the United States and Japan and, especially in the case of Quality Circles, have now found acceptance throughout the world.

Worker involvement techniques supplement the other quality-related activities and can never be expected to replace them. So the best quality strategy is most likely to be one of Total Quality Control. In such a programme, engineering, statistics and motivation theory are blended into a complete approach, providing the best of each individual component discipline.

References

1. PETERS, T. J. and WATERMAN, R. H. (1982) *In Search of Excellence,* Harper and Row, London
2. BENNETT, D. J. (1981) 'Quality and Reliability', in *Operations Management in Practice* (ed. by C. D. Lewis). Philip Allan, London
3. LOCKYER, K. and OAKLAND, J. (1981) 'How To Sample Success', *Management Today* (July)
4. SHEWHART, W. A. (1931) *Economic Control of Manufactured Products,* Van Nostrand, USA
5. DODGE, H. F. and ROMIG, H. G. (1929) 'A Method of Sampling Inspection, *The Bell System Technical Journal,* Vol III (October)
6. CALLAHAN, J. M. (1981) 'US Automakers Now Heed Teacher of Quality Control', *Christian Science Monitor* (23 December)
7. MURDOCH, J. and BARNES, J. A. (1974) *Statistical Tables for Science, Engineering, Management and Business Studies,* Macmillan, London
8. BSI (1972) *BS 6001: Specification for Sampling Procedures and Tables for Inspection by Attributes,* British Standards Institution, London
9. DODGE, H. F. and ROMIG, H. G. (1959) *Sampling Inspection Tables (2nd ed)* Wiley, New York
10. HALPIN, J. F. (1966) *Zero Defects,* McGraw-Hall, New York
11. TATE, W. C. (1965) 'Zero Defects: How to Motivate Perfection', *Plant Administration and Engineering* (December)
12. INOHARA, H. (1973) 'Transferring "Foreign" Ideas: The Zero Defects Movement in Japan', *European Business* (Spring)
13. SASAKI, N. and HUTCHINS, D. (1984) *The Japanese Approach to Product Quality,* Pergamon Press, Oxford
14. HUTCHINS, D. (1980) 'Why Does Britain Want Quality Circles?', *The Production Engineer* (February)

15. THACKRAY, J. (1982) 'The Quest for Quality Work', *Management Today* (March)
16. HUTCHINS, D. (1981) 'How Quality Goes Round in Circles', *Management Today* (January)
17. SCHONBERGER, R. J. (1983) 'Work Improvement Programmes: Quality Control Circles Compared with Traditional Western Approaches', *International Journal of Operations and Production Management*, **3**, No 2
18. DRURY, C. G. and FOX, J. G. (1975) *Human Reliability in Quality Control*, Taylor and Francis
19. CROSBY, P. B. (1979) *Quality is Free*, McGraw-Hill, New York

Chapter 10

Service operations

10.1 The concept of a service

Recent years have seen the rapid expansion of service producing activities rather than those which are directed towards the production of physical goods. But what is a 'service'? How does it differ from a manufactured product, and why is service production growing in importance?

One simple definition of a service activity could be that it arises when the output from a production system does not have a physical form. In many ways this is true, but, as is often the case when such a simple definition is employed, numerous exceptions can be found which confound attempts to understand the wider philosophy.

Take, for instance, the specialist in metal finishing. He takes in another company's products, paints or plates them, and returns them to their 'owner' (the customer). The output from the system is physical, material is added (paint, etc.), yet a *service* is being provided to the customer. So what is this example – manufacturing or service? Most official statistics would place such companies firmly within the *manufacturing* sector, yet their activities are little different from those of a laundry or an electrical retailer's repair department, both of which would lie within the service sector.

It is apparent from these examples that service production could often involve the processing of material and that the output from a service system is sometimes a physical product. It also demonstrates that the classification of enterprises into manufacturing and service *sectors* can lead to misunderstanding regarding the nature and activity of a particular enterprise. Restaurants and fast-food outlets are, for instance, in the service sector yet their goods producing activities are clearly significant. Likewise computer manufacturers and oil companies would be classified as being in manufacturing although many of their customer-directed activities, such as training, consultancy, repair and maintenance, all qualify as services.

199

An important distinction must, therefore, be drawn between service *industries* and service *operations*. A service *industry* is one which, according to some economic criteria, has been categorized into the service sector. A service *operation*, on the other hand, is one whose activities focus on providing for the customer a change of condition or a benefit. Thus, service and manufacturing operations can be found in both service and manufacturing industries.

In a service operation the customer or something belonging to the customer is taken into the production system. This process in which the customer participates is called the *service delivery system*[1]. Unlike manufacturing, where the marketing and production functions can be considered separately, marketing and production interface in the service delivery system. For this reason production must be thought of in terms of the generation of a bundle of 'facilitating' goods and services for simultaneous consumption by the customer. If marketing and production are thought of as separate there is a distinct danger of sup-optimizing and thereby reducing customer satisfaction.

Figures 10.1 and 10.2 serve to illustrate the difference between manufacturing and service operations. *Figure 10.1* shows manufacturing, whereby raw materials are converted to finished goods which are supplied to customers. *Figure 10.2(a)* shows the type of service operation where the customer is a participant, entering the service delivery system and leaving when the service is completed.

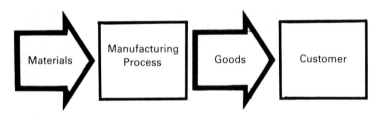

Figure 10.1 The structure of manufacturing operations

Figure 10.2(a) The structure of service operations where customers participate

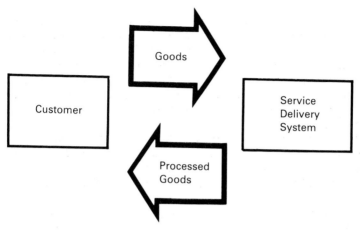

Figure 10.2(b) The structure of service operations where customers' goods are processed

Figure 10.2(b) is the alternative form of service where the customer's goods enter the service delivery system for processing and are subsequently returned to the customer.

10.1.1 Managing service activities

Having described the nature of service operations, the question of service management may now be dealt with. There is a school of thought that recognizes little or no distinction between managing a service operation and managing manufacturing. This assumption rests on the premise that particular types of service system have a more or less direct manufacturing equivalent. This premise supposes that service operations can also be classified into job, batch and flow systems having the same demand patterns as previously described for manufacturing in Chapter 3.

Indeed there are, no doubt, cases where a service could be described as being produced using a job system, such as the small village shop which sells almost anything, or the restaurant which offers an 'a la carte' menu. Similarly services are sometimes delivered by a batch system, such as a fast-food outlet or a hospital out-patients department. The idea of services being delivered using flow production principles may even be demonstrated in cafeterias and some types of fast throughput retail operations such as catalogue shops.

The possibility of classifying services in a similar manner to manufacturing enables them to be managed in much the same way as a factory would be organized for the production of physical goods[2,3]. In this way routine production management techniques for forecasting, stock control, scheduling, work measurement, etc. can all be transferred directly into the service environment and put into immediate operation. Clearly there are many instances when such an approach to service management is valid since services often employ inventories of facilitating products and are sufficiently regulated to enable established factory management techniques to be used.

On the other hand, it is often argued that closer examination of the nature of service operations will yield a significant number of distinct differences which justifies a more unique approach to their management.

These distinct characteristics of services that have been identified may be classified into four areas: intangibility, perishability, heterogeneity of the product, and simultaneity of production and consumption.

Intangibility is of greater consequence to the designer or marketer than to the producer of services since its main effect is on the way a service is presented or advertised; although one production aspect which is affected by the concept is that of quality.

The quality of tangible products can be measured and comparisons made with an agreed standard. On the other hand, due to their abstract nature, intangible products are more difficult to measure and their quality can often only be determined by the sense of satisfaction gained by the consumer. In fact, there is a danger of organizations trying to control the quality of services by just concentrating on measurable aspects while neglecting the parts of the service which are judged subjectively. Clearly this could lead to a mistaken impression of the degree of customer satisfaction being offered. The quality of a bus service, for instance, cannot be assessed only by the promptness of its vehicles, and a restaurant cannot be judged by the amount of food presented on its plates.

Moving on to perishability, one argument that is often made about end-services is that they cannot be inventoried. A manufacturing plant with capacity limited to one hundred units per week can produce for stock when demand is low and thereby meet the requirement for two hundred units which might occur during some week in the future. However, the one-hundred-bed hotel cannot cope with two hundred potential residents who wish to stay on a particular night, nor can the one-hundred-seat aeroplane carry the two hundred hopeful passengers who attempt to check-in for a flight. In fact, the only way in which a service, or more strictly an element of the service, can be inventoried is when a facilitating product is produced in advance of its consumption. This might occur when meals are prepared and then later sold from a vending machine or when banknotes are sorted prior to their being issued via an automatic cash dispenser.

The heterogeneity of services results from the fact that no two customers are the same, their differing requirements and expectations necessitating that each service provided differs in one way or another. Services should not, as a result, be completely standardized and any attempt at standardization should only be done up to a certain point. Thereafter some 'customization' should be possible to meet the needs of each particular customer.

Service heterogeneity, like its intangibility, also leads to problems of quality control. Most quality control techniques depend on the measurement of some feature which is then compared against a standard. This approach can only be used for various elements of the service where standardization is acceptable and possible. Elsewhere control must be exercised in different ways using, where necessary, opinion surveys and value judgements to monitor and evaluate the level of quality being provided[4].

Simultaneity of production and consumption probably constitutes the most fundamental difference between service and manufacturing which militates against the use of established techniques. Simultaneity normally demands the presence of the customer or his goods in the service delivery system so it should naturally be located close to the customer. It is this geographical proximity that limits the scale of operation of a service system making it difficult to achieve the sort of economy of scale which can be found in manufacturing. So, hospitals must be located close to the section of the community which they serve, banks must have branches in every large town and insurance companies must interface with their customers through local agencies.

Closeness of the delivery system is less important in certain information-based services since modern postal and telecommunications facilities enable some degree of centralization. Similarly retailing can be located remotely by the use of mail order techniques, though there is a danger that the resulting loss of customer contact may lead to a reduction in the level of service being provided.

If all these unique features of services are considered together with their widely varying nature and scale, then the gulf immediately becomes apparent between the conventional wisdom which applies to manufacturing and the realities of service management. Sometimes the difference is recognized and an approach is formulated based on techniques peculiar to services, such as franchising and computerized information systems which can simulate a personal acquaintanceship[5]. But there still remains a wide gap between theory and practice which in time must be closed.

10.2 Services to the production system

So far this chapter has concentrated on the service activities which occur outside manufacturing, although it was mentioned earlier that service operations occur within manufacturing industries as well.

Such services may include maintenance, personnel administration, management services and cost accounting. They could not exist in their own right since they all depend on a demand from the 'customer' (i.e. the production system) to justify their retention.

The *maintenance* function obviously makes an important contribution to the efficient operation of the system's physical facilities. In many ways the maintenance function within manufacturing industry is similar in its operation to an after-sales service and repair department within the retailing sector. The 'customer', whether the purchaser of a domestic appliance or the production department in an engineering company, demands quick and inexpensive repairs to a high standard and one of the major responsibilities of any maintenance function must be to provide these as part of its total activities.

A further feature of industrial maintenance is the provision of planned or preventive maintenance. This is carried out to reduce the probability of failure and/or to minimize the cost of failure when it does occur. Planned maintenance is less common in retailing though for some products, especially motor vehicles, its merits are recognized. The effectiveness of planned maintenance is very much determined by how it is applied. It must be selectively directed to specific parts of the system at pre-determined times and requires the collection and analysis of performance data before any planning is carried out[6]. Arbitrary or wholesale application of planned maintenance could incur high labour and parts costs without a commensurate saving in failure costs and, in some extreme cases, the activity could do more harm than good by reversing an improving reliability trend.

While planned maintenance can yield advantages compared with a policy of repair following breakdown, it is still only one approach to improving overall maintenance efficiency. Other improvements can be derived from the design of the maintenance organization and the examination and modification of work practices. In this regard maintenance can be viewed in much the same way as the production function which it services.

Just as production can comprise two sets of activities, system design and production control, so maintenance may also be sub-divided. Again, planning and control is just one of the sets of activities while design of the system is the important prerequisite which must be approached in such a way that the subsequent activities are able to achieve the best possible results.

One fundamental issue which must be addressed regarding maintenance organization is the question of centralization versus decentralization. In most enterprises of a relatively small size it is obviously of no inconvenience to operate a centralized maintenance function. A team comprising all the required skills will be located in a position where there is no problem in quickly responding to a repair call and where travelling time is tolerably low.

Larger organizations, on the other hand, can encounter considerable difficulties if a policy of centralizing maintenance is adopted. Firstly the downtime period of plant is likely to be extended while the maintenance personnel are travelling to a breakdown, and secondly this non-productive time adds to the operating costs of the maintenance function. In such a situation maintenance faces the dilemma experienced by all service operations wishing to provide for a wide geographical spread of customers. So, in much the same way as a retail organization will open a new outlet, the maintenance function is likely to become decentralized.

Decentralized maintenance involves setting up a number of maintenance teams in locations which will reduce the total time spent travelling to and from each job. A local team will often be based in a particular production department which may be using a unique process. If this is the case, one of the problems of decentralizing, that of possible duplication, might be avoided. Where standard machines and processes are used, on the other hand, a complete range of skills will be needed at each location, thereby negating much of the cost advantage to be derived from decentralization.

This problem of skills provision and duplication is often exacerbated by the system of strict trade demarcation that exists in many traditional industries. In the UK, one such industry with a long history of trade demarcation is steelmaking. A typical steelworks would have dozens of different trades working within the maintenance function, each of which would specialize in a particular aspect of a repair or overhaul job. The deficiencies associated with this practice were recognized when designing a new steelmaking plant at Redcar where it was aimed to operate with manning levels comparable with the best plants in the world[7]. The majority of Redcar's maintenance force of over nine hundred were decentralized with less than three-hundred-and-fifty being based in a Central Workshop. However, this policy needed to be linked with a change in the working practices arising from the separation of skills.

JOB: CHANGE DROP THROUGH GATE ON GROUND ORE BIN FEED AIR SLIDES

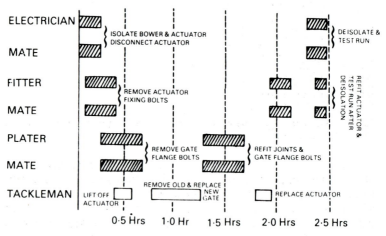

Figure 10.3(a) Manning requirements for a maintenance job using traditional working practices (Flegg & Prout[7])

Figure 10.3(a) shows an example of the manning requirements for a maintenance job using traditional working practices. Four trades are used, three of which are accompanied by 'mates'. All seven persons attend the job for its 2.5 hour duration, the total requirement, therefore, being 17.5 man-hours.

The changes to be adopted at Redcar were based on the introduction of Group Working Practices. This required that maintenance workers should acquire some knowledge of each other's jobs, and to be flexible in their application. The multi-skill group concept, when applied to the maintenance job described in the example, would result in the manning requirements shown in *Figure 10.3(b)*. Here it can be seen that only two unassisted trades are now required for, again, 2.5 hours duration. The total manning requirement has, therefore, been reduced to 5 man-hours, a saving of over 70%.

<u>MAIN TRADE</u> - BOILERMAKER

<u>ASSISTANCE</u> - FITTER <u>OR</u> ELECTRICIAN

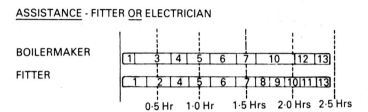

1. ISOLATE BLOWER & ACTUATOR DISCONNECT ACTUATOR
2. UNBOLT ACTUATOR
3. UNBOLT GATE FLANGE JOINTS
4. SET UP LIFTING TACKLE & LIFT OFF ACTUATOR
5. SET UP LIFTING TACKLE & LIFT OFF GATE
6. SET UP LIFTING TACKLE & LIFT ON NEW GATE
7. SET UP LIFTING TACKLE & LIFT ON NEW ACTUATOR
8. BOLT UP ACTUATOR
9. CONNECT UP ACTUATOR
10. BOLT UP FLANGES OF GATE
11. DE ISOLATE AND TEST EQUIPMENT
12. STANDBY EQUIPMENT FOR TEST
13. REMOVE TACKLE & TIDY UP

Figure 10.3(b) Manning requirements for maintenance using multi-skilled group concept (Flegg & Prout[7])

Such a change in working practice seems outwardly to be obvious and simple to adopt. In practice, however, this is unlikely to be the case since it goes against the conventional procedures which are seen to protect jobs and, as a result, are usually defended by the trades unions. Multi-skilled working will also require additional training so that the main trade of each worker is supplemented by sufficient extra skill for the ancillary work to be carried out competently and safely.

The agreement at Redcar on Group Working Practices was only reached after three years of negotiations. As a result, new procedures were implemented for identifying and analysing the task content of each job before instructions were given and manpower allocated. The agreement also included the provision of flexibility training which, because of the large numbers involved, was carried out at a number of centres throughout the region in which the plant was located. Training was mandatory and broken down into a number of modules which could be selected according

FITTERS		ELECTRICIANS		BOILERMAKERS	
DAYS	MODULE	DAYS	MODULE	DAYS	MODULE
3	FLAME CUTTING	3	FLAME CUTTING	5	USE OF M/C TOOLS
5	ARC WELDING	5	ARC WELDING	10	ELECTRICAL APPRECIATION
10	ELECTRICAL APP.	5	USE OF M/C TOOLS		
5	USE OF LIFTING GEAR	5	USE OF LIFTING GEAR	5	USE OF LIFTING GEAR
23	TOTAL	18	TOTAL	20	TOTAL

Figure 10.4 Flexibility training required to permit group working practices in maintenance (Flegg & Prout[7])

to existing skills and the necessary additional requirements. *Figure 10.4* is an example of the type of flexibility training provided.

Although this particular form of group working is unique to the type of activity carried out by maintenance workers, its underlying philosophy is in fact similar to that already described under 'group technology' and 'autonomous working'. In both these cases the principles of division of labour and functional specialization were seen as contributing to a reduction in overall efficiency rather than improving it. Group working in maintenance is based on the same argument and extends the grouping philosophy to cover the complete range of production systems, including the job system, of which maintenance is an example.

Personnel administration is one of the service activities of an organization which has applications across all the functional areas where human resources are employed. In manufacturing organizations the largest proportion of labour tends to be located within the production function so the services provided by personnel are of importance in ensuring that the human resource is managed and utilized in the best possible manner.

Many of the activities which are now regarded as requiring the services of an 'expert' personnel function were often in the past carried out by line managers within the individual departments and in smaller companies this often still remains the case. Indeed, even in larger organizations there is an increasing tendency to devolve certain responsibilities among the functional managers and even among the workers themselves. The case of Volvo's Vara factory described in Chapter 6 is an illustration of this.

Despite this trend there still remains a need for a professional, independent service of the type found in most larger organizations. The personnel specialists in such a function will provide services in areas such as employment, counselling, wage and salary administration, safety, welfare, training, and industrial relations. Rarely, however, will complete responsibility for all aspects of personnel management rest with the specialist personnel administrator. Most managers typically play a large role in the selection of employees, especially at higher levels. Furthermore, an operating manager is in a key position to determine how well employees do their jobs[8].

An examination in detail of the various areas where professional personnel expertise is applied will reveal a number of reasons why they should be dealt with by separate specialists. Employment matters, which include recruitment and dismissal involve a range of tasks which are both time-consuming and often require a knowledge of manpower planning techniques, employment law and recruitment and selection methods. Each of these requires a great deal of specialist expertise to be conducted properly. Manpower planning, for instance, can require a high degree of quantitative skill since many of the modern techniques are based on complex mathematical models.

Employment law is becoming increasingly pervasive and now includes such aspects as racial and sex discrimination, misrepresentation, employment protection and so on. Recruitment and selection requires the use of media advertising and selection techniques may include psychological testing, character appraisal, etc.

The need for and extent of employee counselling is likely to vary widely between organizations since its benefits are often difficult to perceive. Formal counselling is relatively new in most organizations, although experiments in counselling formed part of the famous 'Hawthorne Studies' which were conducted at the Western Electric Company in the USA (see Chapter 1). Counselling may be of two basic types. Firstly, it can be offered as a response to some of the problems which occur whenever individuals are working in complex organizations. Secondly, counselling may be carried out as part of an overall plan to improve the general human relations climate and maximize the employee's contribution to output. Such an approach is based on the theory that counselling is a motivator and can also enable employees to be matched to jobs for which they are best suited.

Personnel's contribution to wage and salary administration is self-evident. This is one time-consuming activity which would preoccupy line-management and is ideally administered centrally so that the routine procedures can be dealt with more efficiently.

The independence of the personnel function is also beneficial when dealing with payment schemes, especially those with a merit rating element. Personnel staff will also be involved in job evaluation in order to ensure that equitable comparisons are made throughout the organization.

The question of safety has already been covered in Chapter 8 when it was argued that a professional approach is called for. Although staff concerned with safety might be located in various parts of the organization, it is more likely that they will be attached to the personnel function because the human aspects side of safety is so important and also since the personnel function is likely to be independent of the interests which might prevail in other areas.

Employee welfare covers a variety of different aspects which range from pensions and sickness benefits through to medical facilities, the 'works canteen', and even the sports and social club. Again, their administration is time-consuming and sometimes requires skill and knowledge not normally acquired by line-managers. Training facilities and programmes are similarly provided, although centralized training would normally only cover the more basic skills. More advanced training may be conducted at the workplace under instruction from a functional specialist or at an outside facility when no in-house equipment or existing expertise is available. In either case the personnel function is likely to direct or co-ordinate the overall training programme.

The last, but certainly not the least important, area where personnel provides a service is in connection with industrial relations. In fact, it could be said that one of the antecedents of the present personnel specialist was to be found in the 'industrial relations officer' whose position was created to deal with 'organized labour' or the threat that the employer's workforce would organize into trade unions[9]. The role of personnel in dealing with industrial relations matters is to provide a service for production managers which relieves them of the need to negotiate directly with the workforce. Issues concerning pay, conditions, grievances etc. would all be handled by the personnel function as the specialists in this field.

A further reason for requiring specialists to deal with industrial relations is the increasing amount of legislation which is emerging and which needs to be thoroughly digested and properly interpreted. A good deal of professionalism exists within the trades unions and most organizations recognize that as employers they should match this within their own negotiating teams.

Management services is the term used to describe services provided to management based on such disciplines as systems analysis, operational research, computing, industrial engineering etc. In many ways, management services complement the personnel services just described, providing a range of quantitative skills rather than those concerned with the human resource. The overall aim of the management services function is to assist management in taking decisions, of both a major and minor nature, using a scientific approach rather than relying simply on intuition. The importance of management services has increased with the widespread availability of computers.

Although logically independent of the computer, mathematical tools used by management services commonly require large amounts of computation for their application, and a large part of their practical significance for management must be attributed to the coincidental appearance of electronic computers at just the time when the techniques called for them[10]. In fact, so powerful are today's computer hardware and software that their use in decision taking has gone beyond the more routine programmed type of decision.

Non-programmed decisions, of the kind which require large amounts of human judgement, can now be taken using computer assistance. Such decisions are common in production management so 'expert systems', as they are called, are being developed which simulate the thinking of the human expert who would normally be needed to reach a solution. The use of expert systems is extending into many areas of production systems design including facility location and layout, process planning, and machine selection. Their use in these areas frees management to concentrate on the wider policy issues which are often neglected while time is being spent dealing with more routine matters.

Cost accounting services are normally provided by the *finance* function of the organization. Finance, along with marketing and production, is a core function so its activities would not in the main be regarded as servicing the other core functions. It was suggested earlier that many personnel activities were in the past carried out by line managers and that today there is a tendency to devolve some personnel responsibilities among the production staff. The same is largely true of cost accounting. Line managers who would at one time have been concerned with product and process costing and budgetary control matters have largely been relieved of these tasks by the cost accounting specialist. Yet an understanding of accounting is still desirable for all managers in all types of organization since they are better equipped to perform their duties when they have a reasonable grasp of accounting data[11].

There are a number of different production activities from

where cost accounting information is derived and a further set of applications to which that information is directed. For the purpose of product and process costing, information is needed relating to material purchases, labour and works overhead allocation. The purchasing department, stores, manufacturing departments, quality and maintenance functions will all need to be examined and their running costs apportioned accordingly. Appropriate cost rates will be calculated for different machines, departments, processes etc. These can then be used to evaluate alternative methods or to choose between different materials, machines etc.

Product cost information can, in addition, be used by the Marketing department to determine profit margins and make pricing decisions. The information can also be used for control purposes. This would involve using the data which had been gathered to evaluate the likely costs associated with future operations. Actual items of expenditure could then be compared with those expected and variances brought to the attention of management so the necessary corrective actions can be taken.

The four service functions which have been described are all necessary to make production operate more efficiently. In many ways they are similar to the type of operation which can be found in the service sector yet their position makes them an integral part of manufacturing. It may be useful from a systems point of view, therefore, to treat such service activities separately. In this way the output and input of such operations can be measured and their internal efficiency monitored and improved in the same fashion as the production system.

10.3 Summary

There are many significant and important distinctions between service operations and manufacturing which call for a unique approach to their management. These differences are not always immediately apparent since a service operation can sometimes involve the manufacture of some physical product. Service operations can also be carried out within the manufacturing sector as part of an organization's total productive activities.

For some purposes service operations can be classified in the same way as manufacturing. This enables the application of some of the more routine techniques of planning, scheduling and inventory control, especially in service operations which are 'factory like'. Many 'pure' services, however, do not lend themselves to this sort of comparison and require an altogether different approach. This is because of the distinctive features that services exhibit which make them dissimilar to manufacturing, i.e. intangibility, perishability, heterogeneity of the product, and simultaneity of production and consumption.

Within a production organization there are a number of functions which can be identified as providing a service to the production system itself. These are maintenance, personnel administration, management services, and cost accounting. They are all staffed by professionals who, by virtue of some specialist skill, are able to assist production management in running their operations more efficiently. Maintenance provides a service which helps to maximize the output from the physical facilities, while personnel and management services make contributions relating to the human resource and decision making. Cost accounting provides information on the cost of processes and allows measurement and control to take place based on financial parameters.

These functions are often regarded as an integral part of production itself but this need not necessarily be the case. They could all be regarded as service operations in their own right which rely on a demand from the customer, in this case production, for 'revenue' generation. Such an approach would enable their efficiency to be more easily measured and improvements to be made in their operation.

References

1. SASSER, W. E. (1978) *Management of Service Operations,* Allyn & Bacon, USA
2. REED, J. (1971) Sure It's A Bank But I Think Of It As A Factory, *Innovation,* No 23
3. LEVITT, T. (1972) Production-line Approach to Service, *Harvard Business Review* (Sept–Oct)
4. HOSTAGE, G. M. (1975) 'Quality Control in a Service Business', *Harvard Business Review* (July–August)
5. THACKRAY, J. (1984) 'Service Managements' Second Coming', *Management Today* (June)
6. KELLY, A. and HARRIS, M. J. (1978) *Management of Industrial Maintenance,* Butterworths, London
7. FLEGG, P. and PROUT, R. (1980) Maintenance Management, Planning and Scheduling by Computer, *3rd National Conference on Maintenance by Computer.* London (19–20 February)
8. MATHIS, R. L. and JACKSON, J. H. (1979) *Personnel: Contemporary Perspectives and Applications,* West Publishing Co, USA
9. THOMASON, G. (1978) *A Textbook of Personnel Management,* The Institute of Personnel Management, London
10. SIMON, H. A. (1977) *The New Science of Management Decision,* Prentice-Hall, New Jersey
11. HORNGREN, C. T. (1984) *Introduction to Management Accounting,* Prentice-Hall, New York

Chapter 11

Implementation and evaluation

11.1 Installing the new production system

The first part of this concluding chapter looks at a topic which is often underrated in importance. The design of a new production system may be based on the most up-to-date knowledge with regard to its organization and could be using the most modern equipment available. Yet often in such cases the new system does not yield the expected benefits due to circumstances which had not been expected beforehand. This is not to say that such circumstances are unpredictable; in fact, many of the problems encountered frequently recur and could easily be avoided. It is more usually a case of the organization not paying sufficient attention to the installation of a system which on paper is sound but which needs careful introduction to ensure the enjoyment of all its advantages.

Installing improved working methods has always been recognized as an inherent part of 'work study' procedure. Here, much depends on the personal qualities of the person responsible for implementation. Active support is required from management and trades unions alike so the qualities required of such a person are an ability to explain clearly and simply what should be done, coupled with a gift for getting alone with other people and winning their trust[1].

Installation of a new method of working can be divided into five stages, i.e.:

(i) Gaining acceptance of the change by the departmental supervision.
(ii) Gaining approval of the change by the management.
(iii) Gaining acceptance of the change by the workers involved and their representatives.
(iv) Retraining the workers to operate the new methods.
(v) Maintaining close contact with the progress of the job until satisfied that it is running as intended.

The desirability of gaining the acceptance of workers and their representatives becomes stronger where changes are proposed which affect the number of workers involved in the operation, which is often the case if the changes are aimed at improving efficiency. In some organizations such consultation is routine where it has been discovered that failure to consult the workforce properly can cripple a new production system soon after its installation.

These simple maxims for introducing new work methods have served well where small changes have been made involving modifications to working practice or the use of a new piece of equipment. Today, however, it is common to find that wholly new and widespread systems of work organization are being proposed or that equipment is to be installed using new technology which requires completely different skills and attitudes.

The dramatic nature of some of the changes now made means that a new approach has become necessary which goes much further than the routine consultative procedures just described. The importance of such an approach has been clearly illustrated via a number of notable examples where new systems have failed to gain immediate acceptance by the workforce resulting in expensive losses during periods of dispute[2].

In this connection the distinction between *consultation* and *participation* is of particular significance. All five stages previously described, by implication, involve some degree of consultation of supervisors, workers and managers. There is no suggestion, however, of the decision-making process involving the active participation of those involved. Consultation usually means merely that the views of others are sought and may be taken into account when introducing changes. In some cases consultation just means 'selling' an idea to the workforce. Participation implies that individuals are involved in, and are able to influence, what is going on within an organization and what is being produced by it[3].

11.1.1 Participation

Although worker participation is often regarded as a fairly recent phenomenon, there are some examples which date back to the early 1900s. Many of these occurred in the USA where Taylor's theories of scientific management, with their built-in preference for hierarchical organization, were fast rising in popularity. In 1923, for example, the Baltimore and Ohio Railroad and the Machinists Union organized joint management-worker committees for the firm's repair shops. Further worker participation exercises followed during the next fifty years though they were still relatively rare compared with the more formal approach based on decision-making by 'specialists'[4].

During the 1970s, however, the idea of worker participation developed rapidly in the USA. Its development was largely led by General Motors which was experiencing labour problems in several plants and decided that a wholly new approach was needed. Early examples of experiments within General Motors include those at Tarrytown, New York, and Lakewood, Georgia. The problems at the Lordstown plant in Ohio have already been referred to in Chapter 3.

In the context of implementation, these problems at Lordstown were highly significant since they occurred in the company's newest and supposedly best-engineered workplace. As a result, General Motors established a national QWL (quality of work life) Committee enabling a high degree of involvement on the part of their employees.

Other worker-participation examples in the US which emerged during the 1970s included those in the Eaton Corporation, Monsanto, Procter & Gamble, Heinz, Armco Steel and Carborundum. In all these cases special programmes were devised, based mainly on some form of committee structure, whereby both workers and management could discuss a wide variety of matters relating to the companies' operations.

The type of participation scheme which has evolved in these US companies involves workers far more in the decision-making processes than does a procedure of consultation. Such schemes do not, on the other hand, provide a genuine situation of industrial democracy since worker committees and councils do not have any legal standing and could still be disregarded by 'management' in favour of some other interest.

A form of industrial democracy which places participation on a formal footing is that of *co-determination*[5]. Like the other schemes, this allows worker representatives to participate in the decision-making processes of firms. It differs, however, by being a right of law and usually allows worker representatives to be elected to the top decision-making forum, the Board of Directors. A further feature of co-determination laws is that they are usually accompanied by additional legal constraints on the right of management and owners of firms. Restrictions on the right to lay-off employees, to choose or modify production techniques, and to close plants are a few examples of such constraints.

Co-determination Acts have been passed in a number of European countries, both Western and Eastern. Notable among the Western European countries are Sweden and the Federal Republic of Germany whose co-determination laws were described in Chapter 2 in connection with organizational aspects of job design. Eastern European examples include the system developed in Yugoslavia where, in 1976, the *Law of Associated Labour* was introduced. This allows employees of any department in a firm to form their own 'basic organization of associated labour' which controls their own business activities and owns its net product. Thus they are rather like co-operatives within a firm, each of which will nominate a representative onto the Workers' Council of the firm.

This Yugoslav model for co-determination is more suited to the communist philosophy, and is patently quite different from the type of arrangement which has developed in the West. Genuine worker co-operatives are still fairly unusual in Western Europe where the majority of enterprizes are either public or private limited companies or state-owned corporations.

Returning to the issue of implementation raises the question of how much more effectively changes can be introduced within a structure under co-determination. This question is not easy to answer since the participation factor cannot be isolated from all the others which may be relevant in order for controlled experiments to be carried out.

For this reason it is not appropriate to compare specific cases from a country which has co-determination laws or other formal means of participation with those from a country which has not. At a general level, however, it can often be observed that more novel forms of work organization and production technology have been successfully introduced in countries where such formal participation has been introduced. In particular, Sweden and the other Scandinavian countries have scored many notable successes involving new systems of organization, while West Germany has advanced rapidly into the new field of flexible automation.

Of course, any hypothesis that participation enables change, rather than preventing it, is likely to conflict with some of the prejudices that exist regarding the nature of industrial relations. There are many who would claim that involving employees in the decision-making process will inevitably not produce the most efficient result due to workers seeking to protect their jobs and thereby creating 'over-manning'. The counter argument is that, provided they are equipped with all the available information, employers and employees alike will reach the same conclusions – in a climate of agreement rather than one of conflict.

When reviewing the role of employees in the introduction of

new production systems it must be appropriate, after considering the practices in the USA and Europe, to look at the situation in Japan. There is no doubt that the Japanese company is markedly different in many ways from its Western counterpart. These differences relate to the industrial context, the labour market, and internal organization[6]. The last two of these are particularly significant since they embrace a number of human and organizational factors which influence success in introducing improvements.

Like many Western firms, Japanese companies employ a system of participative decision-making where, in the Japanese case, a number of people directly involved with a particular situation get together to analyse problems and propose solutions. However, the Japanese approach to participation must be seen within the context of a number of other features which can be summarized as follows:

(i) A humanistic philosophy is articulated and promulgated at all levels of the organization.
(ii) Hiring procedures try to select those applicants who have the same values as the organization.
(iii) A well-planned policy of job rotation helps integrate employees into all areas of company life.
(iv) Work is structured so that it fits into the culturally accepted norms of group activity.
(v) Work areas and attitudes are structured around an open system of communications that allows both for a great deal of vertical information flow from the bottom up and a significant amount of horizontal communication.
(vi) Many corporations use a system of long-term employment and social benefits.

These features illustrate the industrial relations philosophy in Japanese firms, though to understand how this philosophy helps the introduction of new production systems it may be useful to look at a separate concept which summarizes this detail: that is that Japanese corporations are run not from the top down but through initiatives generated at the bottom and passed upward.

Moreover, the average employee at any large firm has a strong loyalty and sense of belonging and has been trained to be ever alert to business competition. A burning desire not to lose out to other firms becomes the ingrained standard, and any employee not accepting this standard is soon made to feel left out[8]. This, therefore, describes the Japanese corporate culture. It is one where commitment to change and innovation is regarded as part of the natural evolution of the firm and does not need to be initiated from the top. The need for management to impose or 'sell' new systems or methods does not exist since their introduction is usually via a common initiative between employer and employee.

There is naturally much that the Western firm can learn from Japanese business practices. A major problem, however, is how to transfer these lessons between different cultural environments so they can be beneficially employed in countries with traditions and values which are less conducive to the Japanese approach. The belief sometimes held that such ideas cannot be transferred at all is, of course, confounded by the fact that nowadays many Japanese firms have subsidiary manufacturing plants in Western countries where many of the management practices of the parent company are employed. Similarly some Japanese working practices are even successfully employed in more enlightened Western companies[9]. In such cases, however, the transfer is often of the *techniques* (i.e. reduced set-ups, KANBAN etc.) rather than of the wider philosophy which leads to such developments in the first place.

A planned approach can be taken to change organizations in an attempt to facilitate participation and enhance organizational success[10,11]. The techniques of 'organization development' (OD) include changing and developing individual and group behaviour as well as changing organization structure and control.

One of the particular features required of an organization in which change can effectively be introduced is the provision of opportunities for individuals to maximize their contribution to the change process. This is a familiar approach across firms who are seeking to promote 'technological innovation'[12]. Such firms are largely interested in product innovation, although the approach is equally appropriate for process innovation. The introduction of a new production system may not necessarily involve the development of entirely new processes. However, most systems are likely to comprise a novel configuration of facilities which requires an equal degree of innovative skill in its introduction.

Before leaving this important discussion on consultation and participation it is worthwhile pointing out that the need to fully involve the workforce is equally true at all levels. The difficulties which are encountered in introducing new systems for production often stem from problems connected with the contribution expected from managers and executives. These problems are not so much of acceptance but rather of awareness and understanding.

It is not sufficient for management to be concerned with the financial implications of the investment. In order that a new system can be successfully introduced its strategic implications must be fully appreciated. Managers must, therefore, be educated in the operational aspects of the production system. In particular, they must be familiar with its effect on quality, delivery, inventory, flexibility, etc. which are all factors affecting the firm's competitiveness in the marketplace.

11.1.2 Planning

The contribution made by both management and other members of the workforce towards introducing the new production system is clearly a key factor determining its success. However, the will to make it succeed, and a willingness to accept the changes, are not in themselves sufficient. Introducing a new production system is in some cases a major project for an organization and requires a considerable amount of planning. During the implementation phase itself, tight control must also be exercised. Items which need to be controlled include the timing of events, costs and the resources being used for installation.

In response to the need to plan and control complex projects a number of techniques have been developed. The most common such technique is probably that of 'network analysis'[13]. This was developed during the 1950s for planning large-scale industrial projects and early users include the Central Electricity Generating Board (CEGB) in the UK, the US Navy (for the Polaris missile project), and Du Pont. The technique has been greatly refined during the last twenty-five years, helped of course by the availability of the computer to assist with the necessary calculations.

A network is simply a diagram showing the sequence of activities required to complete a project, which in this case would be the installation and introduction of the new production system. Activities are normally represented by arrows and events by circles (nodes), an event being the start or finish of an activity. In many cases an activity cannot commence until others have been completed. For instance, a floor might need to be prepared before a piece of equipment is installed. The network is, therefore, a diagram showing precedence and serves a somewhat similar purpose to the type of diagram used for planning flowlines in Chapter 5. In the flowline network, however, the tasks were represented as nodes and the arrows showed their relationship. A simple illustrative network is given in *Figure 11.1* which shows the set of activities required for the introduction of a new production system.

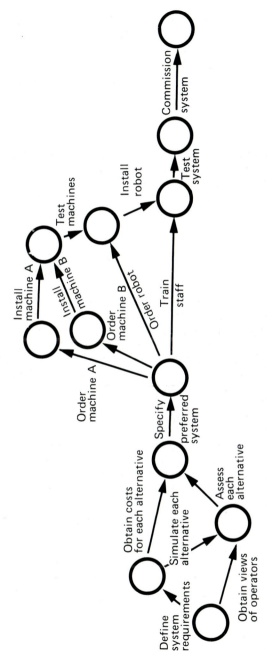

Figure 11.1 A simplified network for the introduction of a production system

The network can be used in a number of ways. Firstly, times may be allocated to each activity and calculations performed to identify the 'critical path' (the chain of activities along which any delay will extend the total project duration). Further calculations will reveal the amount of 'float' on the remaining activities (the amount of spare time available without delaying the project). These float calculations are useful for resource smoothing purposes. For instance, if a particular resource is limited (e.g. only a fixed number of maintenance staff are available for installing the machines) then activities may be shifted within the bounds of the float. If sufficient float is available, the activities requiring the limited resource can, therefore, be phased without extending the project duration.

Yet another variation on the basic network analysis technique is the use of multiple time estimates. Calculations are usually performed using a fixed time for each activity, but clearly there may often be occasions when a rough estimate only can be given. In this event an optimistic, pessimistic and most likely time can be given for such activities. The total project duration can then be represented in terms of a statistical probability distribution in which case the risk of incurring penalties can be assessed and the appropriate action taken.

Finally, before leaving this section on implementation, it would be sensible to mention cost control. The justification for a new production system will doubtless be based on a comparison of the benefits with the cost of the project. If the cost is exceeded then the change may have not been worthwhile. Budgets must, therefore, be formulated for all the direct and indirect costs associated with introducing the new production system.

A list of possible items would include the cost of the physical facilities, the cost of the organization's own labour and contractors' labour, materials used in installation, lost production while installation was in progress, etc. Allowances would need to be made for inflation, particularly where introduction was to be phased over an extended period of time. Routine techniques of budgetary control could be used where actual costs are compared against those expected and variances identified and investigated. Alternatively more effective overall control may be achieved by combining the control of costs with that of the physical activities by linking in with the project network analysis[14].

11.2 Evaluating a production system

The evaluation of a production system should take place at two stages. Firstly, the proposal must be evaluated prior to any decision being made to proceed with the project. Secondly, the actual system should be evaluated after implementation to ensure that the planned benefits are being achieved. This second, monitoring, role for an evaluation is necessary in order that modifications can be made to the system should its performance be affected by unforeseen factors or circumstances. Future systems can also benefit from the lessons learned in the second evaluation.

The precise nature of the method by which the system is evaluated will differ for the two situations described above. In particular, the proposal evaluation will contain an assessment of the project's feasibility and the likelihood of its objectives being achieved. It will also contain an assessment of the financial case which has been made for the investment, applying, where necessary, risk and sensitivity analyses. These will judge the financial viability of the project in the event that any assumptions do not hold, or if forecasts do not prove accurate.

A project feasibility analysis is basically an investigation to ensure that the new system is a viable proposition. It may be conducted in a formal manner or the study format can be informal, depending on the size and importance of the investment. It will make an assessment of the market, material needs, the availability of the required labour, the provision of services and the overall costs of plant, equipment, labour and raw materials[15].

A formal feasibility analysis would comprise a number of stages. In the first stage, general questions would be asked relating to the broad choice of processes, methods, etc. This would lead on to the intermediate stages where the degree of detail would increase. Here the questions asked will relate to more specific items concerning the market, technical and organizational factors. The final stage would be where cost implications are introduced in readiness for the financial assessment. The latter stages may, where appropriate, also contain a social audit to ensure that the proposed system design is consistent with the values and culture which prevail or are likely to prevail within the lifetime of the system.

When the financial evaluation is carried out a number of approaches are available[16]. These may vary from the simpler techniques such as 'pay-back period' to more sophisticated methods which take into account the time value of money such as 'net present value' (npv) and the 'discounted cash flow rate of return' (dcfrr) or 'internal rate of return' (irr).

These last two methods are particularly useful if the project life is likely to be long or if the pattern of cost or income is subject to fluctuation. Their approach is based on the idea that money spent or received some time in the future has a different value at the present time (i.e. the cash flows should be discounted using the relevant rate of interest). The choice of interest rate is a matter for careful consideration. It may relate to the cost of borrowing or to the return on other investments, depending on the organization's precise financial position[17].

If the values of the variables in the proposed investment are estimated accurately, then the result of the financial evaluation can be taken with a high degree of confidence. However, such a situation does not often occur in practice and it becomes desirable to have a measure of how sensitive the calculated outcome is in relation to possible errors in the initial estimation[18]. A sensitive project is one in which the ultimate outcome is likely to change significantly following a relatively small change in the value of one or more of the variables involved. If the values of the variables can be changed over a wide range without significantly changing the outcome, then the project is said to be not so sensitive. Sensitivity analysis requires the construction of a model from which the effect of changing a variable can readily be ascertained. The model can be represented graphically or a computer can be used to recalculate the range of outcomes for a given set of values of a chosen variable.

Risk analysis is somewhat different from that for sensitivity since the amount of variability which must be considered should be greater in order to take account of totally unexpected events. A number of approaches are available[19]. For instance, probabilistic cash flow models can be constructed which describe the relationship between a chance occurrence and the eventual outcome. Alternatively, a decision tree approach or simulation could be used when a more complex range of probabilities is encountered.

When eventually the new system is installed and has reached its planned level of activity (there will usually be a 'running-in' period during which it will operate at below its optimum level) the second evaluation can take place. The overall objective of this second evaluation is to confirm that the system is providing the financial return that was previously predicted. The actual procedure whereby this financial assessment is achieved is one where a number of factors are monitored, each of which will contribute to the costs and revenue associated with running the system.

In practice many organizations spend considerable sums of money on new systems yet largely neglect the post project evaluation, relying on crude productivity measures to judge the success of the system. It is true that to monitor all the relevant factors requires time and effort, and itself incurs further costs in employing staff to conduct the necessary studies. Nevertheless these costs will probably be negligible compared with the total cost of the system and the benefits of a thorough evaluation will often be more than justified. For instance, a change in the expected level of quality has implications in terms of reworking, inspection costs and relationships with suppliers, as well as changing assumptions that may have been made concerning the market and demand for the product.

In no way could an evaluation which only monitored, say, added value per employee, identify such a subtle shift in direction. Conversely, measures such as added value, and sales revenue may be influenced by factors other than those under control within the production system. For instance, a design change may result in the

Area of performance	Possible factors to be measured
Customer Service	– Percentage of orders delivered on time – Percentage of items supplied ex stock – Average lateness of orders
Physical System	– Machine utilization – Output – Downtime – Average repair time – Set-up time
Labour Resource	– Utilization – Output per labour hour – Absenteeism – Labour turnover – Number of disputes and hours lost
Materials	– Rate of stock turnover – Utilization – Work-in-progress levels – Obsolescence
Quality	– Percentage defects and scrap – Warranty costs – Customer returns – Customer complaints – Amount of reworking – Inspection costs – Audit results
Purchasing	– Cost of orders placed – Replenishment lead time – Delivery shortages

Figure 11.2 Evaluation of a production system – quantifiable measures of system performance

use of a less expensive material, meaning that the added value would increase independently of any changes in the production system.

The precise list of factors which should be monitored in the post-project evaluation will depend on the particular type of system under consideration. It will also depend to some degree on the strategic objectives identified when formulating the original justification. For instance, if improved delivery performance was a major requirement then factors affecting this, such as set-up time, should be the subject of close scrutiny.

A number of quantifiable measures is given in *Figure 11.2*. They are grouped into a number of areas of performance to provide a focus when deciding on their relevance. There may also be non-quantifiable factors which need to be included in the evaluation. These are probably best assessed via an 'audit checklist'[20]. Such an approach is appropriate for factors such as skill flexibility or job enrichment aspects, which would be difficult to quantify sensibly.

11.3 Summary

The realization of the benefits to be derived from designing and installing a new production system is not just dependent on the specification and organization of its component parts. It also depends greatly on the quality of implementation coupled with a thorough evaluation. Implementation is important because the most technically sophisticated systems can still fail due to unforeseen circumstances such as employee acceptability. Evaluation is important so that corrections and modifications can be made should any of the factors contributing to system performance not be meeting expectations.

Many of the problems of implementation stem from organizational as well as individual resistance. Resistance from individuals can be countered in a number of different ways depending on the particular circumstances. Generally though, they depend on providing greater involvement of employees in the system design process.

This may be by consultation or by allowing worker participation to a lesser or greater degree. Sometimes this is legislated for by some form of co-determination Act, as in the case of several countries in Europe. In Japan, on the other hand, participation is regarded as part of the corporate culture enabling novel production systems to be introduced relatively smoothly and with maximum co-operation between employer and employee.

The problem of organizational resistance arises where the organization structure is not conducive to change. This often occurs where the structure is too rigid and bureaucratic, preventing the emergence of 'change agents' or 'champions'. A programme of organization development may be appropriate. This would be aimed at changing the structure to allow easier introduction of new systems and procedures.

Apart from the problem of overcoming human resistance, there are a number of other planning and control aspects connected with systems implementation. The network analysis technique can be used in this connection. It can identify the critical path of activities, and the float associated with the remaining activities. It can be used for resource smoothing and may be modified to take account of multiple time estimates. The planning and control of financial expenditure could also be linked to the project network.

Evaluation of the production system should take place both before and after implementation. When carried out beforehand it forms part of the justification process and will comprise a feasibility analysis together with a financial assessment, probably using the discounted cash flow technique. A post-project evaluation is equally important since it is necessary to ensure that the planned results are being achieved. It will involve detailed monitoring of the factors which contribute to overall system performance, using both quantitative and qualitative measures.

Designing production systems is not just a matter of specifying machines and equipment together with new work methods. It forms part of a total manufacturing, marketing and financial strategy so must be closely linked with the plans and controls associated with all the business functions.

References

1. ILO (1979) *Introduction to Work Study,* International Labour Office, Geneva
2. GROOM, B. (1985) 'Vauxhall "Dalek" Strike Threatens Astra', *Financial Times* (10 May)
3. STYMNE, B. (1980) 'Design Principles for a Participative Organisation of Work', in *Economiç and Industrial Democracy,* **1,** Sage
4. DE VOS, T. (1981) *US Multinationals and Worker Participation in Management,* Quorum
5. PEJOVICH, S. (1978) *The Co-determination Movement in the West,* Lexington Books, London
6. CLARK, R. (1979) *The Japanese Company,* Yale University Press, USA

228   Implementation and evaluation

7. LEE, S. M. (1982) *Japanese Management, Cultural and Environmental Considerations,* Praeger
8. HASEGAWA, K. (1978) 'Japanese Corporations and Crisis Survival', *Japan Echo,* **V,** No 2
9. VOSS, C. (1984) 'Japanese Manufacturing Management Practices in the UK', *International Journal of Operations and Production Management,* **4,** No 2
10. ROBEY, D. and ALTMAN, S. (1982) *Organization Development,* Macmillan, London
11. TAYLOR, D. E. and SINGER, E. J. (1983) *New Organizations from Old,* Institute of Personnel Management, London
12. TWISS, B. (1974) *Managing Technological Innovation,* Longman, Harlow, Essex
13. LESTER, A. (1982) *Project Planning and Control,* Butterworths, London
14. STAFFURTH, C. (1980) *Project Cost Control Using Networks,* Heinemann, London
15. CLIFTON, D. S. and FYFFE, D. E. (1977) *Project Feasibility Analysis,* Wiley, New York
16. DE LA MARE, R. F. (1982) *Manufacturing Systems Economics,* Holt, Rinehart and Winston, UK
17. ALFRED, A. M. and EVANS, J. B. (1965) *Discounted Cash Flow,* Chapman and Hall, London
18. PILCHER, R. (1973) *Appraisal and Control of Project Costs,* McGraw Hill, Maidenhead, UK
19. STEVENS, G. T. (1979) *Economic and Financial Analysis of Capital Investments,* Wiley, New York
20. SKINNER, W. (1978) *Manufacturing in the Corporate Strategy,* Wiley, New York

Index

Lanchester Library